"Martin Buser's *Dog Man* i
break, and triumph. This is
story of a hard-working Swiss immigrant's voyage from poop scooper and dog
handler to record setting four time Alaskan Iditarod Champion. Buser takes
readers down some rough and dangerous trails, through life and death trials
for both himself and his team, and along the way reveals the powerful camara-
derie and fiercely competitive battles that took place between Anchorage and
Nome. *Dog Man* reveals how Buser's racing innovation, support from family
and friends, and love for his dogs carried him to victory."

— Don Rearden,
author of *The Raven's Gift*

"If you like dogs, the Iditarod, or Alaskan adventure, this is a book for you.
Martin's tales of his adventures on and off the trail are remarkable. I enjoyed
the read as much as the pictures."

— Jeff Schultz,
Official Iditarod photographer,
author of *Chasing Dogs*

"There is never a dull moment in this book which spans Martin's career of more
than 30 years. Martin is a dog man; he truly loves his dogs. He shares the moments he was on a magic carpet ride, as well as when he hits rock bottom. His
family is always at his side. His admiration for Alaska – the land and its people
– runs deep. Same on the trail; Martin is the real deal. He is always considerate of his peers. This book is the real deal for the avid mushing and Alaska fan.
Enjoy reading one of the best books written about life in the last frontier."

— Sebastian Schnuelle,
Yukon Quest Champion,
seven-time Iditarod finisher

DOG MAN

CHRONICLES OF AN IDITAROD CHAMPION

Martin Buser

Raven's Eye Press
Durango, Colorado

Raven's Eye Press
Durango, Colorado
www.ravenseyepress.com

Buser, Martin.
  Dog Man/Martin Buser.
  p. cm.

1. Nature -- Alaska
2. Dogsledding
3. Iditarod
I. Title

ISBN 978-0-9907826-3-6
LCCN 2015933000

Cover & photo page design

ELLE JAY DESIGN

Interior design

Edited by Sean Patrick Williams, seanpatrickwilliams.com
Cover photo © Jim R. Kohl/IditarodPhotos.com

For information on Martin Buser and visits to Happy Trails Kennel and B&B, please go to buserdog.com.

Printed in the United States of America
1 3 5 7 9 10 8 6 4 2

Dedicated to all the people that have ever had the pleasure to be influenced by a dog. Near or far, warm or cold, dogs have lived with humans and bettered us throughout.

Table of Contents

NOME WHITE
MOUNTAIN
SAFETY   ELIM   KOYUK
GOLOVIN
              SHAKTOOLIK   NULATO
UNALAKLEET   GALENA
                 KALTAG   RUBY
              EAGLE
              ISLAND
          GRAYLING   CRIPPLE
     ANVIK   OPHIR   TAKOTNA
SHAGELUK   NIKOLAI
     IDITAROD   McGRATH
                            ROHN
                        RAINY PASS
                           SKWENTNA
          FINGER LAKE   WILLOW
             YENTNA
                         CAMPBELL AIRSTRIP
                         ANCHORAGE

IDITAROD TRAIL

JON VAN ZYLE © 2000

JON VAN ZYLE

I know exactly where my limits are;
I step over them every day.

March 11, 2014
Somewhere along the Bering Sea Coast…

I need to be the lead dog. When the going gets tough, great lead dogs emerge. When the going gets impossible, the two-legged leader needs to take over. The complexities of this challenge had simply become too much for the dogs, and I needed to assume the leader position. I willed my body to the front of the team and wrapped my fingers around the gangline. Leaning into the wind, I took a step forward. Inches. I took another step. Inches again. A gust of wind threw an uppercut my way and I was on my back, gangline in hand. I mustered all my strength and stood up. Stepping on the bare tundra, I discovered some traction underfoot, so I zigged and zagged in hopes of staying near the trail, but the wind kept knocking me off my feet. Mother Nature had always been the most formidable competitor, and this time was no different – this was a bareknuckle boxing match between Life and Death. For thirty agonizingly-long minutes I tried in vain to lead the dogs along the trail. The all-too-palpable intensity of the wind blew forcefully enough that we could only head out to sea, but that wasn't part of the plan.

Forward progress became impossible. I simply could not stand up in the wind and walk; it had nothing to do with my injuries and pain but everything to do with the strength of the storm. If anything, the pain kept me alert. It occurred to me to try and crawl to Nome, but crawling for thirty-five miles did not make much sense. I laid the sled down and gathered the team into a doggie pile on the leeward side. They cuddled together as if they were puppies. Some actually whined to tell me they were scared. I unfurled my down sleeping bag and huddled with them, stroking each dog to comfort away not just their fears, but also my own.

From my now several days long out-of-body experience, I marveled at how little space twelve sled dogs, the sled, and musher could occupy when everyone wanted to stay out of the wind. We stayed like that for several hours, the wind sucking away at our body heat. When I had to leave the group to relieve myself, I stashed my sleeping bag in the sled to make sure it would not blow to Russia. *What a mess.*

While outside of the huddle, both the wind and I agreed to use this opportunity to explore the idea of going downwind and out on the sea ice to determine if things had improved. In less than a hundred feet my question was answered. Travel was not yet possible, and I had to get back to my team. Venturing away from the dogs was easy in a thirty-knot wind; venturing back only reaffirmed my decision not to try and crawl to the finish. I gave everything I had to get back to them. Once returned to the huddle, my down bag again proved its worth after I draped it over the team.

I decided not to try and move until full daylight in the hope that either the storm would die down or daylight would help clarify the trail to the dogs. Our only option was to wait; we were going to "rest" here for a while longer.

How long can we last? I took a mental inventory of the situation: We were still reasonably warm, well hydrated, and had enough food with us to last a day or two. And there was that button on the tracker.

Shivering in the screaming winds several miles from Safety, I entertained the thought of pushing for HELP. But who was going to come and rescue us? Who was going to travel *into* this impossible situation? If we couldn't move, who could? I didn't want to jeopardize any potential rescuer attempting the impossible. I needed to remain focused, but I was drifting in and out of sleep…

Running From Petunia
March 1958

I was born in Switzerland and was a lederhosen-wearing lad for the first few years of my life. My family consisted of my two older sisters Barbara and Regula, my mother and father, and me. My father was an orthopedic surgeon, my mother an operating nurse. They both worked for a company that started hospitals from the ground up and had traveled quite a bit before I was born, living in Africa and elsewhere. My parents worked in these new hospitals but also helped the local doctors and nurses become proficient enough to run their own show. When I turned six, we moved to Persia. Nowadays we call it Iran, but at that time it was known exclusively as Persia. I played with the local kids, and conversed with them enough that Farsi became my first foreign language. While we lived there I spoke fluently, but that's all gone now.

We loved animals, and we brought or bought them everywhere. We all took care of the chickens. My oldest sister Barbara had a donkey, I had white rabbits, and my middle sister Regula had a goose named Petunia.

Petunia hated me. We were the same size, and she saw me as a threat because of it. We stood eye to eye, and hers were filled with evil and hate, as far as I was concerned. I was just a little one, and too afraid to stand up to her. She roamed freely, all was her domain, and she was the queen. Regula carried that spoiled goose wherever she went.

I stayed on high alert. Whenever I went outside, my mission was survival. I snuck around corners and looked left and right to make sure Petunia wasn't out. Normally, if I didn't spot her, I was home free. One time, though, I must have let my guard down, because she sensed my presence and came galloping around the corner. Imagine that, a galloping goose. I screamed for my life and ran, and her wings fluttered wildly when she caught me and latched her beak right onto the middle of my back, trying to teach me not to invade her territory. I re-learned this lesson on several occasions.

My father hired some workers to build a pool in the yard, and the day they finished was a happy day for all the kids. Soon after, during another Petunia Watch, I felt two arms lift and toss me into the air. I floated high in the sky, and when I looked down, no ground stood beneath me, only water. I was headed into the pool, involuntarily, and gravity made sure of it. *Splash.*

While drowning, I looked up and saw a goose torpedo in my wake. Regula had enacted her grand and hilarious scheme to throw me into the pool then throw Petunia in after me. As I sat on the bottom of the pool contemplating life, sucking water, and generally not having a very good time, I tried to figure a way out of this predicament. Goose feet splashed around, and every now and again a goose neck dove down to look for me. At this point I realized the goose was not my size, but twenty feet tall. It was a giant, it had somehow become the biggest goose in the world, and it was out to get me.

As Petunia tread water above me, I formulated my escape route. With no time to waste, as my life was on the line, I went for it. I rocketed off the bottom of that pool and hit the ground running. Petunia tried to give chase, but from that moment forward I was The Flash. I ran from place to place, never looking back to see if the goose was coming, because that would mean I was afraid, and to be fast you had to be fearless. I found my stride that day. Ever since, I have loved being in front.

MY FIRST SLED

MOM AND ME

ME, SIX YEARS OLD,
WITH REGULA
MY SISTER

REGULA, ME, AND
BARBARAS DONKEY,
IN PERSIA

MY SISTER BARBARA,
ME, AND MY DAD

The End Of My Regular Life
Spring 1974

Whistling a little tune, I zoomed across the back roads leading out of Zurich. I must have hit forty miles per hour. My moped technically topped out at around thirty to thirty-five, but I tinkered with it to give it more zip. It was a Sunday morning; I was a sixteen-year-old teenage punk without a helmet, and my destination was two villages over in Effretikon.

The day before, I happened upon a strange situation. I sat on my moped, ready for my daily dose of adventure, when the skeleton of a Volkswagen Beetle barreled out of the woods and stopped right next to me. Nothing remained of the original car except the steering column, the steering wheel, the seats, and a set of brakes. Most surprising of all, several dogs were pulling this vehicular anomaly.

Caked from head to toe in mud, two people sat in the front seats wearing painter's jumpsuits. Using their fingers as windshield wipers, they wiped off their goggles and unleashed two of the brightest smiles ever witnessed by Man. My jaw dropped. How could somebody so dirty be smiling so big? I walked over to them.

"What are you guys doing?" I said.

"Well, we just finished training our Siberian Huskies, our sled dogs."

"Wow," I said.

"If you would like to come with us tomorrow, you are more than welcome," they said.

"Definitely," I said.

That was the beginning of the end of my regular life.

The moped ride to Effretikon took twenty minutes. From then on I became a grab your books and go, see you later type. Outside of school, every spare moment I had I worked with and for them – Marcel and Monica Huber. Marcel was one of the few full-time military officers for the predominantly volunteer Swiss Army, and Monica worked as a veterinarian who operated a one-room clinic from their house. In the old country kennels, you weren't allowed to keep more than four or five dogs in one place. They solved this by maintaining a two-part racing kennel. Some of their dogs lived in their home, some lived in the yard. At the edge of a nearby forest – where the training trails started – they kept a fenced-in yard with several pens holding one or two dogs each. I tagged along on all the training runs and did chores. At the end of each day, I threw my leg over my trusty moped, gave it a kick-start and cruised home, leaving a long dust cloud in my rearview mirror.

It was the seventies, and still within the heyday of purebred dog racing. The oncoming era of the mixed breed had yet to arrive in Europe. The racing breeds were the Siberians, Malamutes, and Samoyeds. Siberians were the swiftest, followed by the Malamutes. The Samoyeds, the most photogenic, were known primarily for their white and fluffy exterior, not their speed. The Siberian mushers laughed at the sluggishness of the Malamutes and the Samoyeds.

Marcel and Monica ran sprint races – everybody with dogs raced back then. Every weekend we drove to Austria, Germany, Switzerland, or France for an open-class race. Most teams ran with ten to sixteen dogs. The same people raced each other constantly, and the results repeated themselves constantly. In the beginning, my chances for racing were nonexistent, but I persisted until my opportunity for glory came knocking.

Standing on the brake at the starting line near the Austrian-Swiss border, I knew I didn't have the fastest team in the ten-kilometer race. Cobbled together from the leftover dogs of a friend of Monica and Marcel's, we were an eager group of good-looking misfits. Regardless, I prepared to leave it all on the trail – this was my big chance. At that moment, revolutionizing the prestigious three-dog Samoyed class shot to the top of my to-do list. The crowd gathered was as large as any three-dog race in modern times.

"Martin Buser…three…two…one…GO!"

I released the brake, called up the dogs, and we took off down the marked trail. Within a few minutes the elation of starting my first race settled down, and I became aware of our relative speed, or lack thereof. The route followed the border of a lake, and it was flat. I started pedaling, but that didn't help, so I jumped off the runners. Young and agile, I ran behind and pushed the sled down the trail. People could see me and I heard cries of "Look! He's running with the dogs!" I pushed and ran as fast as those three Samoyeds all the way to the finish line. We didn't win. I don't know where we finished, but I enjoyed it all, except for one thing: I wanted to go faster. I knew right then my Samoyed racing career would be short-lived; it was time to race Siberians.

Before my Siberian Era could begin, I needed to complete the last of what I called the "command performances" – join the Swiss Army. Growing up in Switzerland meant that in your early twenties you went through basic military training. It's part of the culture and it's mandatory. After that, it's similar to the Army Reserves, except in Switzerland the entire nation has joined.

The military offered several different schools of training. One of the toughest troops was the Grenadiers. In the United States, the Marines are a good comparison. They even share the same motto, "Semper Fidelis." Then apart from that were the Mountain Grenadiers – the ultimate champions of difficult terrain. Bad to the bone, they were the Swiss equivalent of the Navy Seals. I became a Mountain Grenadier.

To qualify, they put you through rigorous physical tests. I had to run and ski and climb to make the grade. The physical demands were high, but since it was mandatory I figured I should try and learn as much as possible. For almost five months we ran long distances, lifted heavy objects, and practiced shooting. I made a few friends, and it was a challenge. But now I needed a new challenge. Five years of part-time recreational mushing had ignited the spark that fueled the dream of living in Alaska for a year. When my military training finished, I began the search for an opportunity to make it happen.

Alaska was a mysterious word to me then. It was a place on the map to be sure, but its real immensity came from hearing people say it aloud. The way they pronounced it suggested something on a grander scale, something ingrained deep in the human experience. It was a word that felt untamed, felt wild, and it grabbed me by my curiosity and refused to let go. In my mind I didn't have an option. Somehow, some way, I needed to find out for myself.

In the meantime, I went back to helping Monica and Marcel Huber. That period of European sprint racing operated under the rule that only purebred "Nordic" breeds were allowed on the race trails. Like any good racers, the Hubers wanted to obtain the best dogs they could. Siberian breeders existed at that time in Europe, but many of the more accomplished dogs seemed to always originate from one or two sources in Alaska. Everybody that ran dogs kept their ears to the ground for news of any dogs or information that trickled in from overseas. Tales of unprecedented distances and kennels with twenty dogs or more were both situations that remained unfathomable to the mushers of Central Europe. In Alaska, people knew of Harris Dunlap for Seppala Siberians, and they knew of Earl and Natalie Norris for traditional Siberian Huskies. Both the Hubers and the locally legendary musher Toni Schmidt had purchased dogs over the years from the Anadyr line that the Norrises bred and sold.

One weekend, Marcel and Monica ran a race in France near the French-Swiss border, and I tagged along. The countries are stacked close to each other in that part of the world, and naturally that meant every race filled with mushers who spoke different languages. A situation arose that weekend where I became a three-way interpreter between French, German, and English. I spoke French and German fluently, but very little English. A Dutch musher named Lou VanLeuweven witnessed this, and knowing I wanted to go to Alaska, approached me afterward:

"Before you go to Alaska you should learn better English."

"I'm pretty bad, aren't I? Got any ideas?"

"As a matter of fact, I have just the place for you to do that. We always have handlers that live with us and help train our dogs. You can be our handler, free room and board, and in exchange I will teach you English for free."

I ended up working there for a year – 1978-1979. Our agreement stipulated that we speak only English. When mine improved enough I mustered the courage to write a letter to Earl and Natalie Norris. One day I received a reply. Excited, I tore open the envelope:

Hi Martin,
Yes you can come and work at our kennel in Alaska. We would be honored for you to shovel our turds for a year.

Sincerely,
Earl and Natalie Norris

I started packing immediately.

SCHOOL PHOTO

HIGH SCHOOL YEARBOOK

MUSHING
IN EUROPE

UNKNOWN

PART OF THE
SWISS MILITARY

BARBARA SCHOOP

Culture Shock
April 1979

April, 1979.

I buckled my seatbelt, leaned my head back against the chair, and closed my eyes. *Relax.* The plane taxied across the pavement to the runway. The roar of the engine grew louder as we sped up, and I looked out of the window just as we lifted off the ground. *Alaska, here I come.*

A direct flight from Zurich to Anchorage didn't exist. My route took me from Zurich to Boston to Chicago to Anchorage. A friend of my sister's – Jeannie Klugman – lived in Boston, and the plan was to stay there with her family. When I landed, they picked me up from the airport. That night happened to be during Passover, and the Klugmans were Jewish. They included me in all the family festivities even though we had met only hours earlier – American hospitality appeared to be real. The next morning I inquired to see if they could and would drive me an hour north of the city, and they said yes. I wanted to visit with a local dog musher: Roland "Doc" Lombard.

In those days, the Central European mushing season revolved around speed, or sprint, racing. The most famous sprint race was the Anchorage Fur Rendezvous. There were several famous personalities that had evolved and become synonymous with success and admiration. Names like Joe Redington and Rick Swenson had yet to become well-known overseas – we idolized names like George Attla and "Doc"

Lombard.

Doc Lombard lived close to Boston, and during my trip preparations I had arranged to spend some time out at his place. Born in 1911, his racing career spanned more than fifty years. He won the Fur Rendezvous eight times, had a parallel career as a veterinarian, and some of his first dogs had been a gift from Leonhard Seppala – one of the heroes of the 1925 Serum Run. I figured the drive out there might prove educational, so I stayed with him and his wife Nellie for two days, just hanging out and picking his brain. Then I went back to Boston and caught a flight to Chicago.

In Chicago, the layover lasted three hours. I walked around the terminal until hunger pushed me into the line at the airport McDonald's:

"Whaddya wanna order, man?" the cashier said.

"What…um…how about a…" I said.

"Listen cat, do me a solid and just pick somethin – the line ain't gettin any shorter, dig?" he said.

"Chee…cheeseburger and fries, please," I said.

Clearly my English was not as good as I had believed. *Do me a solid?* For the first time since leaving Europe, I hadn't understood a single word. My order came out; I grabbed it and headed back to the gate. I reboarded the plane, thinking that I had a lot to learn. *At least I have a window seat.*

As the plane took off in the direction of Anchorage, in Anchorage another plane took off in the direction of Chicago. Somewhere over the Canadian Rockies our two paths crossed. Staring through a window in the other plane, a couple headed for Europe. The flight manifest listed them as "Earl Norris, Natalie Norris."

At the baggage claim in Anchorage, I found my suitcase and carried it outside. Within a few minutes a green Chevy truck pulled up. The driver slid the steering column gearshift into park, and two people stepped out. By the looks of them, they were my predecessors.

"Are you Martin Buser?" they said.

"Yeah, that's me."

One of them tossed the truck keys towards me and I caught them.

"Here's the keys. The house is at mile 66.5 on the Parks Highway. Have fun," they said, before promptly walking inside and taking the next flight out of state, never to be seen again.

In that instant I became solely responsible for nearly 200 dogs. *Holy moly.* Luckily, I possessed an international driver's license and a youthful dose of Gung-Ho. The Norrises spent the next four and a half weeks lecturing in Europe, and they counted on me to feed, scoop, and water their dogs every day. That spring I spent upwards of twelve to fourteen hours per day doing dog chores. When Earl and Natalie returned, I recognized them from a picture I had seen in the hallway.

Gone To The Dogs
Fall 1979

The chores kept on through the summer, but I managed to travel a little bit. After the Norrises returned, I bought a car – a two-toned metallic-brown Ford Elite. With an advertising slogan like "Styled to keep you out of the crowd; priced so you can enjoy it now," how could a guy go wrong? This big and beautiful two-door gas-guzzler ran on a V8 engine and screamed 1970s America. For 1500 bucks it even came with a leather interior. Most importantly, the car provided me with a valuable asset: the freedom to go places.

In the fall we started the training season with the same exact rig that I had used in Europe – the stripped down chassis of a Volkswagen Beetle. Earl maintained a small fleet of those skeleton cars. We hooked up sixteen to twenty-two dogs and ran the dogs on the dirt trails in Willow. During September we ventured up to two miles at a time; by October the distance increased to three miles. In early November we repeatedly ran a swift eight miles with a big string of dogs and a heavy load; a few weeks later we dared to take a six-dog team fourteen miles on an out and back along the unmaintained Nancy Lake park road.

The entire time I interacted with the dogs as best I knew how and adopted a mouth shut, ears open approach. I wanted to learn as much as possible and only had twelve months in Alaska to do that. Basically I was just a kid, but after several months it became clear that my years of volunteer time working with Siberians had given me a solid footing.

The Norrises liked my approach.

Halfway through the winter training season, we sat around the dinner table and discussed the various races coming up:

"Maybe we should have a team in the Iditarod. Would you have any interest in that?" Earl said.

The Iditarod? Earl just asked me to race the Iditarod – the world's longest dogsled race. The race had existed for only seven years, with many mushers falling short in their attempts. Those that did finish took as many as four weeks to travel from the start in Anchorage, then across the vast wilderness to the finish line in Nome. Never in a million years did I expect that offer to come – it was totally out of the blue. I didn't come to Alaska to run the Iditarod; I came to have a one year adventure. I was a Swiss boy who had every intention of going back home and working and continuing with the military and all that, but I recognized a no-brainer when I saw one:

"Sign me up!" I said.

"Great. We will give you a good team, but probably not the best dogs because I am going to run those in the Fur Rendezvous," Earl said.

With renewed motivation, I pivoted my focus from the poop bucket to thoughts of the trail. My work day ballooned from twelve up to sixteen hours per day. I asked a million questions about sleds, harnesses, dog food – how little I knew then would not became apparent until thirty years later – and happily spent all my time bonding with "my" dogs. I even did one "hundred miler" in February – a fifty mile run the first day, followed by a night off, then a fifty mile run the second day. The Iditarod was advertised as only 1100 miles – that felt sufficient.

In Over My Head
The 1980 Iditarod

The start date crept up on me before I knew it. Hopefully the training had prepared both the dogs and me properly for the trail ahead. We would find out soon enough. Friends and family back home heard that I actually dared to run the Iditarod – the playground of those famous mushers Rick Swenson, Susan Butcher, Herbie Nayokpuk, Dick Mackey, Emmitt Peters, et al – and a few of them decided to send me various supplies, including clothing. I appreciated all of that, of course.

When the morning of the race arrived I woke up to the sound of my alarm. It was time to get dressed. A handmade silk set of long johns acted as my underlayer. The longjohns consisted of two pieces – a top and a bottom. On my legs I also wore a pair of midnight-purple boiled-wool pants. They were thick and plaid and patterned. Over my silk top I stacked a couple of Filson wool shirts. For my feet I slipped on wool socks, then mukluks with removable felt insoles. Earl had worked with the military doing rescues and recoveries via dog team, and his connections gained me access to the military surplus provider that sold the mukluks. If wet conditions called for a different pair of footwear, I kept a pair of white Korean War era "bunny" boots stowed in the sled. On my head I sported a grey, felt-lined, Dutch military cap with a sewn-on Iditarod patch. I had obtained the hat from my friend Lou the KLM pilot years before, and a year later when it went missing I entered a period of mourning. I looked like an old-fashioned lumberjack, but that was just the base.

A neighbor of Earl and Natalie's, Robin Chlupach, designed and made my parka. She sandwiched a layer of quallofil in between the nylon canvas outside and the wool-lined inside, then topped it off with a stout fur ruff. Robin also coached me through making a pair of quallofil-insulated, quilt-lined wolf mittens and wolf hat. Wearing everything but the kitchen sink, I appeared the picture-perfect Alaskan adventurer. *Am I in over my head?*

Sixty teams showed up to try their hand at the big race; we didn't know it yet, but two out of every five would fail. My dogs were 100 percent AKC registered Siberian Huskies – one of the few purebred teams. Most teams ran mixed-breed Alaskan Huskies – the term for any double-coated dog that loves to run and pull. I called them "Iditarod Huskies." Bred in native villages for the utilitarian purposes of trapping and transportation, "Iditarod Huskies" were a diverse group of single-gaited trotters sometimes referred to as "scrub" dogs – short legs, short body, thick coat, and great appetite. Mentally and physically tough, they existed on very little and still held their weight – we called them easy "keepers." All the competitive mushers believed this trotting husky to be the ultimate long distance dog, and their race records proved it. Ready for an adventure, my ambitions didn't include challenging any of the contenders for the title.

I stood on the runners, eyes wide and ears shut. The announcer must have counted down, but I didn't hear it. The next thing I knew my fourteen dogs were flying around the streets of Anchorage, with me in tow. Right turn here, left turn there – I held on tight down the Chester Creek Trail. Fans watching the start of Iditarod 1980 witnessed us traverse along the foothills of the Chugach Mountains all the way to Eagle River. Once there, a four-hour countdown clock started ticking. Now the challenge became trucking myself and the dogs to the Wasilla restart on time and without breaking down or getting stuck in traffic.

The first few years of Iditarod competition saw the race run from the start in Anchorage to the finish line in Nome without interruption. The early races led the teams briefly along Alaska's only major highway, and the dogs actually ran on pavement for a small section or two. The combination of the growing popularity and the evolving logistics of the race soon brought that to an end. In the 1980s the teams raced to Eagle River, then trucked to the restart at what is now Settler's Bay Golf Course.

The sensory overload of being a rookie contributed to the stressful blur that became that first day of racing. I managed to arrive without delay to the restart. We hooked up the dogs again, and I took off rip-roaring down the trail for the second time. The chaotic energy pushed me through the night and past Skwentna and Finger Lake. During the snaking descent en route to Rainy Pass my mind settled down, and I recovered some semblance of self-awareness.

Cresting over Rainy Pass, the highest point of the race, I stopped and put three dogs in the sled bag to rest on the way into Rohn. The thinking was those dogs needed a break, and the reduced power would make for an easier descent. Either that or their weight would exponentially increase my downhill momentum – it's hard to say. Once the dogs were loaded I pulled the hook and started to dance with the Dalzell Gorge. The trail soon turned fast and loose, and I lost control. A tree jumped in the way and my runners collided head-on with the trunk. *Crack.* I righted the sled and inspected the damage. A few busted birch stanchions, but nothing that a little lashing couldn't fix. Besides, my big basket sled had plenty of stanchions. I limped the sled into Rohn.

Having departed for Nikolai, I made it over the glacier and through the woods to the newly named Farewell Burn, where 345,000 acres of charred devastation welcomed the dog teams to the snowless region just north of the Alaska Range. The 1977 Bear Creek fire had burned an area just under half the size of Rhode Island – the largest wildland fire in

Alaska's history – and now the challenge became how to cross.

The landscape consisted of thousands upon thousands of burnt trees fallen flat for as far as I could see. The optimal route to the next checkpoint was anyone's guess – the trail simply did not exist. Several miles ahead, another musher ran into trouble and called for help. That musher's name was Norman Vaughan – the same guy who drove dogs in Antarctica in the 1920s during Admiral Byrd's first expedition to the South Pole; the same guy who drove dogs at the 1932 Winter Olympics representing the United States at mushing's first and only race on the world stage; the same guy who drove dogs for search and rescue during World War Two. Now seventy-five years old, Norman Vaughan was in distress on the Iditarod Trail. The only problem was that his call for help took the form of firing a flare gun into the air, which subsequently caused the Farewell Burn to burst into flames. Again.

The hardest part about driving dogs through the world's largest game of pickup sticks was not the lack of a trail, but having to literally blaze a new one. The other mushers all chose their own paths – I saw teams as far as a mile to either side of me. We were the chimney sweep cavalry, fighting our way through the formerly mature forest. The fiery horizon had not been a part of anybody's training program.

The relief I felt in Nikolai imprinted me enough that less than a decade later I would name my first-born son after the village. My dogs and I appeared unrecognizable upon arrival. Ash blanketed each dog from nose to tail, and my sled bag needed to be beaten like a household rug. My teeth tasted like I had snacked on charcoal briquettes, which was close to the truth. Charred spruce flakes painted my hands black from clearing away multiple truck loads of fallen trees. The soles of my mukluks had worn through with so many holes that I practically stood in my socks.

At the checkpoint, the community turned out in force. A huge fire heated water for all, which saved both time and effort for the mushers.

Local trappers sold fresh beaver carcasses, stacked to the sky on freight sleds, for five dollars apiece. The dogs rested comfortably in the midday sun, and my exhausted body looked forward to supposedly better trail conditions. We took a long break and regrouped. I took my mandatory twenty-four hour break in the next town of McGrath because that was the only place Earl could reasonably fly himself, based on commercial flight availability. He wanted to see how his sprint dogs were doing.

The mercury plunged between Ophir and Ruby. Rumors spoke of seventy below. Those temperatures were exceptionally cold, even for a young and athletic and oblivious musher like me. I shivered and struggled to Ruby, where I parked the team, fed the dogs, and walked inside to warm up. At the table sat another musher who looked just as miserable as me – his name was Ken Chase.

Ken Chase, an Athabascan Native, was one of the early Iditarod pioneers. He had raced in eight consecutive years up to that point, and eventually became one of the rare mushers to race in four different decades. His trusted lead dog Piper knew the trail almost better than Ken did. Piper was cream-colored, almost all white, and 1980 was his eighth Iditarod, but not his last. I think Piper ended up running ten times. The bond between Ken and Piper blew me away, and I marveled over the level of trust and confidence they shared. When Piper finally retired, Ken just said, "Well, I guess I gotta train up another lead dog." Piper had been his only leader! Every year, Ken put him in lead in Anchorage, and the dog led all the way to Nome. Piper even knew where the next open water spots would be on the Yukon River, which would prove to be great for hydrating the dogs. Ken knew all the best places to camp – a major factor for the now bygone ritual of building a fire, drying out, and making tea and coffee. Sitting in Ruby in extreme subzero temperatures, the thought of continuing my rookie race under the tutelage of Ken Chase and Piper sounded like the smartest decision I could make. Inside the checkpoint, however, we sat by the fire like two cold, tired, and hungry dog mushers:

"I think I am going to quit the race," Ken said.

"That sounds like a pretty good idea," I said.

"I know too many people here," Ken said. "Why don't we go to Galena together and scratch?"

"I like that plan," I said.

We couldn't scratch at Galena because on the way to Nulato there was a liquor store called Last Chance. Ken didn't drink, and I didn't want to purchase anything, but the owner was a good friend of Ken's, and we dropped in for a visit. Hundreds of miles from the nearest city, the proprietor had received his liquor license with the unspoken understanding that nobody could make a business profitable in the middle of nowhere. Fortunately for us, the naysayers were wrong. We drove our dogs down the cold and windy Yukon, keeping hope alive knowing there was a place to go inside downriver. We walked into the store, sat down, and watched the news. The owner had a satellite dish, the heat was up, and we instantly decided to stay there for a brief eight hours to catch up on world events. At some point we realized that Last Chance liquor had never been designated as a checkpoint. Nulato wasn't far, so we would keep going and scratch at Kaltag.

Within thirty minutes a dog team approached heading the wrong way. We stopped our teams and dropped our snow hooks. It was Warner Vent.

"Ken, did I leave my wolf mittens at Last Chance?" Warner asked.

"I don't know, but I would look behind your back," Ken said.

The mittens twirled behind his parka. Our rest had lasted a full eight hours, with Warner leaving long before we arrived. Almost to Kaltag, he couldn't find his mittens and mushed back to get them. It looked like somebody had dipped into the supplies a bit too much and needed to fill up the tank again. Warner didn't finish the race that year. Back then, some mushers never made it past Last Chance.

At Kaltag, Ken discovered that if he scratched that he would have to break trail for 200 miles downriver to his home in Anvik. That felt like a lot of work just to quit. He suggested we mush to the Old Woman Cabin located on the portage to the Bering Sea Coast. A good break there would get us to Unalakleet – a far superior location to bow out of the race.

The talk of perpetually scratching at the next checkpoint continued to Shaktoolik and beyond. The wind delivered a cold message as we crossed the Norton Sound, and we showed our appreciation by cussing every step of the way. After that, the wind blew from behind, and conditions became marginally better. Our running joke of stopping ended up being just the motivation we needed to keep going.

In long-distance dog racing, sometimes you inadvertently fall into the same traveling pattern as another musher. You end up getting to know each other, and it can be comforting to have a trail companion in difficult circumstances. It's known as a "trail marriage," and friendships formed under those conditions usually last for a lifetime.

At White Mountain, Ken wanted to camp for a bit longer than I did, so we split up for the first time in a week. I faced the last seventy-seven miles on my own. My dogs and I glided smoothly over the snow and tundra – by this point the incredible dogs had established a rhythm they could maintain for a month. Soon I saw the lights of Nome, and before long, we turned onto Front Street. After more than 17 days I could actually see the finish line. My dogs trotted under the burled arch, I put the hook down, and somebody handed me a microphone:

"I'm here, I'm done with the Iditarod, I'm single, and I'm available."

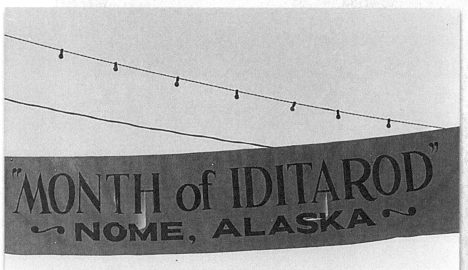

BANNER IN NOME

MY OFFICIAL
FINISHER'S PATCH

I Want To Go Faster
The 1981 Iditarod

The next year in the 1981 Iditarod I took another team of dogs from the kennel. Having finished twenty-second in my rookie run, we decided that I stood a good chance at cracking the top twenty. *Could Siberians be competitive after all?*

Earl and Natalie had not been ultracompetitive for a few years in the Fur Rendezvous, in large part because the Alaskan Husky had become the undisputed champion of the speed circuit. Both sprint and long-distance dogs fell under the term, but in practice they appeared much different. The sprint Alaskan – distance mushers called them Hounds – had evolved to be faster, sleeker, more athletic, and longer-bodied than the trotting Iditarod Husky. The swiftest of Siberian Huskies had been relegated to the back positions on the speed circuit, but what about head to head with the long-distance Iditarod Huskies? Everyone wanted to know if Siberians could still compete in the longer distances like they had during the post Gold Rush era – it fell to me to find out. By the time the Iditarod rolled around, Earl and I had trained up all the best dogs in the Norris' kennel and brought them to the start line.

As it turned out, the Siberian Huskies' destiny did not lie in ultracompetitive long-distance dog racing. Hybrid vigor proved too powerful, like everywhere else in the animal kingdom. I finished nineteenth in fourteen days and some odd hours – a new Siberian standard. If you can't win, maybe you can be the fastest Siberian team

– that was the thinking. Everybody is a statistician, and can formulate new theorems to make themselves feel better. That is much harder to do during a race – especially a thousand mile, two-week-long one. I entered the race with high hopes, but by the twenty-four hour break my dreams had long since been dashed.

During my childhood my parents had put me through eight years of private flute lessons. I didn't go pro, but I did develop a technical proficiency in whistling. Most people can't carry a tune. By the halfway point of the 1981 Iditarod, I was all whistled out. These were the days before portable audio entertainment, and I desperately needed a new way to pass the time on the runners. You don't have to train an "easy" command with Siberians – that's their regular speed. Our traveling times finally fostered an idea: I could read while going down the trail! I read everything I could get my hands on – battery packages, candy wrappers, parka patches, checkpoint flyers, for days on end. Over and over.

When I finally got to Nome, I took a blood oath never to race with Siberians again. I just could not stand going that slow. I wanted to go faster. To do that I would have to start my own kennel, which presented a dilemma: How could I accomplish that with a tourist visa?

MY 1981
IDITAROD
TEAM

TALKING TO
ORVILLE LAKE AND
FORMULATING
A PLAN FOR
THE FUTURE

The Proposition
April 1981

The truck pulled off the road in front of me. I moseyed up to the window.

"Where are you headed?" the driver said.

"Eureka," I said.

"I can get you as far as Nenana. Hop in," the driver said.

I tossed my bag in the back and jumped in the front seat. Heading north up the Parks Highway, I mentally prepared to ask Susan Butcher to marry me.

During the spring of 1981, I had come up with a grandiose idea: I wanted to become a competitive dog musher. Achieving that goal required a new set of circumstances. For two years I had subsisted on renewed and extended tourist visas, but building a dog team and traveling back and forth to Switzerland felt unworkable. Winning the green card lottery seemed far-fetched. I needed to stay in Alaska, I needed a job, and I needed to learn more.

Susan Butcher stood out as one of the most hard-working, successful, and driven dog mushers. Plus, she was single. After two thousand miles on the Iditarod trail, never once had I seen her team. Her chances of winning grew larger by the year, and I thought she might see some mutual benefit in teaming up with somebody like me. I dreamed of a business proposition – I could work with and for her in exchange for a marriage that enabled me to stay in Alaska year-round. She lived way out in Eureka, north of Fairbanks. Right after the Iditarod, in April, I made plans to go up there and ask her. The Ford Elite sat in the shop – a normal occurrence for that car. Traveling north meant hitchhiking.

"Thanks for the ride," I said.

"No problem. Good luck!" the driver said.

I grabbed my bag and started walking. My hitchhiking efforts had landed me in the town of Nenana, more than halfway to my goal of Eureka. That night I stayed at former Iditarod champion Jerry Riley's. We caught up with each other and shared trail stories. While telling him of my lofty intentions, the phone rang.

"Hello, this is Jerry."

"Hi Jerry, is Martin Buser there?"

"Yes he is, hold on just a second."

He handed the phone to me.

"Hello, this is Martin."

"Martin, this is Fred. Do you want to climb Denali?"

What a rude interruption. My friend Fred Agree had tracked me down to tell me he had a group of twenty-one German climbers coming to summit Denali, but he didn't have a German-speaking guide. Having completed two Iditarods, trained in the Swiss Army, and maintained fluency in German, I guess I qualified. It sounded like an adventure, but what about my planned proposal to Susan? This was my twenty-four hour break on my grand hitchhiking journey. I couldn't just give up now, but was this Destiny calling?

"I would love to," I said.

"Great. When can you get here?" Fred said.

"Tomorrow," I said.

So much for the proposal. The next morning I hitchhiked south to Talkeetna.

The lack of a German interpreter had resulted from an unfortunate situation. The climbing company started under the auspices and ownership of Swiss immigrant and world famous mountaineer Ray Genet. Tragically, he lost his battle with hypothermia coming down the summit of Mount Everest. In dog mushing circles, Ray played an integral part of Joe Redington and Susan Butcher's ascent of Denali by dog team a few years prior. All of this happened not too long before Fred contacted me by phone, and I seized the opportunity to help.

Two climbers from New Zealand filled the roles of lead guides. I took care of the stragglers. Several days of effort brought us to twenty-thousand feet at what is called "the football field," with most of the original twenty-one ready to summit. My primary focus turned to Pierre, the lone straggler. Making it to the top required you to stash most of your gear at the football field and carry as little as possible to the summit and back. 320 feet were all that stood between you and the top of North America, but the low oxygen levels at that altitude turned even the best of attempts into a slow-motion scamper.

Pierre frostbit his hands on the ascent. He wanted to try and summit, but he just wasn't able, so he and I hung out as the summiting party charged to the peak. When everybody came back, the main guides insisted I go ahead and summit while they waited with the group and took care of Pierre. I declined. He was my responsibility, and besides, I was now a Sherpa. This new job would bring me to the summit the very next week. Not a big deal. My mind raced with thoughts of climbing Denali in the summers and running Iditarod in the winters. I led Pierre back down, with no regrets.

My job as a climbing guide ended soon after. The company was wading through an understandably wild time, but I harbored no ill feelings about any of it. Unexpectedly, that became my only Denali trip. Today, my house stands atop a hill facing north. Sometimes I stare out at the mountain, thinking of my unfinished business.

MY DAYS AS
A SHERPA

AT THE DENALI
"FOOTBALL FIELD"

Living In The Bush
Summer 1981

During my rookie Iditarod, Ken Chase had extended me a standing offer for a place to stay should I ever visit the village of Anvik – his home – on the Yukon River. Within weeks of climbing Denali, I took him up on it. What initially began as a visit eventually turned into a summer-long course on the traditional rural Alaskan lifestyle.

Days after my arrival we started preparing for the commercial salmon fishing seasons – both sockeye and kings. First we put the fish wheel back together and secured it to the shore. A fish wheel operates similar to a watermill – two large mesh-framed baskets sit opposite each other on an axle, with a framed paddle section sitting halfway between each basket. Every ninety degrees there is either a basket or a paddle. As each section dips into the water, the fish wheel is continuously powered by the downstream river current – like a perforated pinwheel in a breeze. The salmon swim upstream and get scooped up in the basket. As the wheel rotates and the basket exits the water, the salmon slide down an angled chute to be sorted or thrown back. Traditionally the fish wheel has been used as an efficient subsistence method for catching fish to feed both your dogs and your family, but a commercial market also exists.

At the time, the Japanese seafood market brought a high price for salted salmon eggs – eleven dollars per pound. Once we did the math and figured out that a full five gallon bucket sold for hundreds of dollars,

41

we adapted our strategy. I stood at the fish wheel and evaluated the fish as they came into the basket. We threw back the males and kept the females – males have hooked and longer jaws. As the females carried the eggs, we separated that out first. Next we sliced each fish down the middle – leaving the tail flesh intact to connect the halves – and scored skin-deep cuts every two inches along the fillets. Lastly we draped all the scored fish over wooden poles and hung them to dry. If the flies were buzzing we built a small fire to chase them away – thus the term "smokehouse." A few weeks later we had smoked salmon, which we bundled and stored for the winter. Much of this later became dog food. Occasionally we ate some for dinner.

After the fish wheel came the commercial king salmon season. For this we traveled by boat south of Anvik. To catch the kings, we either drifted on the river or set net in an eddy. The market wanted both fresh kings and processed fish strips. This part of the season didn't last long, but fishing for Chinook provided variety.

Moose hunting season arrived in August. Every day that summer I learned something valuable, and during this period I discovered the true importance of hunting for the Native people of Alaska. Living off the land involved more than just procuring meat.

"A moose walked in that direction," Ken said.

"How can you tell?" I said.

"Because the tracks tell a story. From where the moose came the footprints are dry. Then it went through the water here, and on the other side the footprints are wet. Don't just look straight ahead, you're missing the point. You have to scan," Ken said.

He taught me to look at everything all at once, not just what was right in front of my eyes. To hunt a moose, you had to think and look and act like a moose. Many similar lessons were passed down until I finally realized that Ken was not just harmonizing with nature; he was a part of it.

My time in Anvik showed me how to be an Alaskan. The village of 100 people had good hunting, good fishing, and great people, all of which contributed to my dream of a wonderful life, except for one thing: There was only one eligible female near my age range. I would like to live in the bush, but I wouldn't like to live in the bush alone. So I moved to Anchorage.

This Land Is My Land
October 1981

The house stood on the corner of fifteenth and Ingra Street – right in the middle of Anchorage's Fairview neighborhood. I rented a room with several University of Alaska skiers who needed a housemate. That specific intersection produced enough noise to worry even the most cautious seismologist – it was arguably the loudest spot in town. Once I got settled, my agenda listed two primary goals: to get a remote parcel staking, and to get a job.

Alaska's remote parcel staking program was organized like the hybrid offspring of a gold claim and a homestead. First you needed to obtain the plat maps from the lands office. Second came deciphering the maps to determine which parcels were being offered and which one you wanted. After that you drove up the highway to the area and hiked in – there were no roads to remote parcels – to scout out the geography and use your compass to find the brass surveyor caps already staked in the ground. If you liked the parcel, you took a pile of small tin squares and hammered your name into them. Then you waited for the staking date to arrive – no markings were allowed beforehand. I wanted a twenty acre parcel in Trapper Creek. When the staking date arrived, I grabbed my machete, a roll of pink tape, and my personalized tin squares and began hacking a path around the parcel – putting up the tape and tin squares as I went – so a state official could walk the border and verify my claim. Once I finished I hiked out, jumped in my car, and raced to the lands office in Anchorage.

The only problem with the remote parcel program was that more interested people existed than were available parcels. To guarantee yourself the land you needed to get to the lands office first – people would stake over each other with no way to tell the difference.

I walked into the office, and to my dismay the line looked congested. I twiddled my thumbs for an hour until the current pulled me to the counter. I handed over my parcel staking information, but there seemed to be a problem:

"What do you mean somebody already filed for that parcel?"

"It appears that Mr. So-and-So came in already and registered that location."

"That's not right. Mr. So-and-So didn't do the work; he must have paper staked over me."

"That's unfortunate, but I don't know what more we can do."

"Well, somebody needs to go out and check! I did all the work; this is my land!"

Sitting on the floor at the back of the room were two young professional women from Anchorage. They were last in line. Like everyone else at the lands office that day, each of them had staked out a remote parcel and come to register their claim – the parcels they wanted were in Big Lake. These two friends had really tried to get there as fast as they could, but unfortunately neither of them had been schooled in the art of using a compass. One of them blamed it on her upbringing in New Orleans, where the four cardinal directions were "uptown,", "downtown," "to the river," and "to the lake." While they waited, they overheard the sound of an irate European man, and one of them – the one from New Orleans – turned to her friend:

"You know, that guy up there is pretty cute, even when he's mad."

Later, I found out the other guy didn't read the guidelines properly and tried to claim the area set aside for the road. His land claim was denied. I got my twenty acres.

A month of filling out job applications finally showed some promise when I got called back by a company called Alaska Children's Services. On interview day I pumped up the tires on my bicycle and hooked up my entire kennel – two dogs – to combine the interview trip with a training run. We urban mushed down the sidewalks and trails across town and parked right in front of the building. The dogs took a nap, and I went inside. When I came back out I was gainfully employed.

Alaska Children's Services was – and still is – a mental health nonprofit that worked with kids who needed help. They maintained three components: a long term residential facility, a short term group home, and an emergency shelter. I initially worked as a night supervisor for the emergency shelter. That job became a good foot in the door, and later they transferred me to the group home setting. From an aspiring dog musher's point of view, this was ideal. At the group home, I worked sixty hour shifts – around the clock – then had the rest of the week free to train dogs.

The job description entailed handling one crisis after another, endlessly, and the stress could weigh you down if you weren't careful. Those of us who worked together quickly became friends. During an on-the-job training session another co-worker – a Danish guy named Knud – and I got to talking:

"Hey Martin, you should come over for dinner this weekend."

"Yeah, that might be nice, what are you cooking?"

"I'm not sure yet, but Linda and I are going to invite a few friends – it should be fun."

"Inviting anyone I know?"

"Well, I don't think you know her, but there's a family therapist who works at the office who will be there, and she is bringing a bunch of slides to show us from her trip to Nome to see the end of the Iditarod. I thought, since you did the race a couple times, that you could help with the slideshow analysis. How does that sound?"

"That sounds right up my alley," I said. "Where is she from?"

"She grew up in New Orleans. Her name is Kathy Chapoton."

After the dinner, Kathy and I became good friends. Our larger group of friends made a pact to go on weekend trips and outings together whenever we had a chance – partly because we were young, but mostly because everyone needed a way to deal with the stress of our jobs. The group soon joined a new organization in town called The Dancing Bears – a square dancing club. To me that sounded about as American as apple pie. But then again, it was an orchestrated physical activity centered around following directions, which sounded about as Swiss as a Swiss Army knife. Plus, if I ever wanted to win Kathy's heart, then I had to prove to her friends that I wasn't a wallflower. The night of the first big dance, I put on my best dancing shoes and drove to the Mountain View Rec Center. I opened the doors and found the group right as the music began:

Call up your dogs and go for a run,
Let's start dancin' and have some fun.
Bow to your partner now corner salute,
Circle to the left, go lickety-scoot.
All join hands and circle to the south,
Pour a little moonshine in your mouth.
Chase that moose, chase that squirrel,
Chase that pretty girl around the world!

Picking Up Speed
February 1982

"They laughed at the Wright brothers, and they laughed at Martin."
Kathy Chapoton

The Fur Rendezvous World Championship was a major event in dog racing long before I ever came to Alaska. Earl and Natalie Norris were two of the founders of the sprint race in 1946, and after I left their kennel I still attended as a spectator. When the 1982 race came around, I developed a method for following all three days of racing.

The first day I watched the live broadcast at home. The local television station had scattered eight or nine cameras along the trail, but the TV commentator paled in comparison to the radio announcer. To fix that, I listened to the radio while watching the television with the volume turned off.

The second day the teams began in reverse order based on the run times from day one. The slowest team started first and the fastest team started last – the most passing always happened on the second day. I stood at the start line and watched the teams take off, and then I drove out to Tudor Road and caught a glimpse of the action. When the leaders ran by me on their way back, I hopped in my car and raced to the finish line to see it up close and personal.

The third day I returned to watching the TV and listening to the radio from the comfort of my couch. The teams kept up a furious pace, even on the final day of racing for twenty-five miles per day. I paid close attention to the screen. As the top teams crossed the finish line, my eyes grew wide. A long-haired blonde dog in George Attla's team was trotting, but this was no ordinary trot. Normally when a dog trots you see a diagonal displacement with one foot always on the ground, but all four of this dog's legs were completely off the ground at times – it was a flying trot! I ran up to the TV to get a closer look and saw that a good number of the dogs were trotting airborne at incredible speeds. *These dogs are going to win the Iditarod.*

It was an epiphany. Those dogs could maintain top end speed but switch their gaits from a lope to a flying trot. I couldn't imagine a more efficient manner of canine locomotion. The Alaskan Husky breed included both the slower trotting Iditarod Huskies and these multi-gaited "Hounds" (their bloodlines did not have much true hound in them at the time, although that would change in later years). If I could combine the two successfully, then it meant the beginning of a new Iditarod Era. Why wear woolen knickers and ride wooden planks when I could wear a spandex suit and ride composite carbon skis, I thought. Right then and there I changed my approach.

I needed to introduce the swiftest bloodlines into my kennel. These were the same bloodlines that noted sprint mushers like Gareth Wright, George Attla, Roxy and Charlie Champaine, and others had spent decades perfecting. Over time, I introduced myself to several of them and offered to raise puppies. An up and coming sprint racer named Jim Welch, author of *The Speed Mushing Manual*, eventually proved to be a huge help toward my goal. We lived in the same neighborhood – Eagle River.

For long distance racing I didn't need the absolute fastest dogs, and clearly Jim didn't want or need the geared down dogs for sprint racing, so we invented a mutually beneficial system. I had more space at my kennel so would raise a litter of his puppies to a certain age, and then when we split the litter he got the fastest two or three, and I kept the rest. This allowed me to bring in the desired gene pool.

As time went on, other mushers got word of my plans. Many of them wasted no time in openly ridiculing my efforts. "Those sprint dogs have bad feet…those sprint dogs don't have an appetite…those dogs aren't tough…those are fair-weather dogs…they don't have the endurance to run the Iditarod." I heard it all, but one thought kept creeping back: I had never seen anybody try it. The late, great Carl Huntington had been both a sprint and distance champion, but that was before racing became highly specialized. Most of my naysayers probably believed I was as much of a fad as the guy who raced Poodles. I believed I was about to set a trend. Either way, I only knew one way to find out. If it worked, then all the naysayers would miss the boat genetically and need years to catch up. That risk I was willing to take.

HOOKING UP
MY HOUNDS,
CLEAN AND
ZABOO IN LEAD

BACK TO
THREE-DOG RACES

The Free Market
April 1982

As my kennel slowly but surely began to grow, the deliberately increased numbers of dogs made it clear that the flashy Ford Elite was no longer the ideal dog transportation vehicle – I needed a dog truck.

I put an ad in the local Anchorage newspaper:

"1976 Two-Toned Brown Ford Elite. Bicentennial Edition. V8. Leather Interior. $1500."

Nobody had to know that I intended to sell the car for the same price I bought it. Several days later I heard a knock at the front door:

"Hi, I'm here about the car that's for sale," he said.

"Great, yeah, it's right out here, let me show you," I said.

We went outside and walked around the vehicle. I pointed out all of the modern amenities it included – from the steering wheel grip to the eight-track player. Within minutes I had hooked my prospective buyer, and he wanted the car:

"It's a great car. I would love to take it off your hands. How much are you asking?"

"The price is $1500, firm."

"You drive a hard bargain," he said, "Can I give you a down payment of $500?"

"That might work. When can you bring me the rest?"

"I get paid next week," he said, "I will pay you the outstanding balance then."

"It looks like we have a deal. Let's shake on it," I said.

"Wonderful. Here is the $500 down."

"And here are the keys."

"I almost forgot. I need the title to legally drive it around town, do you have that?"

"Sure do," I said, "It's in the glove compartment."

"Perfect, I'll see you next week," he said, as he drove away.

"See you then, have a good day," I said.

Rookie mistake. Of course I never got the $1000 that he owed me. He had immediately recognized my inexperience in the car sales department, and when it came time to make his move, he didn't hesitate. He took me for a fool. There was no paper trail to our agreement and he held the title. The Ford Elite had been swindled. I still ended up using the money for a dog truck, albeit not as nice a dog truck as I had envisioned. I even spotted the car out and about Anchorage a few times and tried to chase it down, but I never caught up with him. Some things were best learned by trial and error.

The Premarital Trial
Summer 1983

"Do you think we have enough space?" Kathy said.

"Yeah, I think it should be fine," I said.

My eighteen foot flat-bottom aluminum river boat didn't look like much, but it did have a forty-five horsepower outboard motor. In front of the motor stood a canopy-covered mosquito tent that I built to maintain sanity while traveling down the Yukon River. We filled the rest of the space with a few bags of clothes, gear, food, and the six dogs – Kathy's labrador and my five sled dogs. At Nenana we pushed the boat into the water, jumped in, and waved goodbye to civilization.

By the summer of 1983, Kathy and I were engaged. Before setting the wedding date, we took off work and embarked on a six-week long riverboat trip. Our plan was to venture down the Tanana River to the confluence of the Yukon and head downriver as far as Anvik, then turn around and head back. It felt like an easy way to leave our worries behind and really get to know each other. I had lived on the Yukon, and Kathy had been overnight camping four times in her life – what could go wrong? We called it "The Premarital Trial."

We didn't see another human being for the first three days. Part of the reason might have been the mosquitoes. When traveling down any river in Alaska during the summer, there are two forces you have to consider: the water current, and the mosquitoes. Out there, we didn't worry about being bitten; we worried about being swallowed alive by the monster that mosquitoes become when they cluster together a million at a time. Whenever Nature called, we answered, but that meant our skin was exposed – the signal for the bloodsuckers to swarm in like a cloud and turn the boat black. Sometimes I steered the boat out into the center of the miles-wide vastness and turned the motor off – we drifted powerless and drank tea and talked for hours at a time. Very few mosquitoes possess enough strength to reach the middle of the river.

Whenever we found freshwater inlets, we veered to where the clear inlet water collided with the murky Yukon River water – an ideal spot for fishing. The fish – mostly Arctic char and grayling – were so plentiful that once the lures hit the water we directed them towards the bigger fish and away from the smaller ones. At mealtimes we filled a bucket halfway and cooked it up for the dogs while simultaneously fishing for our own food. Later, the dogs became so plump that we had to steer into sloughs and catch pike – a less oily fish – because the char and grayling tasted too rich and the dogs refused to eat them. Our supplies included several bags of dog kibble, but we never needed them.

Every night we pulled ashore to make camp. We let the dogs run loose then set up the tent. It was summer, so the days were long and the nights were short. If it looked dark out, we stayed in our sleeping bags. In the mornings – after breakfast – we repacked everything, then rounded up the canine crewmembers before shoving off.

An incident arose one morning when one of the dogs returned after an obvious porcupine encounter. Upon closer inspection we determined that the quills filled not only his mouth but went down into his throat. His justifiably agitated behavior made it impossible to just reach in and grab the quills – we had to innovate. I dipped into the maritime medicine cabinet and found several minibar-sized bottles of liquor. Once the whiskey anesthetic calmed him down, I carefully plucked out every last one of the sharp offenders. He was back to normal within a few days.

The day before our arrival we encountered another boat and received the news that a search party was underway - a boy had fallen overboard. It was Ken Chase's son. Everyone with a boat on that section of the river was looking for him, and we immediately joined in the efforts. It was a tragic situation.

The next day we arrived in Anvik – the downriver trip had taken only a week. I introduced Kathy to Ken, and then we offered him a hand in getting the fish camp up and running. We ended up living at the camp and putting up another fish wheel – running it just like I had during my summer there. When that was done we drifted for king salmon. While we were preparing for the return trip, somebody discovered the body of the drowned boy. We stayed for the funeral, then left right afterwards. On our way out, Ken gave me three puppies as a parting gift.

Now we had nine dogs. Our journey upriver quickly became overwhelming. The power needed to fight the current proved to be a mighty foe for our humble motor. We could barely push the current. Landmarks became our baby steps. One day we started with a distinct set of rock formations to our left; I gassed the motor at full throttle for a few hours; when we looked to the left again the rock formation was still there – we were going nowhere. It might as well have been a treadmill. I began to steer back and forth all the way across the river to find slivers of slower water that we could creep forward against. When that started showing signs of progress, the motor began sputtering. Every time that happened we aborted the mission and dashed for shore to regroup and try again. It took several days before we accepted that the "Love Boat" would never make it all the way back to Nenana. Frustrated, we turned up a slough that took us to Manley Hot Springs – more than 200 miles by road away from our intended destination. Within two miles the slough felt like a hot bathtub, and lush green grass lined the riverbank – it was an oasis. We pulled into Manley and tied off the boat. I made a phone call to our friend Knud and asked him if he could do us the enormous favor of driving 500 miles, picking up our boat trailer, and coming out to get us. He obliged.

Knud showed up twelve hours later. We hooked up the boat to the trailer, boxed all the dogs, and started driving back to Anchorage. Kathy and I had just been through six straight weeks of challenges. The trip had been pleasant and stressful at the same time. We had survived as a team. Like everywhere else in life, the highs and lows were stacked very closely together. When we got home, the first thing we did was set the wedding date. Well, maybe the second thing. The first thing we did was take a bath.

JUST LIKE THE
AFRICAN QUEEN

OLDING A GRAYLING

CATCHING DIN

STANDING ATOP
FISH WHEEL.

FISH WHEELS
ON THE YUKON

PULLING IN
THE GILLNET

HANGING OUT
AT FISH CAMP

KEN CHASE

WEDDING INVITATION
PHOTO, TAKEN
IN ANVIK

KEN CHASE

Getting Hitched
August 1983

"Rise and shine! Everybody up – it's wedding day!" she said.

"Mom, it's only six-thirty, we are trying to sleep!" I said, still under the covers.

Refusing to listen to her baby boy, my mother stomped around the house and rang a giant Swiss cowbell. Swinging it by its ornate and multi-colored collar, she forced every last person out of bed. On the side of the bell were engraved our names and wedding date: Kathy Chapoton & Martin Buser, August 27, 1983.

We lived at the end of Eagle River Road in a small house we bought with our friends Knud and Linda. Overnight in one of the two bathtubs, Knud had marinated a lamb in red wine and spices. In the morning – just before the showering swarms descended – we evacuated the lamb outside to roast on an open spit.

Upon inspecting the backyard we ran into a problem. The little bridge that provided access over the creek appeared to be unstable – the wood felt rotten. On the other side of the water sat the intended location of our noon wedding. The hour hand on my watch pointed to the eight. Only four hours remained until the guests showed up, and there weren't enough hip waders to get everyone across. Knud and I started building a new bridge – we finished at 11:30. I had thirty minutes to get ready.

I showered, put on my suit, headed back outside, and walked over the new bridge to my designated spot. Waiting in anticipation, I took it all in. Fully-bloomed fireweed blanketed the ground. A small gathering of friends sat in a couple rows of chairs – several of them had flown from Europe to attend. The sun stood high, and by all accounts it was a glorious day. Having setup an impromptu stage, the square dance band began playing *Here Comes the Bride*.

There she was. My soon-to-be-bride floated down the aisle wearing a simple, little-house-on-the-prairie style wedding dress that Knud's wife Linda handmade. Kathy looked radiant.

The pastor – John Gavin, the executive director of Alaska Children's Services – officiated the vows:

"Martin Buser, do you take Kathy Chapoton to be your lawfully wedded wife?"

"I do."

"Kathy Chapoton, do you take Martin Buser to be your lawfully wedded husband?"

"I do."

After a fair bit of dancing at the reception, the time came to throw the bouquet. Instead of the traditional flowers, Kathy held a decorated Alaskan cabbage. She turned her back to the crowd and launched it skyward. As it came down, our friend ShooShoo Salasky jumped up, snatched it from the air, and took a bite. Then I swept Kathy off her feet and whisked her away to a far distant land – the Hotel Sheraton in downtown Anchorage.

Our friends had planned a multi-stage you-don't-know-what-you-are-doing-but-be-ready-for-anything sort of a trip as our honeymoon. At each stage of travel we found a brown envelope that told us where to go next. The first night's clue told us to bring our rain gear and meet our friend Phyllis in the hotel parking lot the following day, just after breakfast.

In the morning we took the elevator down and found Phyllis standing next to the "Love Boat" – the same riverboat that we had traveled with on the Yukon River – hitched to a trailer with instructions to head south along the Seward Highway as it wraps around the Turnagain Arm and stop at the Girdwood gas station.

We searched the gas station until we found another envelope. The instructions inside told us to load the boat onto the Alaska Railroad and ride the train through the two and a half mile long Whittier Tunnel – the longest in North America. On the other side we launched the craft into the ocean.

Our clues sent us to Pigot Bay with orders to camp for a few nights under the roof of the A-frame forest service cabin located there just above the rocky shoreline. The view from the porch could not be more magnificent – the cabin sat nestled back with a view out into the Prince William Sound and was surrounded by steep mountains on three sides.

The first day we frolicked about in the fjords, spending hours picking wild berries. Then we cruised around the sound before returning to the cabin for the night. We perused the cabin log – always a good read – with plans of writing our own entry, but as we read through the most recent records they all told of a bear hanging around. Not thinking much of it, as bears are common in Alaska, I started to look out of the cabin windows and noticed something worrisome – the windows had scratch marks all over them.

As we laid out the bedding on a bunk so we could retire for the night, a brown bear ambled up to the front porch of the cabin and helped himself to the cooler that held our diligently collected berries. I found it entertaining to have a four-legged visitor, and I sat back and observed his peculiar behavior. The bruin finished off his fruity snack by sinking his teeth into our cans of Hamm's Beer – delivered direct "from the land of sky blue waters," of course.

Once refreshed, he moseyed on over to our boat. We heard clanging and banging as he tossed our gear around and devoured the salmon heads we had packed for fish bait. Kathy openly declared her anxiety, but it still had not occurred to me that we might be next on the menu.

Then the bear turned around. With his appetizer round complete, his nose led him back to the cabin – from our perspective it looked like we were slated to be the main course – and he began to claw against the walls and windows while grunting.

"Do something! Don't you have a gun along?" Kathy said.

"Yes dear, but the gun is in the boat, do you want me to go and get it?" I said.

In the midst of our first marital argument the beast ripped off some of the wood trim as he tried to get to the sweet Louisiana treat inside. That ended our bickering – we flew up the ladder leading into the loft of the sixteen foot tall cabin, slamming the little trap door shut and holding each other in a tight embrace.

We thought we would be safe up there, should the bear actually come inside and try to have a nibble. To survey the situation, we leaned over and peeked out of the small triangular window at the top. As we pressed our faces against the flexible plexiglass pane, a big nose rose up and met ours from the outside. We froze as the moisture from both the behemoth's and our exhalations condensed on opposite sides of the now slowly fogging up window. The bear stood on his hind legs, staring straight into our eyes. The height of the window meant he was a good ten feet tall, but at that moment we believed him to be greater than thirty, and certainly taller than Sasquatch.

I recommended – with emphasis – that Kathy make as much noise as she could while I banged together whatever we had to scare the animal off. She closed her eyes, put a finger in each ear, and screamed and yelled at the top of her formidable lung capacity.

That did the trick. The bear grimaced from the impact of the shrill sound and retreated back to the boat for one more helping of dessert. Then he wandered off into the woods. We never saw him again.

Needless to say that night did not turn out as romantic as one might have thought. In the morning we assessed the damage – all the berries, beer, and fish had been taken. Most of our gear lay strewn about the beach, except for the gun, which leaned untouched against the steering console. *How considerate.*

"What do you want to do?" I asked my bride.

"What do I want to do? Are you kidding? We are not staying here another night – no way no how! I'm not about to be featured in the Anchorage newspapers under the headline 'Honeymoon Couple Eaten By Hungry Grizzly!'"

Fair enough. We fired up the boat, said goodbye to the brown envelopes and the planned honeymoon, and we haven't taken instructions from anybody since.

THE MOMENT
OF TRUTH

WITH OUR SWISS WEDDING BELL

SQUARE DANCING

NEWLYWEDS

THE BEGINNING OF
OUR SCAVENGER HU

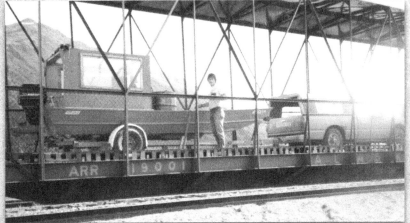

ON THE TRAIN
TO WHITTIER

THE CABIN
AT PIGOT BAY

What It Takes
March 1985

In March of 1985, I still didn't have enough dogs to run the Iditarod. The the morning that the race began we – Kathy and I, along with our friends Art and Bonnie Church – hooked up four small dog teams and mushed en masse up the Susitna River, then overland to the foothills of Mount Susitna. We pulled off the trail, assembled two tents, and built a fire. Our camp sat within sight of the Iditarod Trail – we wanted front row seats to the first day of the race.

That night while shivering around the campfire we noticed our dogs' ears perk up. We glanced at the trail to see a powerful twenty dog team glide past like a freight train. This was no ordinary group – they passed us swiftly, silently, and without slowing down. It was Susan Butcher. Several minutes later the next team ran by, followed by another team a few minutes after that. Eventually the entire field came streaming through; we stayed awake all night watching. Then we packed up and mushed home.

When we got back we heard the news that Susan scratched. Less than three miles from where she passed us, her team encountered a moose. The moose turned aggressive, stomped the sled to pieces, and attacked the dogs. There was nothing Susan could do; she had a twenty minute jump on the next team – Dewey Halverson – and didn't have her gun. When Dewey finally caught up he shot the moose, but it was too late. Two dogs had been killed and several more were severely injured;

was an absolute worst-case scenario.

The race continued without her. At Rainy Pass a storm froze the action for two days. The teams battled back and forth all the way to the Bering Sea Coast, where a forty mile per hour windstorm froze the race again. Libby Riddles got sick of waiting and took off first for Koyuk – challenging not only the storm but lingering stereotypes. She made it across the Norton Sound holding a six-hour lead.

At the same time, I drove north towards Fairbanks. On a mission to pick up a few more foundation dogs for my growing kennel, I spent a couple of nights at Charlie Champaine's house in Salcha. We sat around chatting for a bit – me, Charlie, Roxy Wright, David Monson, and Susan Butcher – until the crackle on the radio yelled that it was time for the daily Iditarod update. Charlie twisted the volume dial louder, and we all listened in:

"Breaking news… breaking news… Libby Riddles has just won the Iditarod," the announcer said.

Dead silence. We stood frozen – even the inanimate objects tried to keep quiet.

Everything changed in that instant. I saw it in Susan's face. For several years running, common knowledge had dictated that Susan Butcher would become the first woman to win the Iditarod. Her race record already included two second-place finishes and four top-five finishes. Everybody believed it was only a matter of time – then Libby Riddles came along and created her own history.

Susan suffered two tragedies – losing her dogs to the moose, and losing the race to Libby Riddles. In Susan's psyche, competition was always around. Normally she tackled her competitors head-on, but in this case she could only sit back and absorb the blow. Most of the drive that can make a person successful happens months away from the action, and right then and there Susan Butcher knew her only option: to come back with a vengeance and win three bloody Iditarods in a row.

The next morning Susan started training for the 1986 Iditarod.

"Can I hop in your sled?" I said.

"Sure, you can sit in the sled bag," Susan said.

That eight-dog team only took us thirty miles, but they radiated professionalism. I sat in the sled bag, not saying a word, and Susan stood on the runners, barely saying anything. It was eye-opening – I saw firsthand what kind of team it takes to win. The dogs pulled continuously at ten miles per hour; they turned left after a whispered "haw"; they slowed down or sped up on command. Susan's dogs readily, willingly, happily, and ably did whatever she asked of them. From that moment forward, every training run I took my dogs on I tried to emulate something similar.

Susan had helped me tremendously, but she didn't realize it at the time. To her, I was a nobody; I wasn't a threat; I was just the guy who had run Siberians in the Iditarod.

Back In The Game
The 1986 Iditarod

Five years of planning, working, and building a kennel culminated with my entry into the 1986 Iditarod. For the past six months I had made preparations, scooped manure, harnessed dogs, unharnessed dogs, worried over which dogs would make the team, and gone on endless numbers of training runs. My first attempt with my own team, with dogs that I raised and trained personally, loomed only a few days away.

I drew the sixth starting position during the pre-race banquet at the glass-walled Egan Convention Center in downtown Anchorage. The quickest team to Eagle River received a free entry into the next year's race, and I planned on starting fast. Fewer teams to pass on the way there meant a reduced possibility of time-slowing tangles. I liked the idea of starting near the front; certainly I preferred it more than the food served at the banquet.

The night before the race, some friends and I went over my checklist: Dog food? Check. Headlamp? Check. Parka? Check. Harnesses? Check. Bunny boots? Check. New sled? Check. Sled bag? No check. Sled bag? *No check.* Twelve hours before the big day and I didn't have a sled bag. Together we scrambled to pull out fabric, make measurements, cut the fabric into pieces, and sew the pieces into shape. Around midnight, my friends ordered me to get some sleep. ShooShoo Salasky took control and completed the project at three in the morning; two hours later we packed the truck and drove to the start line.

Now it all came down to me, my sixteen dogs, and a hopefully unbreakable toboggan sled. *Would my theory on breeding sprint dogs with distance dogs ring true?* I mushed through town and across the foothills to Eagle River. The transfer to the restart in Wasilla occurred without incident. The trail then ran along the Knik flats to Knik Lake where it turned westward toward the great beyond.

Within twenty miles, the high flow rate of adrenaline through my veins distracted me as we shot past a turn and barked down the wrong trail. I was joined briefly by Dewey Halverson and Don Honea, who quickly turned their teams around after realizing their mistake. I recognized the detour and decided to use the isolated offshoot as my first three-hour camping spot. The dogs ate well and curled up for a nap; I tried to do the same by lying on top of my new sled bag, but the first day jitters prevented any shuteye.

Now back on the main trail, my headlight cut through the moonless night, and I recognized two friends from Chugiak. I pulled up to their camp for a quick hello. They offered me a home-baked batch of chocolate chip cookies; I accepted, and then continued on.

En route to Flat Horn Lake one of my lead dogs, Spider, remembered the way to his former home with musher Sue Firmin. We briefly debated the merits of paying his buddies a visit but concluded against it. Maybe after the race, I told him.

The dogs sensed the tangible trail excitement and ran too fast, so I stood on the brake to slow them down to a trot. It worked, but they still pulled hard enough that we shot a snowy rooster tail behind the sled all the way to Skwentna.

I declared my mandatory twenty-four hour break when I arrived at Finger Lake. It was common practice to declare this long layover at every checkpoint; whether the musher decided to stay the duration or leave early and declare again down the trail was totally up to them. Weather changes and equipment problems contributed to most plan deviations. The combination of the first day rush and trying to stay calm had tired me out – I completed my full layover before leaving.

My dogs and I then crawled up Rainy Pass and dropped down the other side of the Alaska Range. I didn't blink as we slid across avalanche shoots, bounced over rock gardens, and barely maintained control until the next checkpoint at Rohn. When I signed in I saw that most of the top teams had taken their twenty-four hour break here; I sat only a few hours behind the frontrunners' pace. *I'm exactly where I want to be.*

After a brief stay at Rohn, we headed out into the dark night to chase the leaders. The bare ground made for rough traveling. Every step the dogs took kicked up more and more dust. Soon the dirty cloud swallowed the front half of my team. Only the back six dogs stayed visible. Sliding across the snowless ground on a suspension-less dogsled provided an opportunity to gauge our speed based on how jarring the ride felt, and it felt like we were speeding up. *Ain't no stoppin' us now…*

Our velocity kept increasing, and suddenly we turned off-trail. The front half of my team had clearly just decided to have the run of their lives. While trying not to fall off the feral rollercoaster, I noticed buffalo tracks. Branches whipped by in the blackness. I heard the handlebar wood crunch under my tightening grip – few things in life can provide as much focus as unexpectedly chasing a herd of buffalo. My main objectives became keeping hold of the dogs and getting out of this alive.

A mile later we came to a stop. The cloud dissipated, and I got my first look at the damage – all the dogs were wagging their tails. They looked back at me – panting, almost smiling – as if to say "Hey, boss, we almost caught them!" I shook my head in humorous disgust and turned the team around. With some effort we found the trail again.

I was back on track when my spotlight landed on the figure of somebody walking towards me. Hallucinations never showed up this early so I stopped the team.

"Who goes there?" I called out.

"It's Bill Cowhart. I've lost my team and am walking back to Rohn to fetch an airplane," he said.

Bill had crashed somewhere up ahead and planned on walking the nine miles back to Rohn. He wanted to hire a pilot to take him out at daybreak to search for his team. The dogs weren't his; they were Herbie "The Shishmaref Cannonball" Nayokpuk's. Herbie had gotten sick before the race, and as a son-in-law, Bill had inherited the chance to drive them to Nome. But not everybody was qualified to ride a rocketship:

"Why don't you hop on and we go look for them together? They have to be ahead of us," I said.

"No, I think the best plan is for me to walk back to the checkpoint," Bill said.

"Okay, well if I find them I will fire my gun into the air three times," I said.

We parted. Shortly thereafter I encountered his tangled team. I parked my team and secured his quickly to a tree. I walked up the trail a ways and – to the dislike of about thirty dogs – fired my gun into the air. Several minutes went by. I walked out and fired my gun a second time. No response. *How could he not hear that?*

With no sign of Bill, I untangled his team and began to tie them safely to trees along the trail so passing teams would not be impeded. My dog, Angel, came into heat at that exact moment, and within seconds one of Bill's dogs took the hint. While they stood locked together, another team came ripping up the trail. It was Rune Hesthammer – he had no choice but to wait. I fired my gun one last time, and as the echo faded, now Angel and one of my own males decided to breed. The waiting game continued.

After the race, Herbie Nayokpuk found out about the accidental breeding and wanted to split the litter. I explained the double-misbreeding situation and told him the paternity test had come back inconclusive. For the rest of our friendship, every time we ran into each other he would say "You owe me dogs from that breeding." It became an ongoing joke. I never determined the father.

Once the dogs separated, Rune and I took off in tandem. We arrived at the notorious glacier; the sapphire-blue ice slanted at a sixty-degree angle. It looked like half a mile to get up and across. I parked my team and helped Rune get going, then followed after.

My dogs clawed steadily over the glacier as I tried to keep the sled from tumbling down the slippery incline. We made it about halfway when my headlamp started to go out like a dimmer switch – I couldn't see much. I balanced on the brake and began digging for my spare. The sled slipped ever so slightly. If the brake failed me, we would all slide to certain destruction, so I scrapped the search for the spare and grabbed a pack of batteries. I swapped them out and clicked on my recharged beam. *Let's get out of here.*

I scraped along and passed a few teams. At midnight I pulled over for a break and was soon joined by two other mushers – Dave Scheer and Dan McEachen. We worked together and quickly built a fire to warm up and dry out our sweat-soaked clothes. After a bite to eat and a chat, we all crawled into our sleeping bags and tried, in vain, to keep warm.

At daybreak we got up and helped Dave work on his sled – one of the runners had completely sheared off. It would be a long way for him to Nikolai. Then I repacked my sled and attached the tuglines to my dogs' harnesses. As I bent down to pull the snow hook, something strange caught my attention, and I studied the team one more time. My stomach dropped. I took a deep breath and recounted the number of dogs – Highway was missing.

I felt miserable. My imagination ran amok with thoughts of Highway being lost forever or worse yet, being torn apart by wolves. Guaranteed disqualification hovered unless we reunited. No options remained except finding him. I bedded down the dogs again and secured them in the woods. Next I emptied the sled, detached it from the main line, hooked up a three-dog team, and commenced the search party.

We headed backwards down the trail for a few miles but didn't come across any clues. I turned the team around, and we ran past the sleeping part of my team. Several miles up we stopped at Farewell Lake Lodge and found somebody with a working phone. I called the next checkpoint – Nikolai – and asked the race officials there to send out a plane to look for my lost dog. If they spotted him, then I would know which direction to travel. Deep down I understood that locating a brown dog within 300,000 acres of brown ground gave no better odds than finding a needle in a haystack.

As I sat at Farewell Lake and contemplated my next move, another dog team pulled up. Excited, I ran out and asked if they had seen a loose dog. The musher appeared incoherent and could barely stand on his own two feet – it was Bill Cowhart. He looked terrible; blood ran down his face. At some point after I had found and secured his team, another musher – Dave Olesen – helped him get going again, but then Bill ran into a tree and knocked himself out. From the looks of it he had almost lost an eye.

"Are you going to be okay, Bill?" I said.

"I'll be fine. No matter what, I'm going to go on and get to Nome," he said.

I left with my three dogs and continued the search. We encountered a passing team, and they reported having seen a loose dog about two miles down the trail. When we got there, sure enough, there stood the somewhat-bewildered Highway. Finally, some good news. I hooked him up then we mushed over and reconnected with my resting team.

Let's try this one more time. I roused the dogs, reattached the tuglines, and counted them. With every dog accounted for, I pulled the snow hook – our first real progress in seventeen hours.

We made it to the lodge for a second time. Bill Cowhart was still there, and he had regained some strength but looked a little shaky. Dave Olesen and I decided to sandwich him between us and travel as a threesome across the Farewell Burn in case Bill's condition worsened. By now our dogs had rested for almost an entire day, and their speed showed it. We bounced over the endless miles of moguls and bare ground like dirty ping pong balls on a washboard.

I welcomed the sight of Nikolai. Getting here meant the worst of the trail had already been tackled. My pace lagged well behind the front pack but my spirits were high. After a hot shower, good food, and good sleep, I left in pursuit of the leaders. I knew the chances of catching them were low, but I stayed positive.

On the hills outside of Takotna I looked back – something I don't do often – and marveled at an expansive view of the Alaska Range, Denali, and the Kuskokwim Valley. I felt humbled by both the immensity of Alaska and the traditional manner with which I traveled through it.

About fifteen miles before Ophir I noticed one of my dogs – Russell – had stopped pulling. I wondered whether something was wrong, as he normally kept his tugline tight. After I pulled into the checkpoint, most of the dogs slept, but Russell just lay there and didn't curl up into a doughnut like normal, so I called the veterinarian over to check on him. The vet listened to his lungs and determined that he had pneumonia. He also suspected that Russell might not be the only case, and cautioned that several of my other dogs might border on the same condition.

I asked the vet what to do, and he told me the best medicine was rest, rest, and more rest. That's what I gave them, in concert with lots of penicillin and straw. After what amounted to our third daylong rest, twenty-five hours in total, the dogs recovered and looked back to normal. The vet gave them the all-clear, and we prepared to hit the trail. I buried any ideas of making money on this trip to Nome; it's difficult to do that from sixty-fourth position. My focus turned to two things: getting to Nome, and keeping the dogs healthy. Careful traveling became my marching orders.

At the halfway checkpoint of Sulatna Crossing – the coldest place in all of Alaska – the thermometer read minus sixty-two degrees Fahrenheit. And there was a breeze.

When it's that cold, everything gets soaked with misery. As you exhale, every single moisture particle freezes to your face, which builds your own personal frost layer. No matter how good your gear, no matter how good your equipment, nothing keeps you warm. You are forced to work. By working in arctic gear, you sweat and create more moisture. Within five or six minutes of working, you get hot and start to fear overheating, because all of the sweat that you create will turn into more ice. If you work too hard the ice can turn you into a popsicle, but if you don't work hard enough you will keep getting cold. You have to find a good balance of working a little bit to keep your blood circulating and your ambient temperature warm. You tend to work a few minutes and then stand on the runners to catch your breath, but not for too long or you will freeze in place. You strip off layers while you work, and put them back on while you rest. At forty below you can throw boiling water into the air and it won't hit the ground as water. At sixty-two below the water barely gets out of the cup. That's what you are dealing with. It's a fine line, and if you aren't careful you can freeze to death.

We continued on to the mighty Yukon River and the checkpoint of Ruby. From there, sandbars and glare ice challenged us for 170 disorienting miles, but we persisted. At Kaltag, several teams' rhythms merged for a break. Without mishap we traversed the ninety miles to the Bering Sea Coast.

In Unalakleet I experienced a nice tradition. Local residents volunteered to house a musher, even if only for a few hours. When I arrived, the checker notified my host family and gave me directions to their house. I stayed at a place called Happy Valley with the Haugen family. The dogs enjoyed their long rest in the warm midday sun, sheltered from the wind by "Haugeybear's" garage, while I enjoyed the indoor plumbing and hot shower. We were truly in the lap of luxury. As the sun started losing some of its power, I packed the sled, hitched up the dogs, and headed out.

The trail to Shaktoolik proved barren and contained little or no snow for forty miles. The plastic on one of my runners wore down all the way to the metal, and the other runner didn't fare much better. I limped into the checkpoint in the middle of the night as strong winds blew away everything that wasn't bolted down. I bedded the dogs down on straw in the corner of a building; they quickly curled up together, taking up less space than your average dining room table. Once they were asleep I detached my sled, pulled it into the school workshop, and got to work on the necessary repairs.

Local trail intelligence dictated that finding the trail in the dark might prove impossible, so all the mushers present decided to join forces and help each other get through the wind by travelling together. At daybreak we lined up eight teams on the ice and made a go of it.

We took turns bucking the wind so that nobody burned out their lead dogs, but the further we got from Shaktoolik the more the wind subsided. The teams began to spread out over several miles. I made it to Koyuk well in front of the other seven teams – for some reason my dogs kept getting stronger and stronger. Briefly I entertained the thought of breaking into the top twenty – the money positions – but I knew I had lost too much time in the early stages of the race.

Before leaving Koyuk I lightened my load considerably to try and maximize our pace over the last couple hundred miles. On the way to Elim my mind started to play tricks on me. With the light sled and the fast pace of the dogs, I saw myself going downhill – not just in my imagination but a topographical decline in elevation. To me, our speed continued to get faster and faster, so I kept one foot pushing hard on the brake. I knew that we were running on the sea ice, but every time I glanced to my left or right, I perceived tall trees. The forest looked to be just out of the reach of my headlight. My brain argued with itself all the way to Elim, where the checkers commented on my strange steering method. As I parked the team the sun began to rise.

The Lincoln family offered me their home to use, and I took them up on it. They served me coffee and pancakes. I had stayed with the same family during my first Iditarod, and this time around we talked of things that had changed and those that stayed the same. From Elim we determined it took an estimated twenty-four hours to get to the finish line. That number inspired me, and I bid them farewell.

The trail followed the coast on the sea ice but soon headed overland and across the long, sloping hills of Walla Walla. Then it dropped down onto Golovin Bay and back on the ice to the checkpoint. I didn't plan on staying long there because just eighteen miles later at White Mountain we had a mandatory four-hour stop, but somebody invited me over for caribou stew. At that point in the race a good meal was difficult to deny.

On the way to White Mountain I passed Mike Pemberton. The brand new lodge there invited all the mushers to a steak dinner; wine was offered, but I refused on the grounds that I wanted to be awake for the last leg of the race. Reports revealed that several mushers in front of us lost the trail on the way to Safety, and some worse than others. I made a mental note to be careful.

One of the things I did to get ready for the race was prepare myself to be constantly thinking about what lay ahead and how to react. Mental alertness is of paramount importance, especially as the body becomes more tired. A wise man once told me that dog mushing is a thinking sport.

The dogs and I made it to the shelter cabin on Topkok Mountain, forty-five miles from the finish. I knew the ride from there to the sea ice would be the last rollercoaster ride of the race. After that the land leveled out all the way to Front Street.

With less than thirty miles to go I pulled out my handheld radio and turned it on:

"Musher Paul Johnson has just pulled into the Safety Roadhouse on the Iditarod Trail," he said.

That was only a few miles ahead of my position. I might have been able to catch him, but I didn't want to push the team. At the checkpoint I needed to drop two dogs: Russell, because he started limping a little after Topkok Mountain, and Jordan, because she had more important things on her mind, namely her heat cycle. Then I walked into the roadhouse, took a seat, and enjoyed a cup of coffee with the checker. As we sat there, he informed me that the trail had been changed and was now about five miles longer than advertised. In the early-morning twilight I took another sip of coffee and smiled. The extra miles didn't make any difference. We would get there for sure now.

I finished the 1986 Iditarod in twenty-fifth place, with a time of fifteen days, zero hours, fifty-three minutes, and fifty-six seconds. The six dogs that finished with me were Angel, Highway, Toby, Bruiser, Squeaky, and Bontero. The veterinarians selected me as the runner-up for the Leonard Seppala Humanitarian Award – the annual prize given to the musher who most vividly demonstrates humane treatment toward their dogs.

THE ORIGINAL
SUPPORT CREW

FROM LEFT,
KEN CHASE,
ME,
KNUD CYRA-KORSGAAF
PHYLLIS GOLDMAN,
LINDA CYRA-KORSGAAF
DOUG PATRICK,
SHOOSHOO SALASKY,
KATHY, AND
LINDA LEADY

THE FINISH LINE,
ANGEL AND BONTARC
IN LEAD

MY GOOD FRIEND
HIGHWAY

Chasing Garnie
The 1987 Iditarod

The wind blew the moist sea air inland and, when combined with all of my worries, fears, and anxieties, chilled me to the bone – downtown Anchorage could be the coldest place in the race. We parked the dog truck right on Fourth Avenue, and the chaos began. Thousands of people roamed the streets.

All the mushers recognized the importance of a downtown start and the publicity it brought to the race, but anxieties always mounted. Too many things could go wrong between here and the real trail. Outwardly, I tried not to appear nervous; Inwardly, I told myself to keep calm. Having been here a few times before made a big difference. I think I got pretty short and tense a few days before the start, but I appreciated all my friends and helpers who put up with me anyway.

We pulled the dogs out of the truck so they could be marked with dots of paint that helped to identify them as part of my team. Then we put them back in the boxes until ten minutes before my start time. One driver let his team scream and lunge for half an hour. His dogs wore their toenails down to the quick, which created a problem for the duration of the race. I didn't want that to happen.

When we harnessed the dogs I noticed something on the side of my dirty truck. An anonymous friend had scrawled the equation "32=3-2=1". Instantly I found a greater appreciation for my bib number, thirty-two. Any method to get to number one, however superstitious, gave me a boost.

During the entire training season I had set my perspective on the big picture and stayed positive; surely all the bad luck of past years had been used up by now, the beginning of the 1987 Iditarod. As I stood on the brake at the starting line, I heard the announcer counting down. Seconds later I pulled the hook and took off.

My eighteen dogs passed team after team, and as they ran I saw them as a single unit. Experience had taught me only to zero in on an individual dog if I detected a problem. My senses told me the dogs felt good, and my lead dogs – Stafford and Jim Cooper – reflected that.

These two dogs could not have been more different. Stafford always acted independently and reliably, and I let her run in front with minimal instruction. Jim Cooper lacked self-confidence and relied on my assurances, but we related to each other without words or physical gestures – our rapport had developed from somewhere in a different dimension. The two worked flawlessly together in front, and I didn't need a radio to tune into them.

We covered the twenty-six miles to Eagle River quickly. Again, a prize awaited the fastest team to this first checkpoint, but I purposefully disregarded it. This year my focus revolved around the finish line in Nome, and nothing else. In Wasilla I changed out of my denim blue jeans and wool shirt, and put on my real racing gear.

My handler Nicolas rode with me for the first thirty miles. The traffic conditions from Wasilla to Knik meant it was safer to pull an extra sled and musher over the multitude of road crossings. After Knik the cheering crowds subsided and Nicolas and the extra sled deliberately detached. The mindset then pivoted to just me and my dogs – alone for the first time.

Physically, we ran alone into the wilderness, but truth be told we never ventured out by ourselves. The machine we became ran on the sum of all the help, good wishes, and thoughts of family, friends, fans, and sponsors. To race otherwise would be daunting.

I chuckled as we passed my wrong turn from the year before. Good dogs. On the way to Flat Horn Lake I directed the dogs off-trail for a break. The dogs weren't tired at all yet and could probably have run another fifty miles without stopping, but that was not the goal.

The art of long-distance mushing lies in knowing when to stop and rest. You don't want to run out of gas, because the walk to the next filling station is long and lonely. The basic rules are simple: stop before the dogs get tired, let them regain the energy they spent during the last stretch, and you can go on forever without slowing down. You have to set a rhythm and pace that are sustainable for a thousand miles, and it's all too easy to go faster than you are capable on the first day.

After making camp I snacked the dogs. Too much adrenaline pumped through all of us to really rest, let alone sleep, and two hours later we hit the trail again. The moon rose on the horizon and glowed almost as bright as the morning sun.

We hustled down the frozen Susitna River and up and over Rainy Pass. We shimmied down the unforgiving Dalzell Gorge into the windswept and snowless country of the Kuskokwim Valley. After slipping past the buffalo stomping grounds near Farewell Lake, we stopped for a ceremonial cup of coffee at a special place I called Highway Bend. The year before, from this exact spot, I had embarked on a seventeen-hour search for one of my steadiest pullers. This time I snacked the dogs in celebration of how smoothly the race was going and gave Highway a special pat. *What a fine dog.*

Riding on the runners across the Farewell Burn proved back-breaking, so I ran with the dogs on the bare ground. This led to sweating and getting damp, and soon I stopped the team and built a fire to dry out. Before trading the comforting fire for the runners, my innate barometer signaled a tremendous shift in humidity and atmospheric pressure. A storm was coming, I told myself. I repacked the sled, and we continued on.

 We arrived in Nikolai – one of my favorite checkpoints – under a much friendlier star than in past years. No major mishaps. I bedded down the dogs and went inside the checkpoint to eat.

I like to think that there are no checkpoints during the Iditarod, only refueling stations. The days and nights can be divided into rhythmically changing patterns of traveling, feeding, and resting. Taking care of your team is the number one job of any musher – the dogs' health and well-being are directly related to how you finish.

To this point, the dogs' enthusiasm had maintained my high energy level and prevented me from sleeping very much. I lay down for an hour nap but a few minutes before my alarm went off, I woke up and got ready to go. Fifty-seven minutes of sleep felt satisfactory.

Some of the dogs seemed to understand the importance of the mission. They hurried to reach the next hill, the next river bend, and the next stand of trees. Before long we ran through the high plains outside of Ophir – bird dog country. Flocks of ptarmigan brought out the pointer in some of my dogs, especially a male named Bruiser. With his tail straight back, his head high, and his tugline tight, he motivated the rest of the team to fly almost as fast as the scared birds.

On day six we reached the halfway point at Iditarod and took our twenty-four hour break. Any of the top twenty teams could still win, but the frontrunners' pace seemed tremendous. Dewey Halverson and Jerry Austin had gambled back at Finger Lake and now led the race. Susan Butcher lurked less than an hour behind in third, and Rick Swenson stayed within striking distance in fourth. Joe Runyan kept resting more than anybody. My team still held their speed, but nobody expected me to contend. I enjoyed that. If we maintained our rhythm to the Yukon River, I thought we might crack the top five.

The team performed well over the hills and ridges that led to Shageluk. As we slid across the low country to Anvik a feeling of nostalgia engulfed me – like I was coming home. I knew many of the people there, and upon checking in, I noticed how much some of the kids in the crowd had grown. At Ken Chase's home I ate a good meal and slept for an hour.

Leaving Anvik I knew that I needed to make up some ground. The time had come to pick up the pace, and a storm approached simultaneously. I dubbed it The Equalizer, because I predicted its path would delay the frontrunners and allow me to catch up. When I pulled out of Grayling, however, the storm mistook me for one of the front five teams and reminded me not to make plans without properly considering weather conditions. The storm grabbed hold of us, and we paid attention as it reinforced the meaning of a headwind. For the next seventy miles we clawed and dug in against the gusting gauntlet as we tried to make headway and keep from getting blown down to the mouth of the Yukon River. Two rest stops later we pulled into Eagle Island, now ten hours behind the leaders – lesson learned.

You can never expect a storm to know who your competitors are, and to hold up or hinder only their progress. A truly competitive strategy must be able to adapt for changes in weather. My plan hinged on a good run up the Yukon, and I didn't have a Plan B. This proved to be a crucial error.

I left Eagle Island only a couple minutes in front of Joe Garnie – the famous Eskimo from Teller. He wasn't happy with me. Earlier in the season my team beat his in a fifty-mile race, and now he wanted to return the favor. For the next three days we waged a friendly war against each other. The games we played could be labeled all-out competition – I snuck out on him while he slept, and then he did the same to me. We drank coffee together and joked at checkpoints, but neither of us wavered from watching the other's every move to take advantage of any weaknesses or slip-ups. The back and forth continued all the way to Nome.

Racing Joe Garnie past Unalakleet and up the Bering Sea Coast proved to be a difficult task – he had the home court advantage. At this point in the race the dogs' energy cycled through ups and downs. During the down swings I tried to stay on his heels and chase, while on the upticks I tried to ditch him with our momentary speed. I didn't gain any ground.

In Shaktoolik I needed a good rest. *But where is Garnie?* Not only did he have the home trails advantage, but he knew all the people. Somewhere in this small village Joe Garnie slept soundly while his many friends watched over me, ready to alert him should I try to leave. He held the upper hand, and it irritated me. I knew that only a bold move could turn things in my favor.

I fed the dogs the warm food that I carried all the way from Unalakleet, then immediately cooked their next meal and filled my coolers. Rather than sleeping in the checkpoint, where the balance of strategy lay in Joe's favor, I decided to leave Shaktoolik and rest at the shelter cabin sixteen miles down the trail. I paraded the team down the middle of the street, enticing every single dog in the village to bark. Once I got out of town I chuckled at the thought of sleepy Joe being shaken out of his warm bed. *Your move.*

We chased each other past Elim. On Golovin Bay I stopped, snacked my dogs, and inspected their feet. The routine stop lasted less than twenty minutes, but I saw no signs of Joe Garnie approaching. I wondered if I had finally gained some time.

Five miles later in Golovin the checker invited me inside for some fresh coffee and beans.

"Sure, I have some time," I said.

I sat near the window in the checker's house and watched my team along the incoming trail. The beans warmed on the stove as I started sipping on a cup of coffee. We began to make small talk when Joe Garnie came bounding into the checkpoint. In less than thirty seconds

92

he signed in, signed out, and blasted down the trail. I jumped up, coffee still in hand, and ran out the door:

"Sorry about the beans, I gotta go, next year maybe!" I said.

I rousted the dogs and gave chase. A few minutes later we caught up to the source of our adrenaline rush. Joe saw us coming and before we got close enough to pass he pulled his team off the trail and gave them a snack. As I went by we both burst into laughter – this was competitive racing.

At White Mountain we checked in one minute apart. After the mandatory break we raced on and traded leads several times. On the last hill before Nome, Joe ended up on the wrong ridge, which cost him some time. For the first time in three days I sat in the driver's seat, and took the opportunity to snack the dogs. When we took off again I could see his team coming up from behind. Forty miles to go.

The word "quit" did not exist in Joe Garnie's vocabulary – I kept looking over my shoulder for his next attack. In Safety I dropped my slowest dog, but before leaving I tipped my sled over and examined the runners. The plastic teetered on the edge of disintegration. I didn't have time to replace it, but if it split down the middle, I would have to. If that happened, we would certainly get passed. With twenty-two miles left I made one more adrenaline-fueled gamble.

I ran and kicked alongside the sled until we pulled onto Front Street. Soon after, both the dogs and my exhausted body crossed under the burled arch. The runner plastic looked like Swiss cheese. Joe Garnie arrived an hour later.

I finished the 1987 Iditarod in tenth place with a time of twelve days, two hours, twenty six minutes, and twenty eight seconds. The seven dogs that finished the entire race with me were Jim Cooper, Angel, Emmitt, Highway, Bruiser, Squeaky, and King.

THE ORIGINAL
DOG TRUCK,
DR. JIM LEACH,
MY ORIGINAL
VETERINARIAN,
ON RIGHT

STAFFORD AND
JIM COOPER IN LEAD,
HIGHWAY IN SWING,
NICOLAS PATTARONI
ON TAG SLED

JIM COOPER

CRACKING THE
TOP TEN,
LED BY JIM COOPER
AND ANGEL

Rocket 88
The 1988 Iditarod

My twenty dogs loped by Susan Butcher without any problem. I didn't look back as we ate up the trail and left her in our snowy dust. Too bad it was only the first day of the 1988 Iditarod.

The last twelve months went by almost as quickly as my team now ran through Anchorage. I had done my homework, and I knew that if I drove my dogs to their abilities then I would get little sleep and only see the front of the field. We passed team after team on the way to Eagle River – starting fifteenth meant not too many teams ahead of us but enough to smell up the trail. Last year we yielded the fastest time and received a check in the amount of the entry fee. This year might end up in a repeat performance, but I didn't wait around to find out.

At Settler's Bay the dogs came out of the truck after their annual four hour long dog box campout. My body shook with excitement. From the real start, fifty mushers and approximately 900 dogs set out for Nome within minutes of each other. We buzzed down the trail to Knik.

The first few hours of the race are always hectic. You wave goodbye to the big crowds lining the trail because you won't see this many people again for more than a week. All the mushers still run with big teams, and the campers mix right in with the competitors. Campers are typically adventurers and rookies whose main goal is to reach the finish line. Competitors want to win. Many intermediate levels exist between the two, and it takes a couple of days for the field to spread out. Until then incidents are common.

The chaos dwindled beyond Knik, and we started to find our rhythm. Within thirty minutes we approached another team. For some reason, the musher – Jacques Philip – either couldn't let me or didn't want me to pass. Unsure if he could hear me, I called for trail repeatedly.

The term "calling trail" refers to the action of verbally requesting the dog driver ahead to stop their team and allow you to pass. The rules state that when one team approaches within fifty feet of another team, the team behind shall have the immediate right of way upon demand – which typically manifests as the approaching driver yelling out the word "trail." The exhilaration of the first day can make that easier said than done.

I got tired of waiting and asked my dogs to make a moving pass. Jacques noticed and tried to stop his team but ran into an equipment issue. Somehow the placement of his snow hook went wrong, and the metal prongs now straddled one of his sled runners. His dogs lunged forward – strong enough to pull the sled with the hook still digging down. It's a long way to Nome with a set parking brake. Jacques tried to pull back against their efforts and free his runner, but the feat proved Herculean. As my dogs and I tried to run by, his eighteen dogs jumped into my twenty, and they formed a thirty-eight-dog ball. Teams piled up behind us with nowhere to go except the soft snow on either side. We disentangled the furry mess, and I hurried off.

My first planned stop came just after Flat Horn Lake. I commanded the team into the trees and fed them the hot meal I had carried in the sled since the restart. A short stop, some trail talk with friends camping nearby, and a nap drew us back into our desired routine. After a couple of hours, teams started dashing by, and my dogs took notice, telling me that if we didn't leave soon they would either uproot the big birch tree I had tied them to or break the gangline. I let a few more teams go by, then gave in to their demands and chased after. At least until Rabbit Lake

I wanted to keep some of those teams in front – my race plan didn't include volunteering for moose patrol.

At Rabbit Lake the dogs still screamed to go, so the checker stood on my snow hook while I retrieved my number one bag – it contained all the supplies and food needed for the next leg. Then we left. I planned to stop alone somewhere outside of the checkpoint; parking an amped up dog team with other teams constantly coming and going seemed out of the question.

We reached Skwentna before daylight, repeating the grab and go routine and camping a few miles down the trail. I still ran with twenty dogs. Every time we stopped, I inspected all eighty of their feet – no small task. I spent most of our rest periods kneeling in the snow, and I vowed only to keep this many dogs so long as the snow conditions stayed smooth.

In Finger Lake heavy snowfall prevented the trailbreakers from advancing, so I declared my twenty-four hour break in case the weather kept us in place. We ended up waiting six hours for the trail to get broken out. Before leaving I banked a few hours of sleep and let several teams lead the way.

Heading toward the highest point of the trail, the weather turned south again. Snow flurries blew about and accumulated, erasing the trail. We came around one corner and nearly ran into a line of fifteen teams stacked up behind each other. Up ahead, the trailbreakers tended to their broken down machines. They looked stuck in the soft snow.

Hundreds of world-class canine athletes don't like to sit around. Within a minute or two everyone ran around the swamped snowmachines and started breaking trail the old-fashioned way. The strongest teams slowly gravitated to the front, and soon it was left to Susan Butcher and me to set the trail. We took turns leading until the trailbreakers zipped past, but they couldn't stay in line behind each other and created a lot of options, none of which felt firm. My lead dogs grew frustrated at the slow going so I pulled them over for a mental rest. During our brief respite the other teams all went by, and I knew that when we passed them again it would be along the most physically demanding stretch of the entire race.

With a well-defined trail to follow, we embarked on the climb up Rainy Pass. The boulder strewn landscape led to quite the sled-saving theatrics, but I couldn't avoid all the obstacles. When a swooshing sound bounced off my ears I looked down and saw my left runner plastic dragging behind. One of the rock punches had completely severed one of my runners, making it impossible to travel. I opened the hood and pulled out my roadside repair kit. Fifteen minutes later we hit the trail with a brand new runner plastic. In the Iditarod you must always be prepared for surprises.

Cresting over the top of the pass it became clear that the trek down would be as slow as the crawl up. Ten teams waited in yet another line, each looking for a manageable route down the Dalzell Gorge. The river at the bottom never froze solidly. Snow slides and avalanches constantly kept big holes open, and the rushing water forever found new ways to take out ice bridges and forge new channels.

One command I implemented this year came in very handy on this section: "Easy down." After hearing these two words, the dogs slowed down, and we deftly maneuvered through the tight and dangerous passages. We slid down side hills, whipped around alder thickets, and bounced over even more rocks as we steadily closed in on the Rohn Roadhouse. We planned to take our twenty-four hour stop at this checkpoint near the south fork of the Kuskokwim River.

During the layover my time filled with feeding, foot control, and equipment checks. I also fit in a few long bouts of sleep, probably my last opportunity to do so before Nome. One of my dogs – Emmitt – had a swollen foot, so I dropped him. That left me with a nineteen-dog team, the largest in the race. Leaving Rohn, I attempted to demoralize everyone by telling them to leave enough room for me to get by with my big team. On the trail to Nikolai I backed up my words and felt like Pac-Man eating up the monsters in front of him – being passed while moving has sent many a dog musher into a deep depression.

When you have a swift team you are able to take longer breaks, at least while the faster teams are sorting themselves out from the slower ones, which mostly occurs in the first half of the race. The slower teams have to put in more moving hours on the trail to keep up, which ultimately slows them down because they are missing the crucial rest needed for a good finish. Over time they will fall behind, and then the racing really begins.

In Nikolai I dropped my female dog, Ringer. Her hamstring felt inflamed, and I always erred on the side of caution. In a few days the injury would heal, but during a race you didn't have the luxury of waiting. Eighteen dogs seemed a little small. Somehow, I managed.

Throughout the race you can drop dogs, but you cannot replace them. Some dogs get dropped because they are tired, some because they get injured, and some because they come into "season" and try to run the wrong way. There are as many reasons as there are dropped dogs. Later on, many mushers may drop a team member because they still have big teams and need to save time at every break. Checking feet and preparing food for sixteen dogs takes twice as long as for eight. You have to play the game correctly, or you will end up with too little power.

After Nikolai my trail routine continued without interruption. I journeyed through McGrath, Takotna, and Ophir without worrying whether it was day or night – they became one. Most of my stops lasted four hours.

A typical four-hour stop proceeds as follows: I command and park the team well off the trail. First, I feed the dogs either a warm meal or a thawed-out meat snack. Second, I start cooking for the next stop, having already made certain to bring more than enough food in the sled to make it to the next checkpoint. The cooking begins by collecting snow or water from a nearby stream and heating it in the cooker. Then while the water heats up I go up the team checking feet, applying ointment if necessary, and assuring any medications stay on by putting on new dog booties. After about forty-five minutes all the dogs are inspected and the water is hot and ready to be poured over the next meal. The kibble and meat and water are usually mixed together to better hydrate the dogs as they eat, but plain water can also be offered as an option. Once the chores are done I put everything back in the sled, secure the load, and jump on top to get a few minutes of sleep. Being all ready to go, I can leave whenever I want. Often I take off a few minutes after letting another team go by because I want to pass the other driver with my well rested team and make them look slow and tired.

My dogs performed well in the heat of the day – it felt warm out – and on the way to Cripple we passed both Rick Swenson and Joe Garnie resting on the side of the punchy trail. Susan Butcher only rested after she saw me taking a break. We made it to Cripple in third place.

Joe Redington – in his seventies – won the prize for reaching the halfway point first and left as the other teams started arriving. He returned not long after, claiming almost impossible conditions, and chose to wait until the trail set up better.

When the mercury drops from above freezing to below, a crust forms on the surface of the snow as any water particles turn to ice. This allows a dog team to glide smoothly over the top instead of punching through with every step. Sometimes the crust is only strong enough for the first couple teams that go over it; everyone else is out of luck.

The trail to Ruby followed an old mining road. The thermometer hovered around freezing, and the sun shined bright – a balmy day for the mushers, but not for the dogs, who preferred much colder. During a scheduled pit stop, Susan Butcher pulled alongside and caught me trying to get a tan. With the heat turned up, I hoisted anchor, and we leapfrogged her a few hours later – favor returned. My happy-go-lucky huskies moved fast, and the warm weather didn't seem to bother them.

Just before Ruby I passed Herbie Nayokpuk on the run. As I arrived into the checkpoint the local people kept yelling "Herbie! Herbie!" They appeared mildly surprised when they realized it was me. The local dog experts congratulated me and said my team looked like the best they had ever seen come into their checkpoint. That fueled my ego even though a lot of trail still remained. I didn't want to jump out in front yet, and on the way downriver Joe Redington and I switched the lead several times.

In Kaltag the temperature dropped, and the winds picked up. Susan Butcher sat an hour and a half behind me. If the current conditions held to the coast then I could widen my lead on her and pass Joe Senior at the same time. No such luck. Nine miles into the portage the trail disappeared. I caught up to Joe as he camped; blowing snow covered his dogs. The trailbreakers – behind us somewhere – had broken down again. The parts they needed were being shipped from Galena, but nobody could say how long that would take.

Along with Joe, two snowmachiners had run out of trail and camped at the same spot. The two grizzled, elderly drivers intended to go to Nome for the finish of the race, and they brought all their worldly belongings with them. Each of their machines pulled a fourteen foot long by four foot wide trailer sled, loaded to the hilt with antique rigid suitcases more properly suited for boarding a steamship. They looked like Alaska's version of the Beverly Hillbillies. Earlier in the day these two characters had gotten stuck several times in the snow drifts. The heavy load they carried made it impossible to get moving again. They had tried unloading and repacking their luggage, but could only progress a few yards at a time, so they decided to camp for the night and rethink their strategy. That's when we met up with them. The four of us sipped coffee together in their makeshift tarp shelter and contemplated what to do. Eventually, Susan joined the circle of wanderers.

The trail needed to be broken out, and if we lingered much longer then Swenson and Garnie would crash the party. We decided to combine forces through the portage – the dog teams took turns out front, and when the snowmachiners got swamped, we helped them get going again. *So much for my widening lead.*

The winds turned stronger and covered our tracks as we went. I felt like a spawning salmon swimming upstream, struggling for every inch gained against the current. Having never been in this position, I wondered how long the dogs could maintain their energy given the conditions. To lessen the mental stress, I switched lead dogs periodically – Angel and Stafford alternated with Jim Cooper and White Boy.

At the Old Woman Cabin, we found ten snowmachining spectators waiting for the Iditarod to near the village of Unalakleet. Right then, I knew we had good trail for the next forty miles, but I also recognized that we were about to enter Susan Butcher Country.

For years now, Susan had flown her team to the Bering Sea coast and trained there for a few weeks every winter. Once those dogs got into familiar territory, they gained the mental advantage of knowing the race was almost over. Instead of increasing my once sizeable lead, Susan and I made it to Unalakleet only eight minutes apart.

The Haugens again proved wonderful hosts – seeing familiar faces always feels good to the weary traveler. After a short visit, a good meal, and a changeover to a lighter sled, I raised the ante by getting out of town. My game plan included resting outside of the checkpoints in order to force Susan away from any possible prearranged help.

As I moved down the trail, I saw two sets of sled tracks in front of me. *Could Susan and Joe have pulled out ahead of me by sneaking out of town?* It appeared like one set headed toward town and the other headed away from town – maybe one of them had forgotten a mandatory item and turned around. Some years local dog drivers went to Nome and tried to stay ahead of the competitors, but I wasn't aware of any this year. My mind kicked into overdrive with the myriad possibilities for the fresh tracks.

At a place called Egavik, I figured it out. A local team must have cruised down the Iditarod trail for a twenty-mile run then turned around at the fish camp, because beyond that the dog tracks vanished. My thirteen dogs and I were leading the race. In my imagination the spruce trees behind me materialized into chasing teams.

The wind picked up again while we climbed the Blueberry Hills. Looking down from the top I realized I needed to put on one or two more layers of clothing – a ground blizzard blew in the distance. Once we got back on the coast, we got our first real taste.

The offshore wind carried variably-sized particles of ice and snow that swirled around and blasted us from every angle. Frequently I stopped and wiped both the dogs' and my own eyes clean from the accumulating ice – otherwise a frozen layer would form and shut off our vision. Above the bottom six feet of the world, the pilots were having the time of their lives with unlimited visibility and little wind to cope with. It was a clear sunny day with blue sky everywhere, except down on dog team levels.

I checked in at Shaktoolik then fed the team and walked my dog Streeper – a quarter hound – to the dog drop area. On the way in she had favored her right leg, and having helped pull me all this way, she deserved to be flown home. I gave her a special blanket and left her with several days of food. Curled up out of the wind, she went to sleep and started her recovery process. The rest of the dogs still ran strong.

My plans called for taking a longer break at the shelter cabin eighteen miles down the trail, and while preparing to head out, I noticed some of Susan's friends watching my every move. Nearby in a warm house Susan was snoozing away, about to be surprised by my early departure. She must not have talked to Joe Garnie.

Going toward the shelter cabin, we ran into the strongest winds yet. Fortunately the storm came straight at us. The dogs dug low and pulled hard in their harnesses. To reduce wind resistance, I ducked behind the handlebar. Just by poking my head above the driving bow, I brought the team almost to a stop. The dogs' noses almost touched the ground as they wedged themselves forward under some invisible object – the blowing wind. Airplanes flew overhead, marking the slow progress of the team and sympathizing with the ordeal. Finally we spotted the cabin.

The dogs deserved the rest, and the weather tempted me to take them inside, but the rules prohibited it – only in emergencies could dogs be brought into a shelter. I made use of whatever relief the little building offered and bed the dogs down behind the cabin, comforting them and telling them we only had two hundred more miles.

A couple of hours later, Susan pulled up to snack her dogs, then threw on another layer and barreled down the trail. My dogs needed more rest, and I let them sleep until nightfall before we headed out onto the sea ice of Norton Sound. Across this giant, frozen bay stood the next checkpoint of Koyuk. The winds raged, and the lights of the village were visible almost immediately, but from experience I knew not to be fooled too early.

The white expanse lasts for about forty-five miles, but the monotony can dupe your mind into believing it is twice that. The worst time to cross is at night, or worse, heading into the evening as it gets dark. Just past the shelter cabin, the combination of wind, temperature inversion, and other meteorological phenomena cause the lights of Koyuk to appear like town is only ten miles away. An hour later, they look forty miles further. Then another hour after that, they seem right in front of you again. The experience can be frustrating, in no part because the wind is typically in your face and trying to push you back to Shaktoolik. If conditions are bad enough you might stop trusting yourself, and if that happens you have to trust your dogs.

As I checked in to Koyuk, Susan Butcher checked out. I had lost some time, but I felt certain that my better rested team was moving faster than hers. I gave the dogs a short break, and then with twelve dogs still in harness, we left the checkpoint in hot pursuit. The winds refused to let up and forced us to fight our way along.

At five in the afternoon we arrived in Elim, and again Susan headed out as I parked my team. My dogs had chipped two hours off her lead in the last fifty miles. If I didn't push now, I might never catch up, so I unpacked any unnecessary gear from my sled and dropped the three weakest links – Bruiser, Nervous, and Gopher. All three stayed behind with only minor foot problems, but the time for babying dogs had ended.

I fed the dogs and shortened the gangline. Afterwards, the ham radio operator came over and handed me a piece of paper. It was a telegram from my new friend Rick Swenson:

> *In White Mountain.*
> *Fast sled, needing a fast team.*
> *Help yourself.*

I chuckled as I pocketed the telegram. "The Master" had just offered me his sprint sled.

In those days, Rick Swenson wanted to win as much or more than anybody else. If he wasn't able to, then the worst thing that could happen was that his arch nemesis, Susan Butcher, would win. It looked like this year he didn't have a shot at the title. He was willing to do whatever it took to beat Susan, and if that meant helping another musher – me – to get across the finish line first, then that was fine by him. If he couldn't do it himself, then at least a Swenson-built sled might win. By rule, two sled changes were allowed, and mushers could not accept help from any one, with one exception – other mushers.

To take advantage of the potential gift, I first had to make it to White Mountain. At six-fifty in the evening – after exactly one hour and fifty minutes of rest – I called up the dogs, and we left Elim.

The trail to White Mountain cuts across the mountains instead of following the sea ice around the long land mass that protrudes into the ocean. The tradeoff is exposure versus mileage. The overland route is much shorter, but its steepness and difficulty of terrain have earned this section a local nickname: Little McKinley.

As we climbed the coastal portage, we became vulnerable to the elements. The dogs and I had a hard time finding, let alone following, the trail. Darkness took over, and the whiteout picked up strength. The winds gusted so strong that I gagged with every breath. The dogs couldn't run five minutes without the blowing snow and ice sealing their eyelids shut. We were blind in a blender.

Regularly I stopped and reopened their eyes by scraping and breaking the ice formations that blocked their vision. Then I fought my way back to the sled and tried not to lose my balance, as well as the team. Occasionally we encountered a wooden marker that verified our heading, but soon the conditions forced me to take the leaders in my hands and walk in front while searching for signs of the trail with my headlight. After awhile, it became apparent that this way of travel was fruitless, so we hunkered in place.

I brought the dogs together in a huddle to keep each other warm. Then I tied down all the mandatory gear and emptied the sled. Intending to wait out the storm or the night, whichever gave first, I opened my down sleeping bag and crawled inside.

Lying in my bag, listening to the wind tug on my equipment, I saw my chances of winning the race drift away with the blowing snow. I also realized that a wrong move could cost me or my dogs our lives. I briefly wondered if Susan was a few miles up the trail and sitting in her bag having the same thoughts, but I knew that her dogs had covered the trail three times already this season. In all likelihood, her lead had given her an extra hour of daylight and enabled her to cross the top of Little McKinley before it got totally dark.

As my thoughts raced in my head, the wind got a hold of my sled bag and ripped it open. Welcome spin drift. Within no time, the entire inside of the sled filled with light, fine snow – Mother Nature's bean bag. I could move my limbs, put them in any given position, and they would stay there. Sleep came in short order and provided relief to my body and my mind.

Things looked a little better in the morning. The wind still blew, but visibility had returned to about the length of a dog team. *Where is my team?* The dogs were completely buried, and I worried that some might have suffocated. I grabbed the gangline near the sled and followed it into the snow. As I pulled the dogs out of their warm igloos, they stretched and shook themselves – ice had formed in their coats that could not be shaken out. I promised them a warm bed of straw in Nome.

We got going and I let the leaders pick their own way down the other side of the mountain. I still didn't know where to find the marked trail, but I knew that if we followed Golovin Bay north then everything would work itself out. Seven shelter cabins, used primarily by local reindeer herders, stood along the bay and led to the village. When I stopped briefly at one of these cabins, a media helicopter hovered overhead then landed near the team. They wanted an interview. The spinning rotors hadn't exactly helped my already windblown body, but I think I managed to form a coherent sentence or two before continuing on.

At Golovin I signed my name on the second line of the checker's sheet, which allowed me to see Susan's arrival time. She had made it through the storm, summited Little McKinley, and checked in last night at ten o'clock. Five minutes later she had moved on to White Mountain.

The emotional rollercoaster that followed surviving a storm then having my dreams dashed proved dispiriting. As I was getting myself back together, Rick Swenson pulled into Golovin. Both he and his dogs looked impressive – they had taken a nice long rest in Elim, out of the wind. We talked briefly, and then I headed out for more.

The trail immediately turned cold; I attributed this in no small part to the impossibility of erasing the ten-plus hour lead that Susan now held over me. Dejected and tired, we checked in at White Mountain.

During our mandatory four-hour stop, Rick and I swapped trail stories; the knowledge gained from being around him would make me a better and tougher contender for the next race. One more stormy night lay ahead, and I realized he would probably beat me to Nome. At least I got the satisfaction of having tried my best to win the race while it was still possible.

On the way to Safety, my lead dog Stafford fought the side winds for as long she could, but eventually gave in and let the current take the team. My young team wondered if there would ever be an end to the trail; the importance of training in similar conditions became clear to me. Then we crossed Topkok Mountain and hit the sea ice for the last time. The wind roared so strongly that whenever I stepped off the runners, the sled tumbled over and over, like tumbleweed on a prairie, with me hanging on for dear life.

During the night we recovered from an airy blast and landed only inches from a huge open lead in the ice. In my disbelief I kneeled down and dipped my hand in to taste the water. *Salty*. I promised myself to stay on a more easterly heading. There had to be land out there somewhere.

Emerging victorious from a long battle, my brave dogs pulled us into Safety. There, we learned that Rick had just left, somewhat sad to take the second place from me. The storm refused to relent and had broken the antennas needed for communication; the people that sat inside the checkpoint building had been stuck in Safety for days, unable to get to Nome. After eating a few sandwiches and drinking a couple of cups of coffee, I readied the dogs and we undertook the last twenty miles of Iditarod 1988.

Usually the adventure ends once you and your dogs cross under the burled arch. Not so this year. Apparently the stress of being married to a musher takes its own toll, especially when that spouse is nine months pregnant.

I managed to get in one good night's rest before Kathy went into labor. We rushed back to Anchorage on the next flight out of town. At the hospital, while my wife did the real work, my body sent me into involuntary naps in the fetal position on the floor. We welcomed our first child, Nikolai Chapoton Buser, at 12:31 AM on March 21, 1988 – three days after my arrival in Nome. He showed up a little early, but I always figured he was just trying to race his father to the finish line. It's just like a Buser to want to push the pace.

I finished the 1988 Iditarod in third place with a time of twelve days, four hours, twenty one minutes, and forty six seconds. The nine dogs that completed the entire race with me were Angel, Stafford, White Boy, Dagger, Neuf, Highway, Jose, King, and Jim Cooper. I was given the coveted Leonard Seppala Humanitarian Award for outstanding dog care, the check for the fastest time from Anchorage to Eagle River, and the Gold Coast Award for being the first team to Unalakleet on the Bering Sea Coast.

STAFFORD
LEADING US
TO SAFETY

ENJOYING THE
NORTHERN LIGHTS

A PROUD PAPA WITH BABY NIKOLAI

A Learning Experience
The 1989 Iditarod

I hopped out of the hot tub and toweled off – my skin glowed as red as a lobster. With my belly brimming over from a delicious meal, I went to bed and passed out like a child. We usually spent the evening before the race in Anchorage. That way, we could enjoy the hospitality of our friends Carl and Diane, as well as avoid waking up at four in the morning to make the trip to town.

My handler MacGill fed the dogs at six a.m., which gave them three hours to digest their breakfast. After a smooth start, we made the mad dash to Eagle River – I drove the front sled, MacGill drove the second sled. When we arrived at the first checkpoint, we all packed up and drove to the restart in the Matsu Valley. As we got closer, I could see that the conditions had changed.

The wind in Wasilla blew like the Bering Sea Coast on a bad day, thundering through town and carrying away all of the snow. The bare ground gave way to nearby lakes that glistened with glare ice. The official restart launched from a gravel runway. *Ready for takeoff.*

I heard the sounds of concrete scraping against my sled runners as we crossed Alaska's only major highway – with traffic blocked, of course – and literally flew over the railroad tracks on the other side like Santa Claus, but with twenty dogs instead of eight reindeer. The aerial surprises probably catapulted most of the second- – sled drivers, but MacGill did 500 pushups a day, and maintained an iron grip. Nothing could shake him. As if that wasn't enough excitement, we then shot onto Lake Lucille, where a fifty mile per hour wind kept flipping spectators off their feet and blowing dog teams in every direction except Nome. Miraculously, we managed to get to the other side of the lake without any major problems, only to find ourselves on an unmarked trail heading towards anywhere – no markers were visible for as far as I, or any of the other mushers, could see.

What happened next was a free-for-all. Several teams snaked through the labyrinth of subdivisions and driveways in search of the main route, which paralleled the Knik Goose Bay road. Once reconnected, the trail turned into one long stretch of polished ice on a slanted sidehill, making it hard to steer the sleds, let alone control a dog team. The weather threw all of the worst conditions at us within the first hours of the race; up to this point the ride had been nothing but white knuckles.

Later we found out that a local resident, mad at the Iditarod over some issue, had removed all of the wooden markers between Wasilla and Knik. Certainly the plan was a success, since having fifty dog teams running circles around the neighborhood was far more efficient than letting them follow an already established path that paralleled the main thoroughfare.

At Knik Lake we traveled into the trees on a protected trail, and I eased up on the handlebar. The dogs remembered the way from previous years and, one by one, started to realize the task that lay ahead. Just as they fell into a regular pace, however, we turned off the familiar course and took off towards Big Lake. *Are we going home?*, the team wondered. Shortly before the lake we passed a batch of "Good Luck" signs put up by my firefighter friends – it felt good to have so much support at home and in the community, and I settled down from the early excitement. At Big Lake, my neighbor Jim had driven the dog truck out onto the ice. After checking in, I cut MacGill's sled free, said my goodbyes to Kathy and baby Nikolai, and rambled on down the trail.

The dogs that made my team this year came from only a few family groups. At the time I didn't yet have the ability to raise many puppies, so I had hoped for a high-percentage turnout of good dogs amongst the littermates. The largest family group included Dagger, Nervous, White Boy, and Ringer. These four young dogs all ran in lead and, with more experience, would later become the core of my team. Neuf, Crack, and Big Su comprised another pod. They were younger than the first group, but at three years old were already running their second Iditarod and gaining lots of knowledge before their prime racing age. Emmitt and Gopher served as my two backup leaders. I had picked up these two brothers from Roxy Wright back in 1985 when they were still pups. This was their third Iditarod with me. My savvy veterans Jim Cooper and Angel had returned, and this year Angel's son Jose made his second appearance on the trail. One of the newest additions was a dog named Tonto whom I had recently obtained from Gareth Wright. Tonto had mainly been taught to run fast, and only fast – this trip would surely make him trailwise. The pride and joy of my team were the brother and sister duo of Highway and Stafford. These two direct descendants of Fur Rendezvous dogs had all the speed needed, and were some of the first Alaskan Huskies that Kathy and I had raised; they were part of our family. The last three Iditarods had taught them – and me – many difficult lessons while overcoming many different situations together, and I hoped to use their skills to upset the competition. Stafford, a little white female, was my main leader, and her brother Highway usually ran behind her in swing with the tightest tugline in the team. Eleanor, named for President Franklin Roosevelt's wife, rounded out the team. She was the daughter of Nervous and Stafford, and although a rookie at two years old, ran like a veteran when in harness.

On the way to the Susitna River we encountered our friend Nick with our yearling team on a training run; they were now relaxing and watching the race on the side of the trail. I decided we should join them and parked alongside. My dogs still had a full tank of gas, as evidenced by their barking, jumping, and pulling whenever another team ran past – a sure sign to get going unless I wanted to be left standing by myself while my driverless team raced towards Rainy Pass. After a short break, I took heed and pulled the hook.

The steep downhill to the Big Susitna River can sneak up on you without warning. This year it consisted entirely of glare ice, but as this area stood well within my training territory, I knew when to anticipate the descent. I commanded the dogs to walk, and we glided onto the river without any problems.

The river trail proved wide and fast. The dogs felt like running wide open, but knowing how long we had to go, I cautioned them against it. We shifted down into a more moderate gear that seemed better suited for a thousand miles.

During the first two days we tried to establish a good pattern of resting and driving. I often found myself in the lead in spite of my long rest times. I didn't aspire to be a rabbit for the field, and en route to Finger Lake I promised myself to let someone else lay down the scent trail.

Upon arrival at the checkpoint I declared my twenty-four hour stop, as was the custom. I planned to complete the mandatory break at Rohn, on the other side of the mountains, but the winds at Finger Lake gusted to the showstopping speed of seventy miles per hour. I parked the dogs under some trees, out of the wind, and waited for the other teams to trickle in.

Hours went by before Rick Swenson and Jerry Austin pulled in, and they too declared their twenty-fours. The checkers then informed us that the trail to Rainy Pass lacked an abundance of trail markers and would be difficult to find in the dark. As the crowd increased, it became clear that most teams intended to stay until conditions improved or someone got restless and volunteered to break trail.

At midnight Joe Runyan made a move. Rick and Susan Butcher followed minutes later. I had been there nine hours by then, and opted to finish my long layover. With my decision made, I would get to leave the next afternoon, well in front of the other teams taking their twenty-fours at Finger Lake. My dogs had other plans, however. By late morning they were barking and screaming to go, and it took all my might, along with the checker standing on the snowhook, to hold them back – they almost pulled me out of the checkpoint ahead of my allowed departure. Finally we blasted off into the Alaska Range.

Typically it took four hours to get to Rainy Pass. The trail snaked along ridges and danced around alders, forcing the dogs to jump over stumps and branches. We were making good time, and most of the team looked light-footed.

About halfway there I noticed that Stafford had a slack line. She had been running in swing, so I moved her further back in the team. Now almost in wheel, she still didn't look so great – a very unusual occurrence for her. I couldn't see any limp or apparent injuries and wondered whether she just didn't like the rough trail.

A few miles before Rainy Pass, Stafford dropped down in her harness. I slammed on the brake and stopped the team, and then I picked her up and put her in the sled. Looking her over again, I couldn't find any visible signs of injury, nor did she let on about any pain. Normally she was pretty wimpy when it came to little aches and pains, and in the past she had always let me know exactly where she felt sore. Not so this time.

We only needed to go a little ways to get to the checkpoint. I kept talking to her as we rushed down the trail, and she was looking up at me the entire time she rode in the sled. She appeared very calm and relaxed.

We soon arrived at Rainy Pass. After parking, I walked up to the other dogs to give them a pat on the head and a warm meal. I called the veterinarian over to talk about Stafford's atypical behavior and asked him to look her over extra carefully. When we walked back to the sled for a closer inspection, we both immediately realized the severity of the problem. Stafford appeared lethargic and barely responded to my voice. The vet picked her up in his arms and ran into a nearby cabin, only to witness her dying moments later.

I was absolutely crushed. Stafford had been my top dog for a few years now. When I had decided to start my own kennel, she had been a part of my first real litter. Kathy and I had raised her from the minute she was born. As a puppy I had carried her around in my shirt inside our home. Only the year before, Stafford had pulled me to Safety and away from the open sea ice, and I couldn't count the number of trying predicaments that she had helped the team overcome, using only her sheer determination. I thought that I had prepared for all possible situations, but not in my wildest dreams had I ever imagined something like this happening. I stayed by her side in that lonely cabin for a long time and tried to pull myself together. I felt like parking myself and the dog team somewhere to hide until springtime. A few years ago when we had searched for Highway for almost a day, we had at least been able to maintain some hope of finding him alive and well, and we eventually did. This time we had lost one of our own without any chance of getting her back.

I left the room as the vets began to do their work. The mandatory, immediate autopsy revealed a blood vessel rupture that had caused Stafford to slowly bleed to death internally. *How could that have happened?* I asked myself. The run to Rainy Pass had been smooth and incident-free. I couldn't figure it out, and I felt like a failure. I hit an all-time personal low.

The days that followed blurred together. I just went through the motions – checking in at Rohn, staying longer than planned, running across the Farewell Burn, pulling into Nikolai, and continuing to McGrath.

Somehow the dogs and I found ourselves sitting in Ophir with the four lead teams. In my two-day-long emotional haze I had let frostbite singe my cheeks, and the searing discomfort forced me to wake up. I realized that hanging up my hat now would be doing an injustice to Stafford's memory and to the rest of my dogs. She had never given up on me, so how could I do anything except try to keep alive her forever forward energy? I decided to run the rest of the race in her honor.

The team picked up on my newfound perspective and within a couple of hours our spirits started to rise. The other mushers sat around waiting for somebody else to make the first move, but everybody ended up leaving Ophir at about the same time. Iditarod – the next checkpoint – stood one hundred miles away.

As we passed each other along the trail, due to our different traveling and resting schedules, we tried to assess each other's teams. I asked and also heard the usual questions – "How long have you been here?" "How long are you going to stay?" – knowing full well that I didn't receive nor did I give an honest answer. Responses like "My, your team looks really tired" or "Gosh, I had a good eight-hour break back there" followed as the moving team passed the resting racer.

Joe Runyan and Susan Butcher raced back and forth to Iditarod and probably spent more energy than necessary to get there. Susan won the halfway silver, with Joe just minutes behind her. DeeDee Jonrowe coasted in right behind them in third place. By the time Rick Swenson and I pulled into the checkpoint, the three lead teams had all finished their chores and their dogs were ready for a long break. The time was ripe for a move.

Rick assessed the situation. The trail in front of us had been put in less than two days beforehand; it would probably punch out a little with each team that ran over it. Rick suggested we use this factor as well as the chance to travel at night to gain the lead. I agreed.

During our short break we needed to convince the other mushers that we also intended to rest for a long time, so we acted like everything was normal and went through the regular routine. At one point Rick even gave DeeDee some of his straw bale after claiming that he had used the rest on his dogs. With the ruse in place, we told the small number of spectators to keep quiet, and then we snuck out of the checkpoint in the darkness. As we headed towards Shageluk we heard the sounds of Joe, Susan, and DeeDee all snoring away in their slumber. Mostly Joe, anyway.

A semi-solid crust of ice topped the trail leading out of Iditarod, but it deteriorated with every dog that stepped on it. We ran for a few hours, and then I snacked the dogs and praised them for their performance. I felt like a little kid sneaking out of the house after bedtime for some forbidden outing. The team reflected my upbeat mood, and for the first time in the race things looked optimistic.

A move like that could decide the difference between winning and losing. My imagination had me already racing back and forth with Rick down Front Street, with me slowly pulling away from him as the finish line inched closer – time would tell. After my dogs devoured their snacks, I complimented Rick on his foresight and let him take the lead.

The traveling conditions proved to be noticeably worse for the following team. My gentlemanly gesture turned out to be a mistake, in no small part due to my inexperience and friendly disposition. Clearly the lead team was spending the least amount of energy on the trail, but at that moment I was just happy to be shadowing such an experienced racer.

Night gave way to dawn and then to daylight. We finally got onto some good trail. Thirty miles from Shageluk, we stopped at a stream to give the dogs a drink. Our strategy had us making it to the checkpoint before the sun gained too much strength and then taking a long break. We only had to travel an hour into the heat of the day before we made it – my team had a little more pep in their step and pulled me into the village first.

By now the other three teams must have noticed we were missing, and I chuckled at the thought of how surprised they must have been when they found out. In my mind I pictured them tripping over each other as they put their boots back on and rushed out after us. My dogs and I ate a good meal, stretched out on the straw, and played the waiting game.

Being jazzed up over the possibilities meant that rest did not come easy. Rick and I sat around hoping for a four or five hour lead – an amount that could carry us for the rest of the race. We learned from the pilots, however, that the other teams were camped fifteen miles outside of the checkpoint. We had gained only about two and a half hours – a bit disappointing – but how badly the trail had deteriorated and how hot it had got for them while they tried to keep up, I could only imagine.

The first team to the Yukon River every year received a seven-course meal. On even years that meant at Ruby, and on odd years it occurred at Anvik. This year the meal was provided – at Anvik – by the Clarion Hotel, who flew their chef out to the village to prepare the fine dining. From previous years we knew that the ceremony consumed a lot of time, but Rick and I only wanted to stay for an hour. To manage that, we had the race officials in Shageluk radio ahead with the message to have everything ready for us when we arrived. Neither Rick nor I wanted to push each other just to win the meal in Anvik; we planned on eating the meal together.

During the entire run from Shageluk we talked back and forth about how it wasn't a big deal which of us got to the river first, and we traded leads back and forth to keep our lead dogs fresh as they broke trail. The last trade put Rick in the lead, and he gained a total of seven minutes on me as we approached the checkpoint. Well, seven minutes and 2500 dollars, to be exact.

I had no idea that the prize included a pile of cash as the after dinner dessert, but Rick certainly did. My lack of knowledge obviously hadn't compelled him to fill me in on the whole story. With a sheepish grin on my face, I joined him in his meal and thanked him for the lesson. I guess that was professional racing all the way.

I left Anvik one hour and seven minutes later, but by then Susan, Joe, and DeeDee had all joined the party. The grand move out of Iditarod didn't pan out.

The pack of five raced up the Yukon River – I called it "the wave." Each racer created a certain amount of energy. We made moves and countermoves, feeding ourselves on our competitors' and our own momentum. We kept each other going, alert and keen by the simple fact of being in the same place at the same time. If you weren't riding "the wave," and never leading nor contributing to the efforts of getting there the fastest, then you had no chance of winning the race.

The lead changed back and forth up the wide Yukon. Nobody yet knew who would win. Most of our teams ran with the same amount of strength, with the possible exception of Joe Runyan. He had managed his team well and still kept a large string of dogs. Having more animals in the team meant that each of his dogs had less weight to pull, which made it easier on each of them. Nonetheless, he seemed unable to pull away as the wave rolled up the river.

In Eagle Island, we each got to enjoy a piece of Helmi Conatser's famous cheesecake. She and her husband, Ralph, lived in a cabin on the island, fishing in the summers and fur trapping in the winters. They ran the checkpoint for many years, but it was Helmi's baking that attracted the hearts of many a hungry dog musher. She baked pies, cheesecakes, cupcakes, and even cooked up a pretty mean moose burger or moose stew. A few years back, when Rick was feeding cream cheese to his dogs, she traded him for two cases of it. In exchange, she promised to make a cheesecake as long as Rick passed through the checkpoint. And I have to say, it tasted delicious.

As we pulled off the Yukon and into Kaltag, the lead five teams all arrived within thirty minutes of each other. Susan and Rick had risen to the top in years past by making moves on the river, but it seemed the rest of us had fought off their maneuvers.

On the first half of the portage to Unalakleet we witnessed one of nature's most beautiful displays. Green and white curtains of Northern Lights that danced in the night were not uncommon, but this show stood out from the crowd. Overhead, a giant red star grew in size, shining bright enough to cast red shadows running alongside the dogs. I couldn't help but notice a single, smaller shadow out in lead. The star's brilliant arms stretched longer and longer until they branched out beyond the horizon and illuminated the trail with a flickering beam of neon crimson. The phantasmagoria continued for hours as the red morphed into green and then white, only yielding to the clear and constellation-speckled sky as I parked the team at the Old Woman Cabin.

Located halfway down the ninety-mile portage between Kaltag and Unalakleet, and at the highest point, there stands a little old plywood cabin in a narrow section of the trail. It's called the Old Woman Cabin. The legend of the local land says that the spirit of an old woman lingers nearby. To help her out, and to ensure safe passage, the custom is to leave a little of your food behind. If the old woman is in need, then she will come and get it. I always put something out for her alongside the trail, and after everything this year I didn't want to leave anything to chance. The legend must work, because the food is always gone the next time I come around.

Just outside of Unalakleet, my trusted friend Highway started showing signs of dehydration, so I stopped and gave him a ride in the sled to the village, then transferred him into the care of the veterinary team. They gave him lots of fluids and a luxurious pile of straw. The next day he would fly to Nome, arriving long before me.

Somewhere on the Bering Sea Coast we were required to take a six hour break. The previous few years we had a mandatory four-hour break in White Mountain, but this particular year we could choose between several locations. This theoretically left a little wiggle room for the various strategies to play out. Ironically, all of the top teams chose to rest in Unalakleet, and most of us changed to a lighter sled. While I waited for my six hours to be over, I watched the lead teams of Joe Runyan and Susan Butcher depart. Joe's team looked much stronger than Susan's.

Once I got back on the trail I sensed that my team was weaker than the two in front of me. On the trail to Shaktoolik, Gopher started having the same problems as Highway, and for the second leg in a row I gave a ride to one of my dogs. As our momentum diminished, I realized that the win sat out of reach, and decided to give the team longer and longer breaks.

It seemed like whenever I got to the coast, somebody turned on the machine that transformed the Norton Sound into a wind tunnel, as yet another ground blizzard obscured the crossing to Koyuk. Temperatures sank. Our traveling speed augmented the wind chill. I layered up with all the clothing I had and ducked behind the sled to try and find comfort, but the only real comfort came in Elim.

Kathy met me there in the middle of the night when the village looked like a ghost town. Not a single soul other than us was awake – creating a very real, very romantic, yet almost eerie atmosphere. Much of that had to do with the cumulative effects of being on an epic journey, but also Kathy's sixth sense for knowing when I needed her emotional support.

After departing White Mountain the dogs and I encountered seventy-mile-per-hour winds. Twenty miles from Safety, after Topkok Mountain, we found a shelter cabin and took refuge. I parked the dogs, handed them a warm snack, and let them sleep – moments later the blowing snow covered them completely.

A musher heading back to Nome had also taken cover in the cabin, but she had brought her dogs inside with her – she wasn't in the race.

I felt tempted to do the same, but disqualification so close to the end didn't seem worthy of our efforts. I sat down in front of the wood stove and fell asleep.

I woke up to the sound of Rick Mackey pulling his team out of the wind to give them a break. Tim Osmar tailed him by only a few minutes, and they both asked me if I had seen Guy Blankenship. *Guy Blankenship?* I realized that I must have really overslept, wasting hours of valuable time. I grabbed my thermos, left the cabin, and started looking for my team.

The snow that blanketed the dogs piled high. From experience I knew that the drift had insulated and protected them, and that underneath they enjoyed a toasty warm bed. I dug them out and they shook themselves off. As we raced towards Safety I turned on my portable radio and extended the antenna upwards. The Nome radio stations gave good updates on who was where, and after hearing that Guy only held a half hour lead over me, I crouched down behind my sled to be less visible on the flat terrain. The announcer said that Guy was still resting at Safety, which meant he must have run almost seventy miles nonstop. *We can't let Guy beat us.*

Guy spotted my dogs and me as we neared the checkpoint and interrupted his break to make the last twenty-two mile sprint. I only stopped for four minutes in the checkpoint – just long enough to give the dogs a warm liver snack – then bolted after him. My dogs shortened the gap quickly, and we passed him ten miles before the finish.

My team of eight dogs picked up their speed as we advanced ever closer to Nome. The rest at the shelter cabin had been the right decision. As we glided down Front Street and our race came to its end, inside I swelled with enormous pride – not only for the dogs that finished, but also for those that contributed along the way. After all, their hearts are what drive us forward and their feet are what carry us step by step through the wilderness.

I finished the 1989 Iditarod in sixth place with a time of twelve days, two hours, six minutes, and five seconds. The eight dogs that completed the race with me were Angel, White Boy, Dagger, Ringer, Jose, Big Su, Neuf, and Jim Cooper. Rohn Chapoton Buser was born on September 18, 1989, and did not challenge his father to the finish line. Not yet, anyway.

JOKING WITH
RICK SWENSON

BRILLIANT AND RED
NORTHERN LIGHTS
OVERHEAD

Gone Fishin'
Summer 1989

"**H**ey boss, I think I see some 'termination dust,'" I said.

The construction season ended when the first snow fell in autumn, and I always raised my hand before anybody else to point it out in the Chugach Mountains. I looked forward to that moment, because that meant they needed to lay people off, and I wanted to go run dogs again.

Both Kathy and I had become burnt out with emotional stress from our jobs at Alaska Children's Services. Dealing with the abuse those kids endured wore us down, so we decided to regroup. Kathy became a teacher and I took construction jobs.

My job had me working long hours. Typically I worked ten to twelve hours per day and got paid well, but as the seasons changed my focus turned to training for the upcoming racing season. That's why I kept my eye out for the "termination dust." I liked construction, but it had one major drawback: I had to be away from my dogs.

After the 1989 Iditarod I contacted Dean Osmar – 1984 Champion – and got hired to join his commercial salmon setnet fishing crew in Kasilof, on the Eastern shore of the Cook Inlet down on the Kenai Peninsula. The job came with the prospect of working for a shorter period of time and potentially making good money, but I could also bring my dogs along and camp out with them for the summer. All the crew lived in wooden shacks on the beach, and I staked my team out right there with me. Earlier that year the Exxon Valdez ran aground and spilled oil all over the Prince William Sound. Several high paying job offers doing cleanup had come my way, but I declined them because I had given my word to go fishing – as a dog musher, you spend everything you have plus a buck, so while money is always a consideration, it is never the primary factor in any major decision.

The Cook Inlet stretches from the Turnagain Arm in Anchorage to the southern tip of the Kenai Peninsula, where it opens up to the Gulf of Alaska and the Pacific Ocean. The western border is lined by a range of several active volcanoes – Spurr, Double Glacier, Redoubt, Iliamna, and Augustine. Fifty miles or more wide, it has the largest tidal range – the vertical difference between high and low tide – in the United States, averaging thirty feet and changing direction about every six hours. That's powerful. Many a pickup truck has been swamped after its driver parked and forgot to pay attention for a few hours. Hordes of salmon swim up the inlet every summer and into one of the many rivers that are their spawning grounds. Once enough fish make it past the mouth of the river, the commercial fishermen are given a window of time to work known as an opener.

In the moments immediately before an opener, scores of open setnet skiffs float on the water in anticipation. With nets stacked neatly inside, you stare at your watch until the exact second the opening begins. Then everyone motors forward in a harmonious fury to get the nets tied as fast as possible to floating buoys anchored by sandbags in specific locations. The force of the current only allows you a couple seconds to tie off the rope ends before the net is whipped out of the boat, so you have to be fast, you have to be accurate, and you have to be cautious – nobody wants to lose a finger or fall into the swift and cold water. The process is repeated until all the nets are out, and the subsequent hours are filled by checking for fish. Retrieving a net involves manhandling it up and over the bow, then hopping on either side and yanking the boat sideways through the water to travel the length of the gillnet as you and your crew pick out the fish. Openers can happen at any hour of the day or night. You have to constantly stay ready, but you can't fish all the time.

Dean enslaved us to be busy at least twelve hours per day. We mended nets, fixed boats, patched up gear, and did whatever chore he could dream up with his vivid imagination. He was a hard driver, but as a multiple Iditarod finisher I could outwork most people, not that anybody there didn't know how to work. They did.

In my spare time I sat by the campfire and built a freight sled completely by hand while we visited with each other. Using local oak, I steamed and bent some wood into the proper shape and length. Then I obtained some ganion rope, dyed it purple, and lashed the sled together. We called my creation "The Purple Monster."

Sitting around with a bunch of rowdy commercial fishermen, I openly pondered:

"How do you guys think that would do on the water?"

Nobody raised their hand. I knew that some of them had waterskied behind their skiffs before, but I wanted to know how a dogsled would fare. My life revolved around mushing, and I saw no reason that the summer should put a hiatus on that. The physics – or our lack of education on the subject – behind whether a dogsled with twelve-foot long, two-inch wide runners could achieve enough flotation to pop out of the water was unknown, so we decided to try it out.

Dean's son Tim – who had run Iditarod and been competitive – also worked on the crew and happened to be a fantastic boat driver. With me standing on the sled, he throttled the motor and we took off, but the sled just couldn't get up and I went face first into the icy water. Had I been able to hang on, it would have become a submarine. We tried it several more times in different fashion – with me in the sled, with long ropes, with short ropes, with two motors, with one motor. We tried every variation we could think of. Nothing worked. I drank a lot of saltwater in those days. We never got it going, but out of our failures a new idea sprung forth: What about a toboggan?

The bed of the freight sled consisted of cross pieces and slats. It was highly permeable. The bed of a toboggan consisted of a solid sheet of plastic. One of the local boys ran up to the dog lot and grabbed one of them. We tied a rope from the boat to the bridle, and then Tim gassed the motor while I stood patiently with an iron grip – the toboggan popped out of the water with ease. We were back in business.

Many of us drove toboggan sleds in the Cook Inlet that summer. Riding one felt a lot like driving a sled on snow, but you had to go faster than a dogteam to be able to jump the waves – probably twenty miles per hour. We got good enough that we could hang on for miles at a time. Some guys only mustered enough courage after consuming a few beers, which made it a little more dangerous for them. Once you bailed you had to have a good boat driver come pick you up right away, because the water pulled you out and chilled you to the bone in a matter of seconds. One of the guys on the crew – Wildman Steve – was known to be a daredevil, and he drove one of those toboggans for so long and at such a speed that it ripped right down the middle. We broke quite a few sleds. Plenty of surprised spectators on the beach hooped and hollered as we skied by, and somebody allegedly even recorded it all on video.

My sled driving skills improved from our recreational endeavors, and the fishing became my annual work. I returned for several seasons, occasionally supplementing by longlining for halibut. Most of the time I got paid well. Sometimes the babysitter ended up with more money than the guy who left, but such was the risk of commercial fishing.

SKIFFS PARKED IN
THE COOK INLET

LOW TIDE
PARKING SPOT

NETS STACKED AND
READY TO GO

Walking In Circles
The 1990 Iditarod

I kissed my family goodbye and called up my dogs. We thundered off into a pouring rain that threatened to turn Big Lake into a bathtub. With darkness closing in and water levels rising, I was glad to have only two teams ahead of me as we transitioned onto the real trail system. Nightmarish tales would later stream in of tangled, driverless, and out of control dog teams trying to hightail it across the lake in two feet of standing water, leaving sopping wet mushers chasing after. Hearing about the chaotic circus, I suspected that the Big Lake checkpoint would get bypassed in the future.

My twenty best dogs had put on the afterburners through the first forty miles of obstacles created by modern civilization, and for the third year in a row we had won the $1200 prize for the fastest time from Anchorage to Eagle River. That surprised me, since our speed felt slow on that warm Saturday morning – temperatures were in the thirties.

My dogs fell into a nice rhythm outside of Knik – led by my experienced leaders Jim Cooper and White Boy – and we now pressed on to the Susitna River. Behind the front two ran my oldest leader, Angel, and her offspring of Jose, Breeze, Fritz, and Jessie. Filling out the rest of the main players were Neuf and Big Su, Cro-Magnon and Beverly, Dagger, Ringer, Nervous, Highway and his younger brother Smokey, Eleanor, Emmitt, King, and Bruiser. I hoped to have the right balance of younger and older, more trail savvy dogs. I knew that some of them would not finish the race, but I hoped that the race would be good to all of them.

At Shell Lake – the location of the famous fan-fueled bonfire and lodge – I found myself in the lead and winning another cash prize. I pocketed the dollars then made the conscious decision not to be caught in the front again until the Bering Sea Coast. Letting someone else lay down the scent on the trail would make it easier on the dogs. This year's plan was to stay behind the leader, rest my team a lot, and benefit from our superior speed towards the end.

Deep snow flooded the trail from Skwentna to Rohn. All the drivers kept their eyes open for moose; nobody wanted to have an encounter similar to that of Susan Butcher in 1985. The soft conditions coerced moose onto established trails where the going was far easier. Some mushers who encountered moose, after discovering that the vocabulary of these long-legged monsters did not include the term "yield," had to snowshoe in a makeshift path to drive their dog teams safely around.

As we clambered up Rainy Pass I noticed a band of 150 or more caribou scattered about, clinging in little groups to the steep side hills like mountain goats. The lead teams had startled the herd and sent the animals darting in every direction. I knew the situation didn't stem from me, given our slow traveling speed from hauling two passengers – Highway and Nervous had worked too hard during the first two days and exhausted their abilities to contribute to the team's efforts. All of our eyes – both the dogs' and mine – welcomed the sight at the top of the pass.

The run to the bottom of the valley down the normally sled-breaking Dalzell rollercoaster had been tamed by the snow, providing a smooth ride to the Rohn Roadhouse. Last year Joe Runyan had gambled by pushing all the way to McGrath for his twenty-four hour stop. This year most of the mushers were prepared to run at least to Nikolai for their layovers, but when we pulled into Rohn the outbound trail didn't exist, so everyone buckled down and took their long rest. Susan Butcher had even planned ahead and flown a cot out to the checkpoint. Having arrived before anybody else, her layover ended first, but when it came time to leave she elected to wait around for nearly ninety minutes and let Tim Osmar break trail, giving him a twenty-minute head start before departing. That seemed strange.

On the trail out of Rohn, Tim encountered a buffalo. Holding back a fresh dog team coming off a day-long break wasn't the easiest thing to do, so he had to convince the buffalo to move. He waved his parka. The buffalo stared at him. He drove his dogs a bit closer to scare it. The buffalo stared at him. He fired his pistol into the air. Still, the buffalo just stared at him. As a last resort, Tim tried to trudge a new trail around, but to no avail. It was a Mexican standoff. After twenty minutes, Susan caught up from behind and yelled "What's going on up there?" The beast must have heard her, because right after that, it took off running down the trail at full speed. Tim later told me, while laughing: "One look at her and he ran." Susan was a force of nature. As to the question of how she knew to let someone else leave first out of Rohn, or if she knew about the buffalo at all, we will never find out. Whatever it was, she was either really lucky or really good. Probably both.

I left the Rohn Roadhouse with the rest of the frontrunners, and we began chasing each other across the desolate Farewell Burn. In spite of the windstorm the day before, the trail was surprisingly easy to find. As darkness fell I encountered a hunter. He was on foot and looking for a buffalo. We had a short chat, and I told him about the tracks a mile behind me.

Most of the night proved uneventful – a sign of good trail. Or maybe dreaming. At one point my eyes pulsated from the adrenaline boost of seeing my dogs disappearing in front of me. In seconds the team dropped out of sight, and the sled soon followed. I held on to the handlebar as we floated airborne over a two-story high snowdrift. The cornice had been created by the now abated storm, and the edge stayed invisible until the last moment. The dogs and I hit the snow at the bottom like a pod of diving dolphins but emerged relatively unscathed. Some mushers were not so lucky at landing. The trailbreakers had marked a way around the drift, but the first team didn't see the slight detour and set a precedent for all the teams in pursuit. Rick Swenson broke a runner on his sled. I'm sure there were others who did the same.

The friendly Athabascan village of Nikolai signaled the end of most of the early race hardships. I had to drop White Boy before leaving – a pretty big blow to my team. Both he and Jim Cooper – my key leaders – would fly home early instead of mushing to Nome. While heading out of the checkpoint, I looked back over the mountains and hoped that my wife wasn't worrying too much.

For the next few days the front twelve teams regularly leapfrogged each other. We only saw each other camped, feeding, or stopped to treat the dog's feet. The team would get sore and eventually fall behind without proper foot care – the continuous chore of checking every toe for abrasions, inspecting closely between the pads, and applying ointments based on trail conditions and temperatures assures further progress.

The lead group coalesced at Sulatna Crossing, or where it was supposed to be, anyway. The checkpoint had never materialized due to overflow, a condition loathed by many bush pilots. As a result we had a wide open parking area without any spectators, media, or race officials. After all the dog chores were done, we gathered in small groups and discussed what lay ahead.

Rick Swenson heated up a hot drink and poured it into his thermos, but he couldn't find the lid to close the bottle. He searched high and low and turned every one of his pockets inside out without success. While doing this, he repeated the words: "It's too early to be rummy dummy, I know I had that top right here." I broke into an uncontrollable fit of laughter. Rick soon gave up on the search and shared the hot drink with Jerry Austin and me, declaring the thermos useless. We stood around talking for a bit until Rick stuck his hand in the main pocket of his bibs and gasped – the thermos top was inside. We cracked up once more, then decided to regain some sanity by joining our sleeping dog teams in a half-hour snore session. Tim Osmar slept so soundly on top of his sled that he didn't notice while a helicopter hovered only a few feet above his head.

In order to keep pace with the leaders, I had been playing a dangerous game of cutting my rest breaks short. Normally I could rest longer than anyone and still be up front, but this year the team didn't look as strong as the other top teams around me. On the Yukon River it became apparent that we were covering less ground. I felt like we were going in slow motion. Soft trail with loose snow on top has never been my favorite condition.

Just out of Ruby I looked over my shoulder and saw a strange, grey, and round cloud on the horizon. It grew steadily until it hovered over the river, spanning from one riverbank to the other. It was no cloud; it was the moon.

In Galena I made the decision to stop cutting rest; that traveling pattern would only end in disaster. The dogs could probably keep up for a couple more days, but would use up their reserves and fall apart somewhere on the coast. I didn't want that, so I got off "the wave" and took a long break – the only sensible thing to do. After a few warm meals, some quality sleep, and a long chat on the phone with my wife, I found myself way back in twenty-first position.

We moved a little faster over the next few days but still rested for long periods. Gradually the energy balance shifted and we started to re-pass teams and move up in the standings again. If the pattern continued, a respectable finishing position seemed possible.

The sun on the horizon of the Bering Sea Coast fought the

oncoming darkness with red and orange flares before retreating. Flashes of northern lights flanked the yellow and gold moon as it rose to prominence. The spectacular sight burned into my memory.

In Shaktoolik, I asked the checker what position I was in:

"If you leave right now, you are number seven," he said.

I couldn't believe my ears. How was this possible? Apparently Rick and DeeDee had both come down with food poisoning from a meal they ate in Unalakleet. They had trouble standing up, let alone driving a dog team. During my rest, however, their health improved and they snuck out of town ahead of me. Luckily I did not run into the same problem.

I left White Mountain with blues skies, no wind, and my headphones on and connected to my Walkman: "She has won again" crackled in over the airwaves. Susan Butcher had just claimed the title for the fourth time in five years. The announcer also issued a storm warning, but with seventy miles remaining I thought my last run would be a piece of cake. I was wrong.

Six miles out of the checkpoint, a light breeze started to blow. My team and I started to climb Topkok Mountain when driving snow and strong winds made it miserable for both dog and musher. By the time we reached the top, we were in a full-fledged storm. The wind drove us sideways, whipping markers out of the ground and making it impossible to see the trail. My lead dog Angel's abilities to buck the wind and find the trail proved to be the only thing allowing us to crawl forward. She had performed well in single lead before, but now, when it counted, she showed herself to be outstanding.

During a well-deserved snack break, Joe Garnie pulled up from behind and volunteered to find trail for awhile. I drafted behind him and gave my only reliable leader a break. Joe lived on the coast, this was his territory, his preferred weather – or so I thought. He kept losing the trail after his dogs gave in to the roaring winds and strayed off the barely visible track.

We soon found ourselves out on the sea ice without any markers – clearly lost. Joe took this moment to utter a few words:

"Well, it looks like the great Eskimo guide has gotten us into a potentially dangerous jam."

His sense of humor could not be deterred, even by the worst imaginable weather.

We stayed lost for several hours into the night, and considered making camp until daylight, but decided to try a little longer. Joe sat on his sled and shined his headlamp in a constant direction while I attempted to walk a straight line out and find the trail. Periodically, I looked back to make sure I could still see the light of his headlamp. On one such instance I tripped and fell over something large. It was my sled. I had walked a full circle, probably no more than a quarter mile, and the entire time it felt like a straight line. *These ground blizzards are really confusing*, I thought.

If we traveled solely on a compass heading we risked missing the last checkpoint. With one last effort before digging in and waiting out the storm, we stumbled upon a fishing shack approximately seven miles from the Safety Roadhouse. From there the trail followed the road. Every now and then we found a trail marker or a bare patch of pavement, until finally we recognized a faint light from a lonely building in the distance. We had found Safety, but might as well have been on Thor Heyerdahl's Kon-Tiki when they first spotted land. Our teams needed a break, and a break we gave them.

The storm raged on, but both Joe Garnie and I knew who held the cards this year. His team was stronger overall, even though with Angel, I had the better leader. At night I could outrun him by finding the trail, but daybreak was fast approaching, turning the tide. The only chance I had of beating him came with a rest and recovery of some long lost speed. Joe and I watched each other constantly as we snacked our dogs, ready to jump back on the runners at any second. We both walked inside for a cup of coffee but didn't dare to remove so much as our hat or parka. Neither of us wanted to be caught off guard. The dogs got ninety minutes of well-deserved rest – not nearly enough, but after twenty more miles they, the real heroes of the race, would get a warm bed of straw and a long vacation. I planned to stay on Garnie's heels to the Nome city limits and then pass him.

Five miles out of Safety, Joe pulled away from us like we were standing still – his dogs remembered the way to the finish. The punchy, bottomless trail dragged on forever; I tried helping my dogs by running alongside and pushing the sled, but I sank in too deep to do any good. We made it to Nome with Angel running in single lead down the final stretch, looking proud and self-assured. Not a win, but the best we could do this time around.

I finished the 1990 Iditarod in tenth place with a time of twelve days, two hours, thirty three minutes, and forty four seconds. The dogs that finished the entire race with me were Angel, Jose, Neuf, Big Su, King, Dagger, Ringer, Fritz, Breeze, and Jessie.

Never Turn Back
The 1991 Iditarod

<u>Part One</u>

The 1991 Iditarod was billed as the race that would break the elusive "Ten Day Barrier," which meant a winning time of less than eleven days. Dick Wilmarth had become the first champion in 1973 by taking twenty days to cross the finish line. By 1990, the improvements of the trail and the competitive advancements of the field had cut that time almost in half, and Susan Butcher prevailed only two hours over eleven days. This year's race started with the idea of setting yet another speed record, but by the fourth day it had turned into a long, hard slog, with each team breaking in their own trail through the fresh snow and drifting winds.

I took my twenty-four hour layover in Rohn because the youngsters in my team needed the break. Joe Runyan, Susan Butcher, Rick Swenson, and many more mushers pulled out and away as I rested there – experience had taught me that we would all be together again. For the next two days I traveled without any of my immediate competition in sight, and sure enough, in Ophir, we all parked within a few hours of each other. The lack of an outbound trail there caused tempers to be tested for the first time:

Susan's big snowmachine sat parked in the checkpoint, and she felt that someone should break trail in front of us. Terry Adkins still had time remaining on his twenty-four hour layover and wanted no part of any efforts to put it in before he could leave. Rick Swenson, arriving a little later, argued adamantly against using any snowmachine that didn't belong to the Iditarod. The race marshal deliberated, then declared that we were on our own – the only trail breaking would have to be done via dog team.

In the middle of all of this, Susan woke me up from my nap:

"Martin, we have to go. Everyone else is catching up with us," she said.

"Go on without me, I'm not ready yet," I said.

Having pushed from Rohn in pretty quick fashion, my team needed a good rest – we would soon plod along en masse anyway. From then on the controversy of who should break trail began, and eventually continued up the Yukon River:

"After you."

"No, you first."

"Ladies first, I insist."

And so on. As part of my race preparations I planned on keeping a cool head and good attitude no matter what. The dogs pick up on the driver's vibes and are strongly influenced by bad moods. I stayed chipper.

The pack reunited again at Blackburn – an oasis on the Yukon River about forty miles up from Grayling and twenty miles down from Eagle Island. At the time, Clint and Vanita Blackburn lived there year-round in a multi-building homestead. Although it was very remote, they enjoyed many modern conveniences, including electricity from a generator, running water, and television. Whenever dog teams stopped by, they treated the mushers to meals, beds, and stories galore. As the couple got older, they started spending their winters away from the river, but always left one of their cabins open and stocked for travelers.

This year, since no one really wanted to be the one forging the first path, we had plenty of time to visit with the Blackburns and tell stories while we waited for somebody to give in and take off. Like a true raconteur, Joe Garnie showed up in rare comedic form. He informed everyone present of his connection to the Eskimo Mafia and the troubles that we could run into further up the trail, promising that a little bit of hush money would prevent a cut gangline, a sick dog team, or even a broken runner – apparently there were some guys he knew that could show up undetected in the middle of nowhere and score your runners so that halfway to the next checkpoint your sled would fall apart. Thinking of his youngest daughter, he told me that if one of my sons ever wanted to take her on a date, they would have to come knocking with 100 good dogs and a sled or else he would not approve. One of his favorite jokes involved whose team he was going to "blubber" – the (hopefully extinct for centuries) practice of throwing seal blubber to your rival's dogs (and causing a massive case of diarrhea) would score high on the Eskimo Mafia scorecard. Rick Swenson almost choked to death from laughing. After some time, the mushers finally started streaming out. The slog continued.

Part Two

"Nothing will stop me now."
– Susan Butcher,
upon leaving White Mountain in first place.

Inside the mini convention center in Nome, a crowd gathered around a large Iditarod race map that hung on one of the diagonally wood-paneled walls. Most of those standing held white Styrofoam cups filled with coffee so black that it bordered on being advertised as caffeinated syrup. When it was cold out, they drank it dark, and everyone still wore their parkas from fear of feeling another Arctic blast each time someone new entered the building.

Stuck into the map were labeled push pins that represented the location of each musher in the race, and all eyes were affixed and waiting for updates. The radio reported outside conditions of twenty below Fahrenheit, with winds gusting as high as fifty-seven miles per hour, and a wind chill of seventy below, or worse. The leaders had left White Mountain in the face of the storm, but rumors were flying that several of them had turned back. Nobody knew who or what to believe. Only one thing was for sure: At least two of them were missing – Rick Swenson, and Martin Buser.

"Hey, you're going the wrong way, girl!" I shouted.

"Well, that depends on who you talk to," Susan shouted back.

Susan Butcher and I were running in opposite directions. In the raging storm, she came straight towards me, stopping only briefly before heading back to White Mountain. I pressed on toward Nome, hoping to find an opening in the relentless white soup of swirling snow and ice chunks.

For many days – up to that very spot – I had compared my progress with the team that would probably be the hardest to beat. Since Susan had won four out the last five years, that meant hers. From Finger Lake to the shelter cabin on the Norton Sound, I had let her be my governor, and our teams were never more than a couple of hours apart. We had seen each other when our dogs were really hot and when they were in their "down phase," as she put it. We both knew our strengths. Often we commented on how different our two teams appeared – her dogs had thick coats, erect ears, and generally compact features while my Big Lake hounds, descendants of some of the best Rondy dogs, had less hair, often fold-over ears, and a rangy appearance. Both teams were equally loved, no doubt. Being fairly friendly and having a happy outlook made it pretty easy to travel amongst my fiercest competitors, and through casual conversation I improved my racing skills. Well, pretty easy when I had a dog team that could stay up there with the perennial frontrunners. This year I had such a dog team, and they deserved all the credit, as these incredible bundles of energy covered greater than 100 miles every twenty-four hours while functioning on up to 10,000 calories per day.

"It's not doable, Martin. What are you going to do?" she said.

"I think I will give it a try."

Our brief encounter ended and I headed up towards Topkok, the last mountain before the long awaited finish line. When Tim Osmar and Joe Runyan both passed me head-on a few minutes later, I realized that all of my skills were about to be put to the test. The knowledge that Rick Swenson persisted somewhere in the storm would not let me turn around.

I had left White Mountain in fifth place believing that I could catch a few teams in the last seventy miles, and here we were, just Rick and me, alone in the storm. Before Susan had turned around, she had been out on the trail with Rick, both of them trying to work together to find the trail. The storm had immediately separated them, and she soon determined it to be impossible. He had no clue that the other teams had turned back. *I know Rick is out there somewhere*, I thought.

As I mushed on, the wind howled from my right side at a forty-five degree angle, and the gusts kept trying to crawl under my right eyeball. Ice particles sandblasted my nostrils and forehead – the stinging on my skin would later prove permanent. Both the dogs' and my own right eyes froze shut. Ice masks formed perfect molds over the dogs' faces – created from blowing ice flakes that glued together with the escaping heat of canine breath. I had never seen anything like that before. The dogs looked like they were at a masquerade ball, only their masks didn't have the thin rubber band to hold them on. I evaluated the situation and decided to leave the protective shields in place – their breathing wasn't impaired, and the next gust formed a new face cup regardless of my efforts.

My sled stored enough food and drinks for at least one day, maybe two with rationing. The storm, with all its intensity, had turned this Iditarod into a survival race. Besides trying to win, I first had to live through it and make sure neither I nor the dogs froze up in the process. Normally in life, a few steps stood between victory and ultimate defeat – that wasn't the case this time. Forward progress came only from strenuous effort.

With zero visibility, I looked in the snow for any ripples left behind from snowmachines – I called these imprints "railroad tracks." At one point a snowmachine came by and left a momentary path for me to follow, but within five minutes the fresh trail had been swept away, and I returned to searching for signs that had been laid down before the storm. The hellacious winds wanted to erase any trace of these older scratch marks, but couldn't finish the job. Those tracks became my lifeline.

I quickly learned to acknowledge the lath that marked the trail only out of the corner of my eye. Whenever I turned my head to the side – even for a second – I lost the way. It happened to me several times, and one time far worse than the others:

I found myself lost at what was probably the top of a ridge, thinking that we had strayed no more than 100 feet off trail. Walking back and forth, still a close enough distance from my team, I tried to focus my already hampered vision through the frozen chaos in hopes of reconnecting with the once marked route. I knew how crucial it was to never leave your dogs under such terrible conditions, but I was unable to find any evidence of where to go. Something needed to be done.

In my sled I carried my own set of wooden markers for just such a predicament. Each marker had reflective tape in a strip at the top. One at a time, I marked my path as I walked out from the dogs by jamming each stake into the snow, never allowing myself to venture out of sight of my last marker – I knew too many stories of people that had lost their dog teams in storms. I staked out as far as I could in one direction, then reversed course and tried it all over again. I did this several more times without success. With all of my abilities, I could not find the trail. Mother Nature had laid her commanding hand down upon us, pressed us to the ground, and told us to "STAY."

Time for a huddle. I bunched all the dogs together in a big pile so they could benefit from each other's body heat. Then I crawled into my sled bag and gave the situation a good long thinking over – *Was Susan right? How long are we going to sit here? Is Rick moving? Will the dogs stay warm enough?* With nothing else to do, I finally found solace in a nap.

Two hours later the wind – now stronger than ever – tugged on my sled bag and violently shook the entire sled, as if to deliberately wake me up to continue my mission. The nap had improved my mental state, and despite my surroundings I felt warm in my Northern Outfitters gear – my only worries centered on the dogs' comfort. Hunkering down in a storm of this caliber sapped almost as much energy out of the team as moving, but heading in the wrong direction could easily make things worse – it was a fine line. With no neutral ground to rest, I decided we had better get going.

The wind speed had increased so greatly that only the glare ice stuck to the ground, and even that looked questionable. Standing upright still felt troublesome, but at least visibility had improved to about twenty feet, or almost half the length of my dog team at that point in the race. Struggling against the wind, I searched once more and found the trail less than fifty feet behind me.

Having already demonstrated that pushing the sled from the back was futile, I went to the front of the team, grabbed the line with one hand, put my head down, and started pulling. Eleanor walked next to me and began slowly learning to put together the many factors needed to keep us on the proper heading. We traveled in such a difficult environment that only the power of reason could propel us forward against the elements. I constantly compensated for the strong side-wind with the weight of my body as the blowing ice tattooed my face with its invisible ink. No dog could handle this weather alone in lead, but Eleanor soon got the hang of it – and so did I. Every tug and jolt on the gangline transferred right up to the front. When a dog stepped over the gangline, I felt it. When the wind toppled the sled, I really felt it – this occurred so often that I eventually just let the sled drag on its side.

Throughout the race I had been looking at myself from the dogs' point of view and decided that I was the "guy with the sled." In their eyes, I was the slowest member of the team – handicapped by having only two legs and traveling on the attached sled. To them I was clumsy and slow, and they often tested that opinion. In difficult passages – such as the Dalzell Gorge or Buffalo Tunnels, where staying on the sled was already a challenge – the gang got together and put the "guy with the sled" to the test. After every command given during the worst sections of trail, the dogs sped up in unison, forcing me to hold onto the handlebars like a towel in the wind on a clothesline, screaming "Whoa, whoa, whoa!" or some other useless utterance of desperation – teamwork at its finest. Whenever they settled down again, the dogs would just look at me with their tails wagging furiously and a gleam in their eyes that said "You are now accepted, but never forget that."

Now "the guy with the sled" was in lead and the sled was dragging along on its side – I could feel my dogs' appreciation, feel their eyes resting on my back, feel their trust in me to get them through a situation that they couldn't quite figure out. We had been close all race long, but now we were one.

Progress came slowly. For seven straight hours I walked in front of the team, and over time we worked out a system that let us steadily cut through the bluster without interruption. Step after step, mile after mile, we continued on. As we crested one more ridge – always wondering if it would be the last one before the ocean – the visibility improved drastically. My heart started to beat faster. The feeling of having made it through the storm – with better conditions in plain sight – was exulting. A few hundred yards more and there it was, the Bering Sea. The dogs accelerated with excitement of their own, and I let go of the line and jumped back on the runners as the team streamed by. Eleanor charged down the hill towards the flat ground.

Wait a minute. *Am I hallucinating? How long has it really been?* I spotted a cabin in the distance and could see a person there, working on something, bending over time and time again. *Is that Rick, putting booties on his dogs, and getting ready to go?* As we approached the cabin the dogs veered sharply to the right to avoid a parked snowmachine. It wasn't Swenson. It was a teacher from White Mountain waiting out the storm with his broken snowmachine. He had been gathering firewood when I pulled into the shelter. It didn't make any difference. I felt overjoyed to be there, and my smile had frozen in place, causing me to grin from ear to ear like a mischievous child.

The teacher informed me that Rick had also made it through the storm and had left an hour and a half ago. The happiness I experienced from hearing that, knowing that we both had survived, manifested as a powerful unspoken bond.

The fire in the cabin warmed me up, and I assessed the damage – the frostbite on my face looked superficial, and would probably peel like a severe sunburn within a few days (I later referred to it as my annual Seward Peninsula facelift, no extra charge). The dogs rested outside while I cooked some warm food for them. Afterwards, I ate my own meal, and had enough leftover "people food" to somewhat stock the cabin for anyone else en route.

Upon my departure, I asked the stranded traveler to be as vague as possible about my whereabouts – especially with regards to when I got there, and when I left – should any of the other teams arrive. Then I turned on my AM/FM Walkman and began listening to the radio.

At the shelter cabin, Rick must have realized for the first time that he might win. Susan, who he had thought was either right in front or right behind him, never showed up. Nobody at all showed up while he was resting, and he probably thought that the other teams had all turned around. But at that moment, if he had his radio on, then he had just been filled in on my uncertain whereabouts, and knew that he couldn't relax just yet. I certainly wasn't ready to give up, so I put on my white wind garments – my stealth clothes – and took off after him.

The radio stations reported mostly speculation on our locations for the first few hours, and I constantly scrolled the little white stripe between the bands up and down in search of more news. Eventually I stumbled on a broadcast telling me that Rick had almost made it to the Safety Roadhouse. *… Where in the storm's name is Buser?...* I saw no reason to prematurely announce myself as I covered the last twenty miles to the checkpoint, so I clicked off my headlight in hopes of sneaking up on Rick before it was too late.

Safety came into my line of sight, only three miles away, as I listened to Rick's live radio interview. My energy picked up when I heard him talking about mushing through zero visibility, raging winds, and cold temperatures – I was less than twenty minutes away and getting closer. Then they announced that he had left the checkpoint more than an hour before airing the interview. Rick must have again left instructions to delay the announcement of his departure – a strategically sound move anyone would have made in his shoes.

Two snowmachiners whizzed by me less than a minute before I pulled into Safety. I dropped my snow hook and stomped on it, and then hopped off my sled and ran into the building to look for the checker. I had to move fast or the dogs would mistake the quick break for a regular stop and lie down for a nap. I didn't see the checker inside, but I did notice the sign-in paper on the table. I grabbed it, scribbled my name illegibly, and dashed out the door. As I reached down for the hook, someone screamed my name. The checker had woken up to the realization that the missing musher was about to take off without his bib number – a required piece of equipment for the finish line. He caught up to me as I slid by and pressed the bib into my palm. Wrong number. I dropped it on the ground then hollered back – facing backwards on the runners – a formal request to please bring the correct bib on a snowmachine. There was no time to waste. A few minutes down the trail the checker brought me the right number. We were already a mile out.

I turned the radio back on to hear that I had been found alive, which was a great relief. Crouching behind my sled, I overheard the siren signal that Rick had almost made it to town. My ears perked up when his team got distracted and briefly bolted down the wrong road. *It's not over until it's over.*

Moments later a snowmachine flew by me at about 100 miles per hour. Seconds after the first one, a second machine whipped past, dodging my legs by no more than two inches. The driver had barely missed me and the sled. His wake blasted cold air onto my dogs and lifted their wind jackets up like cheap umbrellas. Surely it had been unintentional, but the point was reiterated: *It's not over until it's over.*

Rick had already crossed under the burled arch by the time I first spotted the city lights shining in the distance. I could only imagine how happy he must have been. As for myself, I didn't know if Kathy would even be at the finish line – before the race we had agreed that she would only meet me in Nome if it looked like I would place well enough to afford the plane ticket. But twenty-seven hours after leaving White Mountain, when my eleven super hounds pulled me up the ramp and onto Front Street, there she stood. My wife had made it, despite the fact that I had been missing for more than a day. Hugs and kisses for everyone – both dogs and people.

I finished the 1991 Iditarod in second place with a time of twelve days, eighteen hours, forty-one minutes, and forty-nine seconds. The eleven dogs that finished the entire race with me were Eleanor, King, Cayenne, Neuf, Breeze, Jessie, Richard, Woolly Wally, Milkcow, Dresden, and Ringer.

Magic Carpet Ride
The 1992 Iditarod

My wife ran out of excuses in 1992. Since she wasn't pregnant, didn't have a nursing baby, and generally couldn't come up with any good reason not to, for the first time in my racing career she joined me on the sled during the first day of competition – the race marshal had mandated that we take a handler from Wasilla until Knik due to the road crossings. It was a fitting start, as all the work behind our beautiful dog team – including several years of breeding choices, training sessions, management decisions, and financial compromises – required her involvement as much as mine. Kathy's nervousness on the sled quickly disappeared, and for the next fifteen miles we talked and enjoyed the visible results of our joint efforts. The dogs performed flawlessly by occasionally passing other teams, and when we arrived in Knik I recruited a handful of officials and spectators to secure the team while I swapped my starting toboggan and Kathy with my real sled and mandatory gear. After a couple of goodbye kisses for her and the kids – who waited for me in Knik – the dogs and I ventured off alone. No more help from this point forward was allowed.

Prior to this year, spouses, handlers, and sponsors had been able to interact with the mushers throughout the race. Valuable information could be exchanged at those meetings, and in some cases physical support may have been rendered, which provided opportunities for potentially unequal advantages. The new rules banned any planned help, and most people viewed them as fair, including me.

Blazing the way forward, we were led by Eleanor, partnered from the outset with D-2, a young leader who showed great potential and whom I was carefully grooming to take the reins when Eleanor retired. Behind them came five of D-2's full brothers, all with great potential – Dave, Hector, Madrid, IBM and Handy Man. Their litter was quickly turning into the best litter we had ever raised, and I was anxious to see what they could do. Their half-brother Tyrone had, at three and a half years old, recently blossomed in training and returned for more. Next to him stood Dagger – the relief pitcher, the jack-of-all-trades, and the father of D-2, or "Dagger Two" and his littermates. Dagger's sister Ringer was once more was the lightest dog in the team, at thirty-nine pounds. Jessie, Cayenne, Breeze, Milkcow, and Dresden, all seasoned veterans and tough enough to make it through the 1991 storm, rounded out the middle. Harnessed further back ran Clifford the big red dog, Neuf the Newfoundland lookalike, Emmitt – the oldest dog in the team at eight years, and Jose – back for his fifth try and filled with sheer dedication and drive. Jose was a fifty-pound dog with a hundred-pound heart. The twentieth dog, Wolfie, was a swift-legged new addition purchased from Clifton Cadzow in Fort Yukon. Last, and primarily riding the runners because he was too slow to keep up with his four-legged teammates, was the guy with two legs. Me. I had gotten in pretty good shape, and expected to help our progress by running up the hills and ski poling along on the level ground.

The trail wound beyond Knik and through the stately birch forest speckled with open clearings. We coasted across the Little Susitna River then turned southwest towards our first three-hour stop at Flat Horn Lake, which bustled with activity. Once there, I parked the dogs well off the trail; teams passed by in regular intervals. Darkness concealed most of the drivers. "Who goes there?" "Who is that?" – Some drivers answered, others did not. The annual cat and mouse game had begun.

The Iditarod is a long, grinding battle, and the race would be no fun without the possibility of someone making a strong move to pull away from the field. Even though it was still early and we had a long way to go, everyone stayed on their toes. The dogs didn't feel tired yet, but experience dictated this to be a crucial stop. I took a thirty-minute nap.

At this stage of the race the drivers typically stay very conservative. There might be a progress-halting storm around the corner with days of breaking our own trail. Nobody wants to double the difficulty by combining the climb over the Alaska Range with terrible weather. Cautious racing was and is considered the most productive in the first days, with rare exception. I often marvel that I can be sitting in the middle of nowhere, sipping a boxed fruit juice while the dogs are sleeping, yet be in a race where every minute counts. I call it "racing relaxed," and it takes time to learn that the rest stops are every bit as important as the travel phases.

Moot point. The dogs soon started screaming and lunging on the lines. I didn't want a busted gangline, so I packed up and got moving. Snow and strong winds joined to turn the trail into a fluff-filled river. The deep drifts swallowed entire dogs as they wallowed through each one, emerging covered from nose to tail in snow before shaking themselves free and diving into the next. The slow traveling came with a high energy cost. Occasionally I waited to let somebody catch up and pass me, hoping to benefit from their trail-breaking efforts, but the wind blew hard enough to immediately erase that idea, and I let the team rest frequently. Daybreak had already passed when I arrived in Skwentna – normally I traveled that section of trail during the first night. Progress came slow for everyone, and we joked that the twentieth Iditarod would take the winner twenty days to finish.

Inside the Skwentna checkpoint, Joe and Norma Delia served all the hungry mushers breakfast, hot Tang, and a spot for a nap. In the corners of the spacious and dimly-lit log house, sleepy mushers sat propped up in rocking chairs, recliners, and dining table chairs. Some looked like they had fallen into their slumber mid-meal, with their hands still holding onto spoons sitting in half-empty soup bowls. The lucky ones got invited to rest upstairs on a mattress-covered floor.

Joe Delia had put up with the dog mushers since the first Iditarod, and probably had more stories to tell than anybody on the vast river system. This year he recounted an incident involving a few summertime visitors. Apparently some tourists had been floating down the Skwentna River in a leaky rubber raft, and became swamped and stranded just above the location of the Delia homestead. Instead of hiking just a couple of miles downriver to the home, they dismantled one of Joe's storage buildings, fashioned a raft out of the wall logs and tin roof, then drifted to the homestead and asked for help. They didn't specify what kind of help, so Joe served them a hearty piece of his mind, after which the tourists were allowed to rebuild the shed and travel back to civilization on a chartered river boat. Joe could be frank, but his humor was rich.

After a nap and a good breakfast, news trickled in of poor trail conditions. All the dogs had been resting for more than six hours, but nobody wanted to make a move. From my parking spot I spotted two recreational teams heading up the river. I gave them a thirty minute head start, then followed their freshly scented and broken trail towards Shell Lake, arriving before anyone else and winning the unofficial monetary award there – I had won the prize several times before, but having determined it unproductive to lead that early in the race, I parked the team and planned for a couple hour break while waiting for other mushers to catch up and pass. I used the big and already hot bonfire to melt snow and make water for the dogs.

It was a good thing I arrived soon after the party started, because the heat and ashes from the giant fire are known for burning a crater all the way down to the tundra. In snow-rich years the crater can become ten feet deep, and more than one out of control dog team has accidentally encountered the hole and been forced to leap across its gap, with the long jump faring far easier for those with four legs than those with only two.

The sun beat down on us as we hiked up Rainy Pass. The heat of the day softened the trail so much that we caught up with the trailbreakers. I expected them to be eight hours ahead, but the same snow that slowed our progress had also virtually stopped the official iron dogs. One machine turned back for repairs while the others hurried to stay in front of the lead teams. The front pack – I was running in fifth place at this point – and the trail crew traded back and forth all the way to Rohn. Not ideal, but at least on the downhill stretches we had an unbroken buffer against the sometimes scary switchbacks.

With a questionable trail ahead, strategies were changed on the spot. Many drivers had planned on taking their mandatory twenty-four hour layovers at a later checkpoint, yet with the trail-breaking crew still in Rohn, some opted to wait and let the trail get broken out first. The thinking was that overnight it would then set up and harden so they could mush into the interior with a fresh team on a firm trail – I thought differently. After a solid eight-hour rest and the assurances that Joe Runyan, Bill Cotter, and Doug Swingley were also all leaving, I bid goodbye to Rohn and took off towards Nikolai in fourth place.

The decision to push proved to be the correct one. The trail had solidified behind the outbound trail crew faster than expected, and my dogs held their speed across the Farewell Burn. Soon we caught the three teams in front of us. *So much for not leading the race.* My team moved along swiftly, so I stopped a few times to let Doug and Joe pass and scent the trail, but no rest seemed long enough, and we kept catching and passing them back. Nikolai drew nearer, and shortly after noon on Tuesday I declared my twenty-four hour layover in the small village. We had covered the seventy-five miles from Rohn in nine and a half hours, including rest breaks.

I parked off the beaten path and shook out a straw bale over the team. Each dog – I still had a full twenty – had their own routine to paw the perfect bedding, so I left that part up to them. Then I removed all their booties and harnesses so they knew it was time to rest. After feeding I prepared for a nap.

The new rules had us park in designated spots and use only the official buildings. The musher building had a phone, a stove, and a shower inside. I made use of all three during my stay. Most of the field had opted to take their layover in Rohn, and the three teams around me – Doug, Bill, and Joe – were already on their way to McGrath. I had Nikolai to myself, and slept soundly through the night, only waking up twice to feed the dogs.

The other racers started arriving at six in the morning. Since I had to stay at least until one forty-five in the afternoon, I would have teams in front of me when I left. The trail reports sounded optimistic, and the lead three had already pushed towards Ophir. Right before I finished repacking the sled for my departure, Sonny Russell arrived with a deep gash over his eye from hitting a tree in the Farewell Burn. Blood poured down his face as he sought out the public health nurse for first aid. Soon after Susan Butcher pulled in with a broken nose and eyes nearly swollen shut from hitting the same branch. Lynwood Fiedler made his bloody appearance moments later. The Burn had claimed several victims, and I felt lucky to have avoided the same fate. As I retrieved my snow hook and the train headed out of town, the thermometer displayed a temperature of minus fifty Fahrenheit (-46C).

The run to McGrath spans fifty miles, mostly down the Kuskokwim River. The trail from there on out is more physically forgiving, but the flatter terrain introduces a different challenge to the driver – sleep deprivation.

True sleep deprivation comes on after a few days on the trail and cannot be combated by the typical remedies tried on your way home from the airport after a long flight. Rolling the window down does not work – you are already outdoors. Splashing your face is pointless since the water around you is usually not available in liquid form. You might try throwing snow down your neck, but that has other drawbacks when you soak your underwear. I shake my head and sometimes even bite my gums to chase away the cobwebs draping over my eyelids. Eventually I give in to "just a tiny little nap" – standing up, while driving the sled. Other times – after pulling over for a break and feeding the team – I have been caught sound asleep, standing in the middle of the trail, with the dogs resting comfortably curled up in little doggie doughnuts. The code of the trail has the passing musher at least poke a finger into the sleeping statues as they go by. If you wake up on your own – usually after your knees buckle and you collapse face first into the snow – your befuddlement is met by the stares of your oh-so-rudely awakened dogs. Once you regain some cognitive ability you rub your eyes and look left and right to see if someone has just passed you. If they have, you can expect to become the butt of a joke in the next checkpoint. If they haven't, then you can hide your embarrassment from the general public.

I cruised through Takotna just slow enough to reach out and grab the free sack lunch before carrying on to Ophir – the springboard to the deep interior, and a strategically important spot. For my entire career I had believed that if you weren't with the leaders in Ophir then you wouldn't be with them at the finish line. But upon my arrival there, both Doug Swingley and Joe Runyan had already rested for five and a half hours and took off for the halfway point at Cripple. They were well on their way, though neither had taken their twenty-four hour layover. I mentally jostled with this new riddle.

The checkers at Ophir supplied all the teams with fresh buckets of clean cold water – a fantastic gift that saved each of us thirty or forty-five minutes of effort. The extreme cold wanted to turn the water into ice as I poured it into my cooker pot, but the raging flame underneath fought back the frozen layer forming at the top. Several minutes later the burning alcohol fire had won the battle and heated all the water thoroughly. I fed the dogs, then walked over to the one-room cabin for a snack, a nap, and some conversation.

Rick Swenson sat at the table picking icicles from his mustache. While openly debating whether to cut the beard for the next race, Susan Butcher leaned across to offer her skills as a barber:

"I could trim that ugly thing for you. I have plenty of practice with David's beard," she said.

Hearing this, I whipped out my Swiss Army knife – every good Swiss boy has one – and handed the little scissor to Susan, who immediately grabbed Rick by the throat and looked him in the eye:

"Do you trust me with a knife?" she said.

"I'm not sure I have a choice. Do what you will," he replied.

She then proceeded to trim his mustache, expertly and neatly, turning him into a better looking musher. The room filled with laughter as well as compliments. Rick and Susan were the best of friends, whether they liked it or not.

The temperature had frozen in place at fifty-four below when it came time to head out in the early morning. The trail crossed the Innoko River three times before Cripple, and the only sounds I heard on the way were my own breathing and the swishing of the gliding runners. Frosty vapors clung to and outlined the dogs' snouts, exaggerating their smiles as their feet stepped in unison. Watching them, I relearned a humbling lesson: They could outwork, outrun, and sometimes even outthink a person, without getting all stressed out. In exchange for their trust and unconditional love, they only wanted to be taken care of, to be loved, and to run. The drive to keep going, to explore what lay ahead, was unequaled in most human beings. Most.

Turning my head to the side as we passed a dome tent, I saw a figure emerge and wave a hand. He said something, but his words didn't penetrate my hat and parka hood, so I just waved back and continued on. It had to be one of the two guys walking to Nome in the annual invitational foot/bike/ski race that paralleled the Iditarod. The thought of it made me shiver. To experience this beautiful landscape without your best friends and to travel three miles per hour instead of ten was a painful notion – even for a musher. If he had brought just a single dog as company, his journey would have been more pleasant.

The dogs sped up after this short encounter. Anytime something unusual happened, the team perked up and pushed the pace, as if to say "Let's go discover something else." My leaders Tyrone and D-2 were especially curious. Whenever we approached another team from behind, they snuck up silently – until they were inches behind the sled runners – then started barking like crazy. With their tails high in the air and their boisterous echoes perplexing the other driver, we roared by like a rocket, never giving the newly passed dogs a chance to trail behind.

We pulled into Cripple having passed everyone except Joe Runyan and Doug Swingley, who were pressing on to Ruby, still without having taken their mandatory long break. My dogs stood in front of the checker – lunging at the lines like they did at the start – while I looked around for a place to park and bed them down on some warm straw. The race officials were struggling to stay warm, so I inquired:

"What is the temperature right now?"

"It's fifty below zero."

Still fifty below? I hadn't noticed. The monolithic Northern Outfitters system I wore was clearly a big improvement over the outfit from my first races. The bitter cold didn't bother the dogs either – they looked fresh, alert, and physically strong. The mental bond we shared obviously contributed as much to their well-being as all the months of training. Once I fed them, they settled down and slept soundly, sheltered amongst the small spruce trees.

As part of my pre-race strategy, I wanted to have a few teams in front. DeeDee Jonrowe left the checkpoint thirty minutes ahead of me, but I made up the gap in no time, giving me a good idea how fast her team was traveling compared to mine. Our dogs passed in the cold night and her head light slowly disappeared behind us as we gained momentum. My team seemed to be on a real high, and it felt like I was constantly adding more dogs to the line. Frequent snacks kept them fueled and happy, while the several short stops I took – to give them encouraging words – turned them on more and more:

I had recently introduced something called the "mental health minute" to my racing tactics, as a way to reinforce good behavior. Whenever the dogs were working at their peak, I would stop the team and set the snow hook securely, then pet each dog from the wheelers to the leaders, telling them how proud I was of them and how good a job they were doing. Once I made it back to the sled, the dogs would inevitably be barking and jumping in their harnesses to press on and get some more work done. Eventually the minute stopped translated into many more minutes gained in overall traveling time.

By the time we crossed the Sulatna River Bridge – a huge and rickety steel structure in the middle of nowhere that dates to the 1920s – the dogs were nearly galloping down the trail. Just on the other side appeared to be the perfect spot for a long break. Daylight had arrived and the team deserved a hot meal, so I parked them well off the trail in case any traffic came by. Then we all ate and fell asleep.

After waking up, I repacked the sled and bootied the dogs. *Where are the other teams?* My dogs Hector and Madrid rolled around in the snow; Jose jumped up and down to get others to play, and the rest of the team barked and wagged their tails. A minute later I noticed a team coming up the road. It was Jeff King. He pulled up alongside us and stopped:

"Look at these dogs, just look at them!" I said.

Jeff stared at me for a second then shook his head and continued down the trail – after the race he would say I looked like an excited little kid wanting to show off his new toy on Christmas morning. I gave him a head start before chasing. Having not rested yet meant Jeff was traveling slower than we were, so when we neared him he parked his team aside for a break. My dogs screamed like banshees as we passed. Proud as could be, we raced on to the first Yukon River village of Ruby.

Someone stood on my snowhook as I signed in. On the check-in sheet I saw that the two rabbits – Joe Runyan and Doug Swingley – had only been there for eight hours. They needed to wait sixteen more hours before completing their mandatory layover. I parked my dogs along a fence and went through my regular routine.

Four hours later I glanced around and noticed that none of the teams who pulled in during my rest were ready to depart. My original plan had me leaving at that point, but I didn't intend on leading quite yet. Not sure what to do, I asked Rick Swenson if he would like to head out with me, but he didn't take the bait and urged me to get going as long as my team was on such a high. Walking over to Joe Runyan, he gave me the same advice. I looked to my dogs for the answer. They were standing up, wagging their tails, rubbing shoulders with each other, playing and mock fighting, and looking me straight in the eyes, as if to say "Let's go, what's keeping you so long?" That's all I needed to know. *Time to make a move.* I broke with my number one game plan and disappeared down the Yukon River.

Along the frozen highway, the telltale tracks of a wolf pack emerged. The wild ancestors of my team – my kennel had begun by breeding with a Yukon River Husky – had paralleled the trail, cut across it, meandered up the steep bank, and romped about in a grand wolf parade. I could see where they had taken naps and played games in the snow. The full account of their day on the river was revealed to me by sight, but my team sensed the same story by smell, and we glided through the wolves' backyard with such a driving energy that I wondered whether the odor had triggered some kind of instinctive memory. Without a whisper – nor the sight of a single distant relative – we pushed on to Kaltag.

The community building that served as the last river checkpoint felt eerily deserted. It was the middle of the night. One race official slept in the corner while a couple of semi-awake checkers and veterinarians tried not to make any noise. After some warm food and a short nap, I got back on the runners with a ninety-minute lead and a ninety-mile portage between me and the Bering Sea Coast.

Halfway through I broke up the long run with a stop at the Old Woman Cabin – the water always flowed from the stream there, even in the coldest of winters. Several fans from nearby villages had traveled by snowmachine and gathered at the cabin to check on the progress of the race. While cooking a meal for my team I inadvertently kissed the flames of the alcohol stove and burned off my seven day old stubble – the thin hairs on my face singed and curled back as they stung my skin and alerted me to back away, forever impeding my ability to grow a beard. Before leaving, I admired the skills of one of the snowmachining nomads as he charged up a steep hill in a semi-whiteout – while pulling a massive wooden freight sled – and disappeared over the horizon.

On the next section of trail I encountered a strong tail wind and decided to make use of a long-held idea. Tying a rope around both my waist and the handlebar freed my hands and I leaned back into the breeze. Then I extended my two ski poles and slid them into the sleeves of my red wind parka. Holding them wide apart from each other, the wind billowed into the garment and created a sail. I chuckled repeatedly as the sled surged forward like a windsurfer jumping over one choppy wave after another. The dogs ran resistance-free and appeared to follow my example by sticking their tails straight up and catching more air – I felt like a conductor driving from the caboose of a floating freight train for the next few hours.

The outline of buildings on the horizon kept getting bigger by the minute. When we soared into Unalakleet, a crowd of two thousand cheering, whistling, and clapping spectators swallowed us like a ground storm – I couldn't even see the wheel dogs. The local children hugged my leaders and climbed all over the sled. Only with the help of the race officials and some local friends was I able to park the team and spread some straw out, although it took awhile to get all the kids on the same side of the gangline so the dogs could rest.

Where is the competition? I hadn't seen another team since Kaltag, but when I inquired about my lead it became clear that the trail intelligence was almost nonexistent – I put the others out of my mind and tended to business. After feeding the dogs, checking their feet, changing the runners, and repacking the sled, I allowed myself to walk inside for a meal. The winner of the high school's cooking contest had earned the chance to share their dish with the first musher to the coast, and unfortunately for them that meant sitting at the same table with a grubby, smelly, sleep-deprived dog driver. My eyes, brain, and stomach visibly and audibly argued with each other over how long to stay awake and how much to eat of the delicious stew and dessert. Finally I gave in and passed out, luckily not landing in the bowl.

Painful leg cramps constantly woke me up during my fitful and shallow nap. In my stupor I jumped up and down to stretch them out – each attempt only provided a temporary fix. The time soon came to check on my dogs. Their looks in my direction told me they were ready whenever I decided to go, but no other team had checked in yet, so I stalled my departure. For the first time in the race, I let myself wonder what was really happening.

By all appearances, none of my competitors were giving chase. I thought that was a mistake. The first team to the Bering Sea Coast needed to be watched. Always. A leader that left unseen from Unalakleet became a ghost to the rest of the field, and that was a serious hurdle to overcome. But was this real? Were we finally about to pull it off? Years of planning, calculating, and hoping had led to this place – two hundred and fifty miles from the finish with a several hour lead. I was nervous, excited, happy, and worried. My emotions had me wide awake, thinking of all the stories of teams running out of gas on the final stretches of the race. Had I driven the team too hard, pushed too much, made mistakes, or were these dogs simply ready to win?

We had been there for six hours with no one else in sight when I pulled the snow hook. Night had settled in, but the TV cameras created a cloud of light around us as the dogs trotted out of town, and we vanished into the darkness.

On top of the Blueberry Hills – halfway to Shaktoolik – I parked off the trail to give my friends a snack and ended up having an out-of-body experience. I saw myself stop the dogs, slowly open the sled bag, leisurely search for the snacks, then walk over to each dog and pet them as they gobbled down their meal. The slow motion continued until I shook myself back into race mode after realizing that I was trying to beat the best and couldn't afford to slip up. They had many tricks up their sleeves, and the last two hundred miles were no cakewalk either, having stopped me more than once in previous years. I slapped myself a few times then hopped back on the runners and hurried on, while pretending that Susan ran two minutes ahead of me and Rick one minute behind. At that level of fatigue it didn't take long before my imagination blurred with reality.

In Shaktoolik I remained fully focused – the race was on and I wasted no time. We headed back out on the trail after only a short rest and no nap. My heart pounded. I had scared myself so good that I could see headlights coming behind me.

Eighteen miles out we passed the shelter cabin where Susan Butcher caught up to me in 1988 on the way to her eventual win. Many hours I had spent in that well-placed cabin, and usually with a group of shivering drivers. I had never traveled the entire coast without a storm so it did not surprise me when I felt the wind picking up as I drove onto the frozen sea ice of the Norton Sound.

The dogs bucked a fierce headwind while making little progress across the torturously long crossing to Koyuk. The illusory outline of the village made its appearance known and toyed with my mental state for yet another year. The tailwind to Unalakleet where I used my sail had ruined me, because tacking into a headwind was not possible on a dogsled.

Koyuk slowly crept closer. And closer. Finally we reached the checkpoint. The welcoming committee loomed large, and the local kids once more engulfed the dog team, keeping the wind at bay as long as they stood around us. I parked the team along the giant fuel tanks near the village generators, which churned and buzzed loudly, grating against my ears.

The Norton Sound crossing had taken a little over six hours. While resting, word came that the next team – Susan Butcher – had just then left Shaktoolik. I had a six-hour lead. I could not figure out where along the trail I gained that much time, but I refused to declare victory – nobody would dare to do that ever again after last year's race – and shortened my team to save some work. Hector, Madrid, and Wolfie stayed in Koyuk. In a possible storm, I wanted as small a team as capable without jeopardizing pulling power, and thirteen dogs provided more than enough.

Soft and bottomless trail stood between me and Elim, so for motivation I imagined the rest of the teams racing towards me on a hard trail and closing the gap. We plodded forward for the next fifty miles until we finally lumbered into the checkpoint. The local residents informed me that the trip to Nome usually took a solid twenty-four hours, but a light snowfall reminded me that accurate predictions were hard to make, especially once the village elders began talking about a storm approaching. I had experienced my fair share of being stuck in storms, so I got out of there before the weather proved anybody right.

The dogs picked up the energy on the way out. The ease with which we conquered the hills and then Golovin Bay showed me that my late season training trip paid off – in mid February I had flown my race dogs to Nome and run them all the way to Elim and back, getting them familiar with the last 150 miles. We charged up the Fish River to the small village of White Mountain for our mandatory eight-hour break.

After parking the team on a big bed of straw, I felt like I had arrived on a "time island." Every team had to stay the same amount of time, so no surprise maneuvers were possible. Still, with my thousand-yard stare I kept gazing towards the incoming trail – how far behind was the next team? The mind games could be spooky. To give the dogs and myself the most recovery, I planned to break the eight hours in half and repeat my regular checkpoint routine twice. That would give me a couple hours of sleep – enough to carry me through the rest of the race. Just as I lay down for a nap, race judge Mark Nordman came over.

"Martin, you have more than an eight-hour lead."

"I'm not sure if I believe it."

Realizing that I might not see another team left me dumbfounded, but helped me sleep more soundly.

The veterinarians carefully checked over each dog, and the drug testing crew gathered samples for analysis. I had shipped a lightweight sled to White Mountain, but I decided against using it. Keeping the bigger sled while heading into last year's storm allowed me to take more supplies and forge ahead – a decision I did not regret. The forecast this time around called for another potentially big storm, so I just changed the runner plastic on "The Tramp" – one of my favorite and most proven sleds, fitted with a trampoline bottom as the bed underneath the sled bag – and prepared for the last seventy-seven miles.

The clock stopped for nobody, and my eight hours soon came to an end. The dogs shook the sleep from their bodies as we set out to tackle our final obstacle. I beamed with the pride of a father at his children's graduation, even though I knew as well as anybody that anything could happen, and usually did.

We left the river and started ascending the Topkok Hills – a place known to create its own weather. In the past I had departed White Mountain under calm blues skies only to get hammered a few miles later to the point of zero visibility. This time the sky showed something brewing, but I stayed ahead of it.

The sound of the brake screeching against the snow permeated the air as we crested the last ridge and dropped towards the coastline. The shelter cabin at the bottom that served Rick Swenson so well last year now swelled with reporters and local travelers, but I parked there only long enough to give my dogs a quick snack and a reassuring pat on the head. Safety sat twenty miles away, and Nome twenty more from there.

In Safety the checker told me of some trail changes for the last stretch, and that I should find it good and wide and well-marked. He was wrong. The dogs crawled through chest deep snow, and I did my best to pedal and push as we plowed our way forward, every step bringing us closer to Nome. I listened intently as the radio in my ears played a familiar tune:

> Well, I just pulled out of Safety I'm on the trail all alone,
> I'm doin' fine and a pickin' up time and a runnin' on into Nome
> There are no sled tracks in front of me and no one on my tail…

Never had the lines to Hobo Jim's song been more appropriate. Pushing ahead inch by inch, I concentrated so hard on watching the dogs that the fact of a probable win did not sink in, and I spent no time celebrating. *It's not over until it's over.*

171

When the road crossing with the first automobile came into sight, I heard the radio announcer declare they had spotted a headlight nearing the town. Butterflies found their way into my stomach; all feelings of fatigue fled my body. A group stood by the side of the road and cheered us on. I recognized the Smyth family – who had just won the Junior Iditarod – among them.

The lights of Nome reflected in the falling snow and soaked the town in a yellow halo. It was almost four in the morning. The temperature hung at thirty degrees, and the wind kept calm. Throngs of people lined up along the trail and my dogs sensed the race coming to a close – they wagged their tails, acknowledged the spectators by looking left and right, trotted onto Front Street, then navigated through the noise of the crowd and onto the fenced-in snow chute. Moments later we crossed the finish line. I dropped the snowhook and walked up to each dog, hugging them one by one. My wife and sons patiently waited under the brightly-lit burled arch. As I wrapped them up in my embrace and gave them great big kisses, Kathy whispered in my ear:

"Well, it looks like you are finally the fastest in the world."

I laughed.

I did, I did, I did, Iditarod champion.

I finished the 1992 Iditarod in first place with a time of ten days, nineteen hours, seventeen minutes, and fifteen seconds. This was the first time a team made it to Nome in under eleven days, breaking the previous record by more than six and a half hours. The dogs that completed the race with me were D-2, Tyrone, Dave, Dagger, Cayenne, Emmitt, IBM, Jessie, Jose, Milkcow, Neuf, Eleanor, and Dresden.

RUNNING INTO RUBY
WITH D2 AND TYRONE
IN LEAD

CROSSING THE
FINISH LINE IN FIRST

TYRONE, ME, AND D2

PERMISSION TO
GO AGAIN

D2 WITH HIS ROS
AND HIS TROPHY

TYRONE, ALWAYS WITH
A DETERMINED STARE

A DAD JUST CAN'T
WIN SOMETIMES.
NIKOLAI LIKED THE
RED LANTERN
MORE THAN THE
WINNER'S TROPHY.
VERN CHERNESKI
AT RIGHT.

1-800-STOP-STAN
The 1993 Iditarod

Once you win the Iditarod, your life changes, and everything you do gets examined under a microscope. Whereas before, if you tried to sneak out of a checkpoint or make a move early on in a race, half the field might not notice. But afterwards? Everyone pays attention, and the scrutiny becomes palpable. You have to be on top of your game from then on out, because you will never again get afforded any slack.

In that way, things got harder, but in other ways, things became much easier. No longer did I have to worry about my trusty old dog truck catching on fire for the fourth time or the transmission failing, because now I drove a new one. Eagle Pack had come on board after the '91 race and provided the greatest benefit imaginable – free dog food – but winning in '92 made it more compelling to attract new sponsors. Being the reigning champion also meant a year of traveling around making media appearances, which was a heavy weight to bear – the amount of time needed to do the role proper justice could have easily led to a diminished training program in the months leading up to the next Iditarod, but I stayed organized as the winter progressed.

In January of 1993 I received an invitation to join the contingent representing Alaska at President Bill Clinton's Inaugural Parade in Washington, DC. It was an honor just to be asked. Of course I accepted, and Kathy and my lead dog D-2 came with me. The overall group included Libby Riddles with one of her dogs, and the Eskimo Dancers from Barrow – the northernmost community in the United States. The day of the parade turned out to be an unprecedentedly cold day in DC, and many of the groups from other states complained. *I think I may be the only one comfortable in these conditions,* I told myself as we walked down Pennsylvania Avenue and waved to the shivering crowds. I had my racing gear on, I felt cozy and comfortable, and the Barrow dancers may have been the only ones better suited. The entire event proved to be one massive cultural exchange – as far as the eye could see, different groups from different corners of the country proudly performed as they made their way past the presidential reviewing stand in front of the White House. After the parade we found our bus parked next to a marching band from New Orleans. They danced and did somersaults and acrobatics right there in the street, then stopped and watched as the Barrow Dancers sang and beat their Native drums as they returned the favor from the sidewalk. You couldn't have picked a more appropriate moment for Kathy – she stood between her two worlds. Even D-2 soaked it all in, pounding his paws while watching.

D-2 had stolen the show and been the clear hero of all my various appearances. It got to a point where I believed he just brought me along to sign him in and out of hotels. During the racing season I was "the guy with the sled," but now I was "the guy with the sled dog." The two of us starred in several commercials. One of them portrayed D-2 driving a big Ford dog truck away from the dealership with me running after, and for the rest of the winter I fielded questions from kids asking "Does D-2 really know how to drive?" He had transitioned quite well to sleeping in fancy rooms and flying in his travel kennel, so much so that he became my first dog to log more air miles than training miles. D-2 loved the attention, and the attention loved him. I should have known that things would be the same at the start of the Iditarod.

When March finally arrived, we charged down Fourth Avenue in Anchorage, and every few seconds somebody called out his name:

"Look, it's D-2! Go get 'em D-2! We love you D-2!" In response, he alternately wagged his tail, barked back a greeting, or kissed his co-leader Eleanor. Whoever said "don't let fame get to your head" never saw how happy it could make a sled dog. They love to be loved.

The gathered crowds lining the streets looked enormous – maybe my perception had skewed because more of the spectators knew my name, but the frequent banners of encouragement warmed my heart. I swelled with pride as we made our way through the city. The dogs' smooth gaits and happy demeanor showed me that I had trained the team right for another year. We were ready to defend the title, and I felt at ease while I waved to the fans.

And then I crashed into a parked car. The snow sparse trail crossed Hiland Road at an acute forty-five degree angle. This type of maneuver in a car would mean slowing down to safely make the turn, but on a dogsled you have to actually increase speed to give yourself enough momentum to swing wide and slide around. A police cruiser had parked right on the inside of the turn and only came into view at the last moment. In the split second I had to react I dumped the sled on its side. The wheel dogs missed the vehicle by inches and the runners bounced across the bumper of the car, whacking it hard. I hung on and dragged behind, scraping up my gear on the pavement. The dogs listened to my urgent commands to stop within a few seconds and I stood up and dusted myself off. *Way to look professional,* I thought. The tow rope to my tag sled driven by my handler Bruno had severed and he was already walking across the street to catch up. I hollered at him to jump into my sled for the last mile into the Eagle River checkpoint. We drove off in a hurry – waiting at a precarious spot risks compounding the problem when the next team arrives – and I looked back to see the next musher, Kathy Swenson, burning up her brand new racing suit like I had done seconds earlier. A few minutes later we packed up and headed to the restart.

Kathy joined me again from Wasilla to Knik. This was her second year in a row to ride with me and gauge the progress of the team. She had been my good luck charm the year before, and my superstitions wouldn't allow me to change anything about the first day, if I could at all help it. We casually carried on for the next ten miles, and as we neared a sharp right turn I calmly commanded the dogs wide and to the left before giving them a "Gee" at the last possible moment – swooping around the turn without the runners ever leaving the ground. Without many words both Kathy and I understood how far we had come in the sport. Gone were the days without a single command leader and when every dog ran with a different gait. The dogs sensed these moments of pride and strutted happily down the trail to Knik, where I dropped Kathy off and ventured out into the approaching night. My mind immediately turned to the serious task at hand.

I watched the dogs effortlessly float over the frozen ground as we silently glided past spectator after spectator in the dark – my headlamp was off. I liked to travel this way. After only a short time, my field of vision grew larger, and I felt the dogs had a better handle on their surroundings, without the glare from behind casting shadows and blacking out the very place they put their feet. As we passed each group of race fans on that first night, I heard calls of "Who goes there?" and "What's your name?" and "What number are you?" The kid in me, taking up a pretty good portion of my being, always looked for an odd reply but I usually managed to yell out the proper name or bib number. Usually.

During my first stop at Flat Horn Lake I looked in my sled bag and noticed a strange parcel. *I didn't pack this*, I thought, as I opened it to discover a toy cellular telephone. A message clung to it: "If I get too far ahead, call 1-800-Stop-Stan." My friend and Iditarod rookie Stan Smith had somehow snuck the toy into my sled bag. I laughed pretty good, but I obsessed over saving weight – initially I planned on burning that plastic phone in my campfire, but I changed my mind and decided to have some fun with it. Being competitive in the Iditarod meant traveling light when you could, but that wasn't the only thing that mattered. Mind games also mattered. I reckoned at about Ophir the frontrunners would all be sitting together waiting for someone to make a move. So I burned the package but saved the phone.

Sure enough, at Ophir, I caught up with DeeDee Jonrowe and Doug Swingley. They were taking their long break and still had some time to rest. I watered and fed the dogs first, then pocketed my fake phone and headed into the checkpoint (keep in mind, nobody but nobody had a cellular telephone in 1993, and those that did couldn't get service in Interior Alaska). Once inside, an open seat next to Doug caught my eye, and I sat down right next to him. My stomach prepared for a delicious bowl of stew, but my mind had its own plan brewing. With one hand inside my parka pocket and one finger on the toy phone, I pressed the button to make it ring.

Everyone in the checkpoint looked up, startled. I pressed the ringer button again, and Doug watched intently as I sheepishly pulled the phone out of my pocket and raised it to my ear:

"I told you not to call in the checkpoints! What? Uh-huh. Yep. I can't really say right now," I said.

I carried on this make-believe conversation for awhile, and then I glanced over at Doug only to see his fork stop in midair as his eyes darted back and forth furiously. He didn't look happy.

"You want to talk to him? He is sitting right here. Okay, okay, I'll let you talk to him," I said.

I handed the phone to Doug, he asked which button to press, and I pointed to the red button. *Music.* I roared with laughter. *Welcome to the big leagues, buddy.*

Doug swore up and down that he had one year to pay me back. I was sure he would come up with a good one, as driven as he was, and I made a mental note to stay on my toes around him. We left the phone at the checkpoint and later were told that several people played similar pranks on each other.

Up until then my team performed flawlessly, and our run times had pulled us ahead of last year's record pace by a couple of hours. Dipping into the drop bags over the last 100 miles had revealed a concern – the unseasonably warm temperatures had temporarily thawed much of the dog food, risking spoilage, but it had refrozen. I didn't think much of it and certainly would never withhold what was most likely safe food from the voracious appetite of my dogs. Within a day, however, I had to seriously consult with the veterinarians about the health of the team and put the first four dogs on medication for a stomach bug, a number that would balloon to eighteen in no time.

The dogs still traveled fast with diminished strength, but not to their full potential. Sick dogs simply needed more rest. I gave it to them, and they gave it to themselves on occasion – en route to Iditarod, and while competing with Rick Swenson and Jeff King for the "First to Halfway" prize, D-2 and Eleanor called a surprise forty-minute timeout in the form of a misbreeding (sixty-three days later we welcomed nine new puppies). Needless to say, I pulled into the checkpoint later than expected.

From then on I tried to race under the "yellow flag" – trying to maintain a decent pace to stay in striking distance but not revealing the overall condition of my dogs. Mushers watched each other very closely, taking note of the condition of other teams. From my own observations I knew that I was not alone in my troubles. Keeping with the frontrunners now required a far greater expenditure on the part of the two-legged dog, and by Shageluk – the last checkpoint before the Yukon River – I needed at least fifteen minutes of quality sleep.

After tending to the dogs, I opened the door to the community center. I didn't want to get trampled, so I set my alarm clock and fell asleep under a table. Twenty minutes later the buzzer sounded. I tried to stand up but failed, knocking myself unconscious on the table leaf. A few minutes later my body snapped into action – the same as if you woke up late for work after a long night and jumped out of bed in a hurry – and I hit the table leaf again. Lights out. When I finally came to I caught myself midway to a third concussion and carefully crawled out from under the table, triumphantly standing up. Then I walked straight into the wall (in my defense, it looked like a door). If it weren't for the sound of laughter I may have crumpled back down and given up. Waking up after twenty minutes of deep sleep at three in the morning was probably the hardest part of the race. If I didn't get up, however, the race would pass me by.

Normally when you get a head injury, the doctors tell you not to fall asleep the first night. At least I had that going for me, since I rarely slept in the second half of the Iditarod. The dogs' condition soon improved, but by then the leaders had gained too much time to make a real difference. We pressed on, refusing to abandon hope – I was the defending champion, after all – and still finished with a respectable placing. Sometimes things just don't go your way. The combination of the spoiled food, the time needed for the dogs to recuperate, my dizzying self-inflicted injuries, and five other teams plainly having a better run all contributed to our inability to repeat the win. It would be real easy to point fingers and complain, but that's not me. There were factors that I couldn't control. That's okay. In high stakes gambling you just never know what will happen next.

I finished the 1993 Iditarod in sixth place with a time of eleven days, zero hours, forty-seven minutes, and thirty-nine seconds. The dogs that finished the entire race with me were Eleanor, D-2, Ringer, Hector, Clifford, Jose, Jacques, Polly Pro, Dresden, Handy Man, and Gravy.

D2 AND ME IN DC

WITH ELEANOR AND
MY NEPHEW,
IDITAROD VETERAN
MARK CHAPOTON

ELEANOR

ROHN LEARNING HOW
TO BE A WHEEL DOG

Catch Me If You Can
The 1994 Iditarod

I crouched deep into my canvas sled bag with a sixty-knot wind howling around me. My friend Nicolas Pattaroni did the same in his as we both tried to hide from the fierce storm with our dog teams. Only ten feet apart, yet we could not hear each other, nor render any help were it required. When we decided to hunker down, I shouted one last thing to him:

"Empty your sled and tie everything down or it will get blown out to sea!"

As I sat in my narrow and icy confine, powerful gusts rattled the sled, and I knew the dogs were having just as hard a time getting comfortable. Being incapable of sleeping in situations like this was not unusual. I waited patiently for the storm to subside, but I had only one thought on my mind: *I am so glad this is not the Iditarod!*

This year's annual training trip to the Bering Sea Coast hadn't gone according to plan. The weather forced us to train mostly between Topkok and Nome, never getting to our usual stops along the trail. When the start of the Iditarod neared, I still had some question marks: Would all the dogs work together on the long runs? Were the proper personalities picked to run together? Was the balance of young and old dogs right? Like every year, it took some last minute contemplations before I chose the final lineup:

Eleanor and D-2 both returned and would lead from the start –

Eleanor could set a moderate early pace while teaching D-2 how to perfect some of his already proven racing skills by running next to him. Dave and Hector initially would run in swing – Dave knew how to lead but in the beginning set too fast a pace, while Hector would migrate about in various positions but never in front. Dagger – the daddy of nine dogs in the team – and IBM would be the first pair of team dogs. Then Madrid and Polly Pro, followed by Spandex and Blackbeard. Behind that the veterans Tyrone and Wolfie, then Jose and Milkcow – I always kept some of the main officers further back in the team. You never knew what could happen. This would probably be Jose's last competitive long race, since he was nearly nine years of age. Red Won – originally "Red One" until he won a race as a yearling – and Clifford – my best dog to train new leaders with – matched well after that. Jacques and Joe would work just ahead of the wheelers. Bringing up the rear were my two petites, Isabella and Dresden – I always preached the benefit of running smaller dogs in wheel as they had less downward forces on their hips. Dresden was a little lazy and certainly not the best of our dogs, but every year she somehow managed to get picked as the last dog to make the team. She would probably again work her way up to the swing position and shine during the last third of the trip – some dogs only showed their best after 700 miles. With this lineup of all seasoned veterans, I expected the miles to stretch out long and fast behind the runners.

A few days prior to the race, Anchorage looked virtually devoid of snow, so the race committee decided to only let us start with six-dog teams downtown, reloading a few blocks later at Mulcahy Stadium – a distance of less than two miles. The run to Eagle River faced the chopping block for the same reason. A blizzard blanketed the city the day before the race, but it arrived too late to rearrange all the volunteers, trail markers, and support personnel. The conditions at the traditional restart in Wasilla also never materialized, and the first real miles of the race were rescheduled farther north to the town of Willow.

We left Willow on a fine Sunday morning, with a soft trail and a blanket of fresh snow. People lined along the race trail for several miles, cheering on the dogs and drivers as they shot past. Since the restart was relocated, the dogs and I now cruised down many of the same trails that I had trained on in the early 1980s before my rookie Iditarod. The first fifteen miles wound around Willow, Long, and Vera Lakes towards the Big Susitna River. We passed teams with ease on the widely groomed trail, making it to Skwentna in good time.

For the next couple of runs, I eased into a predictable and repetitious trail routine – the dogs settled easier into a good pace when they knew what to expect. Four to five hours of runtime followed by an equal amount of rest had, in previous races, helped me establish a sustainable rhythm to compete for the win as we approached the finish line. While the dogs ran I steered the sled and worked on the runners by pedaling or running when the team went slow enough, enjoying the spectacular scenery along the way. Whenever we stopped, my work really started.

Many rookies and less savvy veterans work too much in the beginning of the race, tiring themselves out unnecessarily, and before it counts. It is important to always have enough energy to be an efficient one-man pit crew for your team. To do that properly requires more than just conserving energy at the right places; it requires good food to power you along the way. It is just as important to refuel your own body as it is to refuel the dogs. Those who have yet to learn that lesson properly tend to lose quite a bit of weight during the race; I usually seem to enter the race with some flab reserves that can then be turned into more muscle as the trip goes on. At the end I might look different, but I usually weigh the same. And that is where my wife is the difference maker.

At each stop, once the dogs are all taken care of, I begin my personal refueling process. I always have a great variety of supplies out on the trail – lovingly cooked beforehand over a several month period. All the meals are either vacuum packed and sealed for quick heating in water, or wrapped in tin foil to be thawed out on top of my stove. Grilled cheese sandwiches, marbled steaks, or butterfly shrimp entrees are complimented by oatmeal molasses cookies, Swiss chocolate, or my favorite, slices of poppy seed cake stuffed with thick slabs of butter. The goodies that I don't eat are left behind and shared with the officials or locals. The word got out during the last few Iditarods how good a cook Kathy is and my "left behinds" have brought many smiles to hungry volunteers. Nap time comes easily on a full stomach. When the dogs and driver are done resting – the dogs always get substantially more rest than the driver – we then embark on the next section before the routine is repeated once more.

With the poor snow cover we had all year the trail proved to be predictably difficult. However, it seemed everywhere we traveled, we encountered a couple of inches of new snow – just enough to cushion the ride, but not too much to slow us down. The ideal amount.

During the first third of the race it was hard to gauge the competition. Every racer employed a different strategy and travel pattern. I pushed over the Alaska Range and into the interior past Rohn and Nikolai, continuing on to Ophir for my mandatory twenty-four hour stop. This was the first time in eleven Iditarods that I went that far before stopping – Kathy had urged me for several years to wait and take it at the halfway point. This time we were almost halfway, and to my wife's credit, I could tell that my team still felt great. The only other team that opted for their long layover at the same checkpoint was Charlie Boulding – the picture-perfect bearded and burly sourdough.

Having dropped an unusually high number of my dogs – six – early in the trip, I suspected that my friends and family back home had begun to worry about me. At one point, Jim Clemenson – my friend that picked up my dropped dogs this year – received four at once. I understood the sentiment. Canine athletes don't fake injuries or fatigue, so I dropped dogs whenever needed. The team could only go as fast as the slowest dog. I knew that those dropped would soon get pampered by the race personnel and later by my helpers back at the kennel. Besides, I had a strong, solid group. The fourteen remaining dogs were high spirited and healthy.

The twenty-four hour breaks came to an end and all the competitors started tuning into each other's progress. The race was on. Dave Olesen from Canada made it first to Cripple and surprised the officials with his unexpected arrival. Dave had one of my dogs in his team – Eric the Red – and was happy with his performance. Several other mushers got there after that. I pulled into the checkpoint in fifth or sixth position with a team that told me they were peaking. As I signed in, I caught a glimpse out of the corner of Jeff King's eye as he looked over my team and then turned away to shake his head in obvious disgust. My jazzed up dogs wagged their tails like puppies as I bed them down right behind the '93 champion, knowing full well things would heat up from here on out. In the meantime I wanted to give Jeff as close a look at my dogs as possible.

The long stretch to Ruby had traditionally been a good time to make a strong push without the competition responding immediately. I knew the exact place my winning 1992 team had begun peaking, and I smiled when I pulled the dogs over in virtually the same spot with a similar feeling of momentum.

Tim Osmar and Rick Mackey soon caught up. The narrow trail wouldn't allow parallel parking, so the two teams passed and parked ahead a little ways. I watched them only very briefly before continuing my regular rest routine and taking a nap. It was difficult to totally relax as the competitive tension built, but the true heroes of the race – the dogs – needed quality sleep to perform at the highest levels.

When I woke up both teams were gone, clearly tempted by the seven course meal and the $3500 check awaiting the first musher to the Yukon River. I took my time and glided into Ruby over an hour behind. Rick Mackey led the pack, but the normal fanfare surrounding the award soon got overshadowed by an unusual rumor – a story floated around that hockey superstar Wayne Gretzky had flown into the village and bought several foundation dogs for his own team from then mayor and former Iditarod competitor Don Honea. The story proved to be a complete hoax, but it went so far as to be published in the Anchorage Daily News, and even 1975 Iditarod champion Emmitt Peters – The Yukon Fox, as he was known during his racing days – allegedly tried to track Gretzky down and sell him a few dogs. Word of mouth could be powerful.

Several teams were still vying for the win. Rick Mackey maintained sixteen strong. Jeff King pulled in with fifteen. Bill Cotter drove fourteen and had been posting very fast times between checkpoints. With all the close competition, I had no choice but to keep a close eye not only on my own team, but on the others around me. For the next 150 miles, the front-runners barreled down the Yukon River in hot pursuit of each other, trading the lead at every checkpoint. My team performed exceptionally well and maintained a swift pace, largely due to the driving energy of one of my best dogs: Dave.

Like in real life, when you have a successful brother, the other kids in the family might be overlooked by the coaches to some degree. D-2 usually stole the show, in part because he looked more "husky" than his siblings – beautiful mask, grey and white face, self-assured demeanor. Dave was every bit as good as D-2, but a tiny bit more reserved. My vision of long-legged, multi-gaited, friendly, outgoing, and fast dogs had started to come to fruition with their litter, and these two quickly became foundation dogs in my breeding program. Eventually Dave would produce more puppies than his more famous brother – Dave's back measured a half inch longer, giving him a tiny bit more reach for every step taken and making him slightly more desirable as a stud. Both were exceptional leaders. Dave had missed every race last year due to a broken toe, but rather than rushing him back into training, I opted to rest him all winter long and have him well again for 1993/1994. When he returned, he had something to prove. During the Kuskokwim 300 in January, Dave set the pace most of the time. He pulled, raced, and outran all existing records as he led us to victory in thirty-seven hours and four minutes (including ten full hours of rest) – the fastest 300 miles ever clocked in a dog race, before or since. I rarely ran D-2 and Dave together in lead – a coach with two great quarterbacks never plays them at the same time – but when I did, it was because I needed to make extra good time on the trail or because I simply wanted to show off. Their combined skills first taught me that the true lead dog – the musher on the sled – didn't necessarily have to rely on just a single super leader. If you bred, trained, and raised them right, you could end up with several. When these two boys ran in front and another team came into sight, they sped up silently until they were close enough to pass. Once on the heels of the unsuspecting driver, they would start barking and yelling. Oftentimes the driver nearly fell off their sled from the unexpected commotion. My team had become known for doing this same thing during my championship run in 1992, and this year many of the same dogs had returned. In 1992, D-2 and Tyrone had been the primary culprits, but this year Dave had come into his own, so I teamed him up with his brother, and they took the surprise tactic to an entirely new level. After we startled a team, Dave and D-2 would quickly shift us into overdrive and race past, ripping down the trail without affording anybody any drafting. It was at those moments that I noticed the key difference – once my team got in front, the two brothers literally bumped shoulders, wagging their tails as if to say "One more down. Let's go get another." Running up the Yukon, I held on and watched them work as we neared the last of the river villages.

We pulled into Kaltag in the middle of the night. I believed that to have a chance of winning it was paramount to be here with the leaders, so it came as no surprise when "The Master" Rick Swenson joined the lead group with Charlie Boulding in tow, both with very good times – ample competition still abounded for the ninety-mile jump over to the Bering Sea coast. I wasted no time and proceeded to water, feed, and baby my team before entering the community hall for some much needed sleep.

After a short nap I strolled outside into the night to check on things. Swenson and Boulding had just finished up their initial chores and were walking inside to feed and rest themselves, but they didn't see me. I approached my resting dogs; they looked up at me with willing smiles on their faces. I felt a tremendous sense of calm as I looked around to see who else was watching. Not a soul. I gathered up the team. *Time to make a move.*

The clock read three a.m. when I pulled the hook. I couldn't believe that the other mushers were still sleeping. As we began to make our way out of Kaltag, my only human interaction occurred when I accidentally ran into an official race cameraman. He wanted to run back into the community hall and grab his camera, but I stopped him. We talked for a few seconds until he realized that I would already be gone upon his return and that his actions would alert the rest of the racers, greatly influencing the potential outcome of the race. I thanked him for his understanding and then headed out under the cover of darkness.

Classic rock played in my headset as we raced towards the coast. About eight miles out, in a narrow passage, I heard what sounded like yelling, but with all my heavy clothing on I lacked the ability to grope for and turn down the volume on my Walkman. As the shouting grew louder and the dogs sped up, I started to worry we might run into a moose at any moment. Around the next turn we flew by a parked snowmachine, missing it by inches, then a sled and another snowmachine, surprising a sleeping film crew waiting for any oncoming dog teams. The yelling had been an attempt at waking the camera guys up, but at this point we waited for no one and raced on by into daybreak.

The Old Woman Cabin compelled me to take my next stop. I collected water from the tiny nearby stream that never freezes and started cooking for the dogs. The television crew soon caught up, and we both sat and waited for the next team to come. The dogs ate their warm meal and slept for two hours. I examined all of their feet. During the entire break I stared down the trail looking for the first chaser, but my rest ended with no team in sight. *Did I catch the others this much by surprise? Are they giving up, or are they playing games with me and camped a few miles back?* I didn't know the answer, but I thought it a mistake if they had decided not to chase after me. My team still had their strength and speed and had proven in prior races this year that they could maintain their pace down the homestretch. I tried not to think about the whereabouts of those behind me as I took off again.

Unalakleet, loosely translated, means "Place Where The East Wind Blows." This time around that description seemed off by 180 degrees – a stiff headwind blocked the way. Typically this stretch afforded some wind mushing, and in '92 I had fashioned a makeshift sail out of my parka and ski poles. In my sled this year I carried a new and improved sail that my friend Lyle Anderson – a lifelong sailor – had built for me. I was eager to try it out, but for about 700 miles now we had encountered exactly zero favorable conditions. Rather than surfing, I crouched down on the footboards at the back of my sled and hid from the wind as much as possible.

Practically the entire town welcomed us as we entered Unalakleet, winning the Gold Coast award for being the first team there. Before I could park, I received the trophy and prize in a short exchange:

"On behalf of the National Bank of Alaska, we would like to present you with this beautiful trophy and these gold nuggets, valued at $2500. Welcome to Unalakleet," they said.

The sound of golden pebbles hitting the brass bottom of the bowl-shaped trophy reminded me of hailstones.

"Thanks, but having all of this set into jewelry for my wife is going to be pretty costly, so I think I better get to Nome first so I can make enough money to pay for that," I said, semi-jokingly.

I bedded the dogs down just beyond the crowd and went through my usual routine. Rick Mackey arrived almost three hours after me, at seven minutes past four in the afternoon. I packed up and departed shortly thereafter at five thirty-one behind thirteen strong dogs – still ahead of record pace, and sending the signal that anyone wanting to chase me down would have to cut rest.

As I raced into the night towards the Blueberry Hills, I noticed a light bouncing off the dogs and my back. I looked over my shoulder expecting to see an oncoming snowmachine or maybe even Rick Mackey catching up, but I couldn't make out the origin of the glow. When I turned forward I still detected the bright presence. Repeatedly I glanced back in confusion. Finally I looked high in the sky and discovered the source of the beam – the Northern Lights danced overhead in a formation unlike any I had ever seen. A round ball of light, similar in shape to the setting sun, shone strongly in the Eastern sky, pulsating brilliantly as it surged and retreated in its intensity every few minutes. Usually the aurora showed up streaky instead of round and concentrated – I committed the vivid view to memory and continued on.

On the next stretch of trail I thought of Bruiser, one of my old hound dogs. Many years ago we had traveled through here and followed a big flock of ptarmigan. Bruiser was a great sled dog, but his ancestry was half husky and half pointer, so when he saw all the birds, his instincts got tickled, and he tried to point – raising his ears, standing on three legs, and sticking out his long tail, all while running and pulling in harness. The combination of his two jobs had been a most hilarious sight. I laughed out loud – I always did, and still do – when we climbed into the Blueberry Hills and past his favorite spot.

The late morning light returned as we mushed along a slow and punchy trail out on the sea ice between Shaktoolik and Koyuk. For several hours the dogs and I wallowed through the soft snow. Hard-packed trail appeared to be only ten feet over to either side, on the left or the right, but we could never quite reach it. I hadn't seen another team for most of a day and thought I had a good idea where my competitors were, yet all of a sudden Rick Swenson's team raced up next to us and effortlessly glided by. I stood on my runners in complete shock as Rick's lead dog, Bluto, powered forward with the rest of his teammates in tow. I could see every whisker on every dog and I watched in amazement when Rick waved to me in his purple parka before slowly disappearing into the distance. The team looked absolutely beautiful, but they were moving far too fast for it to be real. My mind had started playing tricks on me. It had all been a hallucination. Normally they happened in the middle of the night, but this one manifested in the middle of the day – sleep deprivation had just made its comically dramatic entrance. If you want to win the Iditarod you have to push yourself right up to the line of delirium, and then step over it. Once you are in the mental wilderness, you must be able to accurately distinguish the real from the illusory and press forward.

Leaving Koyuk, we mushed into the next night alone and with a healthy lead. I drove the sled with my light off to see more of the surroundings – the star-peppered sky provided a distant backdrop for the aurora's now snaking and multicolored dance just overhead. We climbed into the Walla Walla hills in pursuit of the natural nightlights, seemingly getting closer all the time. The dogs, sled, and I cast long, exaggerated shadows as we rose and fell with the changing terrain. The horizon stayed clear and cloudless, and the temperature plunged. We covered mile after exhilarating mile. Between Golovin and White Mountain my body began to give in as I battled back one of the most intense sleep attacks ever felt. No matter how hard I tried, no matter what I did, I couldn't stay awake. *Trust your dogs.*

"D-2, I'm going to have to sign off for a little bit, you are in charge," I said.

I tied myself securely to the sled and allowed my eyes to close. As soon as I relinquished control, a peaceful feeling washed over me, and somehow I sensed the presence of all the family, friends, fans, and children who had wished me well; I felt warm and protected as if traveling in a sheltered cocoon.

I woke up just before White Mountain, pulling into the checkpoint with a feeling of inner peace, rarely experienced. As I tended to the dogs, reserving a special pat for D-2, a reporter interjected:

"How long are you going to stay?" he said.

How long am I going to stay? What? Where am I? Every team had a mandatory eight-hour rest in White Mountain, but that question flustered me momentarily with the fear that my dogs had taken me back to Golovin – they hadn't. The resulting adrenaline boost that now coursed through my veins helped me take care of the dogs in swift fashion.

Rick Mackey checked in about four hours later. We chatted for a brief moment, both realizing that the time separating us was likely too much to overcome in the last seventy miles, barring any unforeseen circumstances. I reminded myself that the finish line was in Nome and nowhere else. Unpredictable misfortunes had occurred many times on the last stretch of trail, but I felt confident on our way out of town.

The first few miles following the final eight-hour break always started like a freight train leaving the station, slowly warming out of any latent stiffness and gradually gaining momentum. Within a half an hour the wheels were chugging along nicely and our rhythm returned. Before long we passed by the spot where only a few weeks earlier Nicolas and I had hunkered down in our sleds in a storm. This time, however, we had the elements on our side. The trail could be seen for miles. We rumbled onward beyond Safety, beyond fatigue, and beyond all previous records. We rumbled onwards to Nome. Dave and D-2 led the way.

I finished the 1994 Iditarod in first place with a time of ten days, thirteen hours, and two minutes. A new record. The dogs that finished the entire race were Dave, D-2, Tyrone, Clifford, Joe, Milkcow, Jacques, Blackbeard, Polly Pro, and Dresden. And me.

TRYING TO KEEP

FAMILY PHOTO
FRONT ROW,
DAVE, ME, & D2
BACK ROW
KATHY, ROHN, NIK

PEOPLE SNACKS

DOG SNACKS

The Fire
June 1996

It was the last day of school. The first week of June, 1996. Kathy had just taught her final class before summer vacation. We wanted to celebrate.

"Why don't we have dinner at The Islander?" Kathy said.

The Islander was a waterfront restaurant located on an island on one side of Big Lake. In the winter, the ice grew thick enough to provide a seasonal road to drive on, and cars parked right out front. On the ice. It wasn't winter. It was a hot, dry, and sunny summer day. We boated across to the restaurant.

As we enjoyed our meal on the outdoor patio, a column of smoke rose far off in the distance, to the north. It looked big enough to know that somebody nearby was not having a great day.

When we got home the telephone rang. It was Lynda Plettner – an Iditarod veteran who lived nearby. She operated the closest big kennel to mine, and she was calling everybody she knew that might have a dog truck:

"Martin, I'm right in the line of fire and I need to get my dogs out of here. Can you help me?"

"I'll be right over."

I started up my truck, hooked up the trailer, and drove over with my new handler Matt Hayashida. Matt had flown to Alaska the night before and still had jet lag.

Lynda lived seven miles up the road. When we arrived she was already frantically helping everyone evacuate her kennel. We started loading dogs right away. My truck and trailer had forty-two cubbies, but it felt so hot outside that I didn't dare put more than one dog in each. We hurried to fill all the spaces. For the lower boxes, many of the dogs jumped right in. For the higher boxes we had to pick them up. Then we headed back towards home.

On the way there we ran into a roadblock. At the intersection of the Parks Highway and Big Lake Road, across from the fireworks stand, sat the parking lot of a local hardware store. It had been established as the command center for fighting the fire. People filled the concrete clearing – firefighters, police officers, evacuated residents. That was as far as we could get.

I needed to get those dogs out of my truck. I feared that they might overheat. A chain link fence surrounded the lumber yard, and it looked like as good a spot as any.

"Let's get the drop chains out and clip the dogs right along that fence," I said.

We unloaded all forty-two dogs one by one, spacing them out evenly. Then I walked over to try and plead my case:

"I live down the road, I want to go back to my house."

"Sorry, we can't let you do that right now. The wind has shifted and the fire is headed in that direction."

"Oh no, that's not good. I need to get back there. My family might be back there, and I have sixty dogs to take care of."

"Okay. Right now we aren't letting anyone go by, but we will try and get you an escort as soon as we can."

Up until that moment I hadn't recognized the gravity of the situation. Fires happened frequently during the summer, and the vast majority turned out to be minor or were contained quickly. But this fire had become a real fire. Only an hour before, we had been sitting at the

Islander enjoying dinner. Now the entire area had been evacuated and more than 150 homes had burnt. Things had changed drastically, and I grew more worried by the minute. Waiting had never been my strong point.

After a few hours they found a forestry truck to guide me home. Matt stayed behind to take care of Lynda's dogs as I followed the official escort. For the first couple of miles the road stayed pretty clear, but I could see as we got closer that we were about to drive through a massive wall of smoke.

When we turned onto the road leading to my property, I thought we had entered a warzone. Trees fell on the road left and right. I swerved to miss several of them. I could barely see for all the smoke, but I could still make out the blinking hazard lights of the forestry vehicle in front of me. My truck engine repeatedly cut in and out because it wasn't getting enough air. It was surreal.

Two miles later the smoke cleared. The fire hadn't reached our home yet. I pulled into the driveway, got out, and opened the front door. Nobody was there. Kathy had left a note on the table:

"Martin, the boys and I are safe. The police came to escort us out. We had five minutes, so I only took what I could carry. I have the cell phone."

I felt momentary relief. My family was safe. But now I found myself alone with all of my dogs, and I had to prepare for the worst-case scenario. The fire was coming. It was still a few miles away, but it was coming.

As in any emergency, a handful of defiant people stayed back and refused to heed the orders of evacuation. One of them was my friend and next door neighbor Bob Jones. He had built his house himself and didn't want to see it go up in flames. I was in the same boat, having only weeks earlier put the finishing touches on mine.

In Alaska, when people say they are building a house, that means they are outside digging in the dirt and swinging the hammer. They are laying the foundation, framing the walls, and trimming it out. Outside of the city, many people literally carve their homes out of the wilderness. We were no different. Our house started out as a basement. Gradually we built a couple of floors on top of it through several years of sweat equity. But I had been a volunteer firefighter, and I knew that despite the effort it took to build, it was never the building itself that people missed the most when they lost their homes. What really mattered were the trinkets, the knick knacks, the pictures, the irreplaceable things. There were several outbuildings on the property, and I didn't want to lose those, but I didn't have any time to worry about them, other than gathering up any valuables from inside. My only chance to save anything came from narrowing the circle of defense. I focused on the main house, filling every available vessel with water – bathtubs, buckets, pots, anything that worked.

The handler cabin on our property was the original cabin that Kathy and her friends built after she obtained the land in the remote parcel staking program. Matt had lived in it for one night. I drove over on my four-wheeler and gathered up all of his belongings in a bedsheet, like a giant knapsack, and then carried them back to the house. At that point I could see that the smoke and flames were less than a mile away, so I started formulating a plan to evacuate my dogs.

Bob Jones and I had kept track of each other during our initial preparations, venturing around on short four-wheeler excursions to establish where the fire was and what escape routes were still open. Now we took one more to determine the best way to get the dogs out and came to a grim conclusion. The road had become impassable. The fire was coming, and there was just no way to get through it. The only way out of the neighborhood, the only hope for the dogs, was across Big Lake.

I would have to use my boat. The Love Boat. The same one from our

Yukon River trip and our honeymoon. Sixty dogs would never fit into an eighteen foot riverboat. *How is this supposed to work?* I thought, but I already knew the answer.

The temperature had been rising steadily since I made it home. It was hot, and getting hotter. The access point to the lake was less than a mile away, in the opposite direction of the fire. I could haul forty-two dogs using both my truck and trailer, but I couldn't use both my truck and trailer because I needed to pull the boat. The truck only had enough space for twenty dogs. I had to decide, without delay, who would get to go and who would get to stay. I chose my twenty best dogs.

My mind clouded over with emotion, but I didn't have the luxury to dwell on them. There was no guarantee that I could come back once I left. If this was going to be it, then I had to give myself a way to recover afterward. I hooked up the boat to the trailer. Then I filled my racing sled with one full set of winter gear – my Northern Outfitters parka and bibs, a pair of boots, a pair of mittens, and a hat – and heaved it into the boat. After that I loaded the dogs and drove down to the lake.

When I got there I parked the truck, pulled the sled out of the back, and pushed it into the water. With everything in it. It was not going to burn in the lake. If I ever made it back, if I was ever able to find it again, then it would dry out.

With the help of a couple of neighbors I got the dogs out and tethered them in the boat using whatever we had. Then I shifted the truck into reverse until it hit the water. Once the boat became buoyant, I hopped in and started yanking on the pull-start while drifting backwards. As the motor kicked on, I looked up at the mushroom cloud of smoke and flames, and then I throttled us around and towards the other shore. I didn't look back. I couldn't look back.

The dogs refused to sit still. They were not boat dogs. This was their first time at sea, and they thought I was taking them on some kind of grand adventure. They were only half right. Several of them kept jumping into the water. I had to pull them back in each time. That slowed our progress.

We made it to the other side – the south side of Big Lake – and all the willing people were there. I had let some friends know that I was coming. Everybody wanted to help.

"What can we do? How can we make this efficient?" they said.

I handed out the stakeout chains and leashes to whoever would take them. Some of the helpers had never handled excited sled dogs before. A few did belly drags as they tried to walk across the yard behind a single dog, but it didn't matter. I needed as much help as I could get. By the time we tethered out all twenty dogs, the once manicured lawn had been transformed into a minefield of digging, barking, screaming canine fervor.

I hopped back in the boat and motored off in a hurry. I hoped that I wasn't too late. The air slapped my face with the stench of burning spruce and birch. In my years of commercial fishing I had learned how to beach the boat without slowing down very much and I employed these skills when I returned – I tilted the outboard motor up as I coasted up the boat launch, locking it into place and using the momentum to walk to the front of the boat and back onto land without missing a step. I jumped in the truck and gassed it to the kennel.

They were still there. The dogs were still there. I repeated the process – loading them in the truck, putting them in the boat, taking them to the other side, and rushing back. Forty dogs were out of harm's way. It looked like I still had time to evacuate the rest.

One problem. I had run out of stakeouts. All the leashes, drop chains, and makeshift tethers were used on the first two groups. *What am I going to do with the last twenty dogs?*

There was an island – Bentz Island. It was no bigger than half an acre and fifty feet wide at the most. The only structures on it were a couple of old boathouses. And it was right in the middle of Big Lake. Perfect.

The last group consisted of retirees and puppies. I shuttled them, along with some dog food, across the water. At the shore of the island I turned them loose. Some of the puppies I picked up and placed on the ground. Most of the older dogs just leaped out. I scattered some kibble around to keep them occupied while I made my exit. As I motored away, I looked back to see some of them splashing in the water after me, but they all eventually turned and swam back. *All the dogs are safe.* With my biggest worry eliminated, I headed back to the house.

The situation then deteriorated. Smoke percolated through the trees. Small pieces of ash and debris sprinkled down from the sky. The power went out. That meant the well pump wasn't working, which meant there was no running water. If I could get a generator then I could wire it directly to the pump. That would get the water flowing again, and if I attached a garden hose to the pump then I might have a chance. I called Kathy and asked her if she could try and arrange anything. Cell coverage stopped minutes later. I needed as much water as possible to soak and defend the perimeter of the house. The hose could be my front line. My only line. But until a generator arrived, if one arrived at all, I had to figure out a backup plan. Fast. All the signs said the flames were getting closer, but the height of the trees prevented me from knowing exactly how far and from what direction. The time had come for another four-wheeler foray with Bob Jones.

To be able to see what was going on we had to drive down the trails or road and find a high spot to look from. A quarter of a mile up the street was a substation of the local volunteer fire department that provided a decent vantage point. We went over to check it out.

My time as a volunteer firefighter provided me with the knowledge of how long it would take to respond to somewhere as distant as our house. When we began to build it, that knowledge became the reason we installed a sprinkler system, because at the time all the fire service's facilities were far away. The substation had been built only very recently.

Given the severity of the situation and the high levels of organization at the roadblock, I thought that the building would be empty. Nevertheless, Bob and I decided to check, just in case there was anything left inside that we could use. We peeked through the windows:

"I can't believe it. Are you seeing what I am seeing?" Bob said.

"Uh-huh. Why aren't they using all the equipment?" I said.

"That's unbelievable. There is no way they are going to be able to use it now. The fire is too close," Bob said.

Inside the building sat a water tanker. It looked like an old semi converted into a 4000 gallon water carrier. I surmised it was full, because there would be no point in having it if you had to fill it up before responding to a fire – that would take too much time. This piece of equipment could easily be the difference between losing our homes and saving them. If the garden hose was a pistol, the tanker was an AK-47. The smoke and flames had already broken through the trees and started to swarm over the back of the building, and if you had asked Bob or me at that moment, we would have both agreed that within a few hours the building would be reduced to a pile of rubble.

"We should liberate it," I said.

"Are you sure about that?" Bob said.

"Yeah, I'm sure," I said.

The heavy metal "man" door around the side had a combination lock on it. I didn't know the code, so I wrapped a chain around the handle and attached the other end to my four-wheeler. Then I drove away. The door popped right off its hinges and dragged on the ground. I hit the brakes and hopped off. We walked into the building.

Opening the door to the cab, we looked inside. The keys dangled from the ignition. Now the six paneled, fifteen foot tall garage door became our last obstacle. Without power the opener – installed on the ceiling – would not work. Our only choice was to try the manual override and then raise the door using brute strength. I climbed on top of the engine to get a closer look. The manual override had been bolted shut. On a regular day, with a couple of hand tools, I could easily remove the hardware. But it was no regular day. We had neither tools nor time. With smoke filling up the building, hanging out at the highest point ranked at the absolute bottom of the list of safest things to do during a fire.

"Bob, I think we have to just drive it through the door," I said.

"We can't do that, Martin."

"What's the worst case scenario – we buy a new door? We can certainly live with that. I don't know how to operate this thing, though, so you should be the driver," I said.

"Well, there's no time to argue. Let's do it," Bob said.

Easier said than done. The building was barely bigger than the tanker – less than twelve inches separated the back bumper from the back wall, with the same situation in front. Bob stepped on the gas pedal. We lunged forward and hit the door. The engine rumbled as the sound of bouncing metal echoed across the room, but nothing happened. No damage done. Bob slammed it into reverse, striking the back wall with the back bumper. I squeezed the armrests as we smacked into the door for a second time – it shook harder and louder, but we were still inside. *If at first you don't succeed, try, try again.* We backed up into the wall once more.

"Just step on it. Floor it," I said.

"I'm going to try a different gear. Hold on," Bob said.

Then he hit the gas. We roared forward, crashing into the door and forcing it to break apart as the truck pushed itself out of the building. The top three panels mangled and bent upwards while the bottom three fell to the ground. We drove over them and onto the gravel pad outside. It worked. I grabbed the radio microphone:

"Tanker 8-2 in service, standing by at Happy Trails."

In the movies the paper maché doors immediately breakaway and explode, sending pieces flying in every direction. In real life all you get are adrenaline and persistence and maybe a little luck. The volunteer fire service didn't have anyone who could drive the tanker. That was why they left it parked. The irony was that the only guy who knew how lived just across the street. I knew that they needed to know the location of every piece of apparatus – that's why I called it in. But rather than having 4000 gallons of water standing by in a burning building, I figured it would be better off in my driveway – all of 600 feet away and ready to be utilized at a moment's notice, should I or anyone else need it. We drove it over.

Within a few hours, my friend Art Church rode up on a four wheeler with a gas-powered generator strapped to the back. After I had called Kathy requesting the generator, before the phones went out, she had contacted Art, who had a spare and agreed to transport it. Then she and Matt Hayashida met him at the roadblock, where they explained their situation to the authorities but were turned back. Undeterred, the three of them regrouped at a lesser used side road and tied down the generator on the back of a four-wheeler. Art drove while Matt sat on the back and held on. The police quickly spotted them, flashing their sirens and ordering them to stop. Art refused, sped up, and took them down a wooded trail. Matt tried to hold on but fell off repeatedly along the bumpy path. He finally gave up and told Art "you just go on without me" as he darted into the trees and somehow found his way back to the roadblock undetected. Art continued on, but the police soon caught up to him again:

"Pull over and step away from the four-wheeler," they commanded on their loudspeaker.

"You will have to shoot me first," Art yelled back.

Then he gave it full throttle into the forest. Eventually he got away and made it through the thick of the inferno on his way to the kennel. Good friends always appear when they are needed. We wired the generator to the water pump, screwed on the garden hose, and cranked it on. Art stuck around to help, starting his own strategic wars around the property.

From that moment on it felt like David and Goliath. Time stopped as I battled back the blaze with little more than my garden hose. The situation grew in intensity and I could hear the sap sizzling. Forty foot tall flames lapped at the doghouses. I knew that nothing would prevent the fire from seeking fuel, so to protect the house I diverted the fire as best I could, deliberately spraying some areas while leaving others dry.

After some time, out of the smoke emerged a local firefighter:

"I brought you another hand," he said.

Covered in soot, I looked over. I recognized the face.

"You didn't bring me just an extra hand, you brought me a crew!" I said.

It was John Schandelmeier – a dog musher (two-time Yukon Quest champion) who worked as a professional firefighter during the summer. When he heard about the fire he drove the 300 miles from his home in Paxson to come down and help.

We got to work, dousing smaller spot fires with buckets of water and rags. We cut specific trees with chainsaws. We stayed conscious about conserving our water. We kept calm and refused to get hysterical. Eventually John took the tanker to help save other houses in the neighborhood.

At some point the main thrust of the fire had gone by, but that didn't stop little smoky areas from bursting back into flame. The work continued. Slowly but surely, the danger decreased. Every now and again I took the boat to go feed the dogs. Several times I woke up on the deck without knowing how I got there – my body had collapsed, forcing me to rest for a few minutes at a time. When the phones came back on, I called Kathy:

"Hi honey, the house is still standing. I am safe, the dogs are fine, but boy that was a really long day," I said.

"A long day? That was a long three days for us!" she said.

Three days? The combination of the midnight sun and the smoke and the severity of the situation had eliminated all signs of day or night. I had worked nearly nonstop for seventy-two straight hours.

In the immediate aftermath, I went down to the lake and retrieved my sled out of the water. Then I took it back to the house and spread all my winter gear across the unburned part of the lawn and let it dry. After Kathy and the boys returned, I went and rounded up the dogs, modifying every single dog house chain to have a snap at either end – to be used as a drop chain should we ever have to evacuate again. The media made their way out to do an interview. My voice had gone out, but that didn't stop me from being portrayed as the fire-truck-stealing villain. For the record, I liberated it. And technically I rode in the passenger seat. No matter. Harry Truman once said "If you want a friend, get a dog." Or something like that. We had plenty of those.

THE FLAMES
GETTING CLOSER

BOB JONES

DRIVING THE BOAT
THROUGH THE
SMOKE CLOUD

BOB JONES

THE VIEW FROM TH[E]
BOAT ON BIG LAKE

THE DOGS ON
BENTZ ISLAND

THE FIRE TRUCK AN[D]
THE BAY DOOR ON
THE GROUND

AERIAL VIEW
SHOWING HOW
CLOSE THE
FIRE CAME

TRADING STORIES
MATT HAYASHIDA
AFTERWARDS

From The Ashes
The 1997 Iditarod

You don't want to fight very often, but when you fight you better make it count. The fight against the fire had certainly been one I was willing to put up with, but when you have a close call, such as it was, you tend to reflect on what is most important. Whereas we had been living in a small clearing surrounded by a mature forest, the fire now left us standing as survivors atop the ash heap, shedding light on the bigger picture. With the periphery burned away, only the essential remained – family, friends, and dogs.

We started the long cleanup process. Chainsaws could be heard for many hours of the day trying to somewhat clear the carnage created by the fire, but at least we were all together. We worked hard throughout the summer and into fall training – in no small part thanks to our great helpers. The team shaped up nicely, and I knew that the 97 Iditarod had potential before it ever began – when the energy around your home is positive, when the aura created by the beings filling it is singularly focused, you know that you are on the right track. I called it "The Unspoken."

The race committee once more relocated the Sunday restart from a snowless Wasilla to nearby Willow. Most mushers and dogs welcomed this change as it avoided the many manmade obstacles that had created headaches in the past, such as highways, driveways, and railroad tracks.

My team this year averaged a youthful three and a half years old with at least one season of racing under their belts. The lightest dog weighed in at a featherweight forty-three pounds, and the heaviest tipped the scales at sixty-five. Seven knew how to lead. Dave returned as my oldest dog, at almost eight years of age, and would be counted on to pass the torch to the new generation. I anticipated that such a young group would not rest well around the other teams, media, and foot traffic, so I camped away from the first four checkpoints. The reclusive routine helped settle the dogs down and left my competitors guessing.

My primary race plan called for satisfying our twenty-four hour mandatory stop at Iditarod, but when rumors abounded of blown in or nonexistent trail, I adapted our schedule on the fly, and we rested in Takotna instead. Coming off the long break, the team shined. Two of my most promising lead dogs, Blondie and Fearless, naturally gravitated to the lead position and made for a hard-driving pair. Given their family history, that came as no surprise.

If genetic memory exists, these two were prime examples – they emulated the best qualities of their older relatives. Blondie had been sired by Dagger, one of the most consistently competitive and toughest dogs I ever owned. Squeaky, one of Blondie's grandmothers, had helped us race Joe Garnie up the Bering Sea Coast on the way to our first top ten in 1987. Tonto, one of Blondie's grandfathers, had been a speed technician for Gareth Wright before making the transition to long distance. Fearless's parents were D-2 and Eleanor. Eleanor had been the true hero of '91 and was the daughter of my beloved Stafford. D-2 loved racing so much that when I dropped him from the 1995 race, he hid in his house at home and refused to look anybody in the eye for several days, only getting happy again when all his team members returned. Fearless's grandmother, Angel, had been an incredible leader during my first five non-Siberian Iditarods and had saved me from more than one predicament. Standing on the runners, I watched Blondie and Fearless set a fast pace for the miles to come. I could see by the way they looked, the way they ran, they way they carried themselves, that the family resemblance was clear.

Just as the team started to really move on the way to Iditarod, the sled tipped over on one of the many jarring bumps. I was violently thrown off, separating me from my team and instilling the fear that they were running driverless along the trail. The force of the fall disconnected my light, and I lay in complete darkness. I tried to stand, but one of my mittens, tied behind my back, had securely snagged on something – I could not get up without first cutting myself loose. I reached for my knife and took a swipe at the string behind me. Finally free, I groped for the battery box to my light and reconnected the headlamp, clicking it back on. My pupils constricted as my eyes settled on a pointed, razor sharp stump that stuck out from the ground, ending a foot away and facing right at me. I was looking Death straight in the eye, and perhaps vice versa. *That was close.* Had I fallen a single second later I would have landed directly on this potentially deadly obstacle. I gathered my senses. My spotlight scanned the full length of the nasty stump and discovered my snowhook balancing, under tremendous strain, on the last quarter of an inch of an exposed root. One sharp claw trembled as it hung on, preventing the team from racing alone after Doug Swingley. At that moment I fully appreciated the quality with which my neighbor had forged my snowhook. I picked the sled up, popped the hook off its precarious perch, and kept going. The team just got better and better from then on. All I needed to do was stay upright.

We left Iditarod in third place with a peaking team. My winning '92 and '94 teams had also coalesced at the same mileage point, albeit on the northern route. I made a strong move towards the Yukon River, stopping in Shageluk for an entire minute, and leaving Doug Swingley wondering what might happen next. He had arrived there twenty minutes ahead of me, just long enough for his dogs to get comfortable on a bed of straw.

My move materialized and handed me a few hour lead. When we resurfaced in Anvik, our reward came in the form of the seven course First To The Yukon feast. From there we sat firmly in the driver's seat – my competitors shortened their rests and lengthened their running time just to keep up.

Punchy trail tried to stall us on the Yukon, but we soon encountered a barrage of wolf tracks, frenzying the dogs' forward. We followed the tracks for many miles until a smattering of giant green eyes reflected against the riverbank. The first wolf stirred from his sleep, raised his head, and followed our progress without worry. The second, third, up to the seventh wolf all awoke, tracking us only with their eyes as they stayed curled up in their beds. What majestic animals – paw prints as big as my hand, perfectly designed for winter travel. Yet there I was with my "small" dogs, the wolves' direct descendants, covering even more ground than these original arctic adventurers. I saw three worlds at once – the wolves, in their wild environment; the dogs, domesticated and dependent; and myself, the partner to the dogs and in a way the reason they could surpass the wolves' natural ability. All three in the same spot and all proud, all strong, all greatly interconnected through time – some of my dogs looked back over their shoulder at me, seemingly winking and nodding their approval of my perception.

As we bounded up the mighty Yukon, we unknowingly slipped into the territory of a second wolfpack. Hidden from view, they accompanied us with their call. At first a single wolf started howling as we passed aside him, but as we progressed further up the trail the entire pack joined in the serenade. The experience proved to be unnerving for RipTide, whom I had to put in wheel – the closest spot to me and the one that made him feel the safest. The rest of my dogs harmonized with their slightly more self-sufficient cousins, bellowing back while on the move.

The next few checkpoints celebrated our arrival as the first team in and out, with the fastest traveling times. Being able to rest more while running less reinforced a rhythm that was hard for others to break. Many had already stopped chasing altogether, but not those mushers named Doug and Jeff.

The Norton Sound crossing had often been a "make it or break it" stretch, but not so this year. With clear, calm skies, and temperatures of thirty below, we headed out of Shaktoolik under a moonless plain aglow with racing bands of green and yellow aurora. Embedded amidst the swirling light show the Comet Hale-Bopp rocketed forward. I could only wonder how many worlds this celestial visitor had encountered in its journey, and I heard only the sound of the runners coasting atop the ice as I stared up, humbled, realizing that 4000 years had passed since this comet previously soared overhead. Its last witnesses may have even been some of the earliest dog mushers, sharing the same sight not far from where we ventured now, looking up as they rode behind an ancient fan hitch.

Remaining privy to this view for multiple nights led me to the outset of Golovin Bay. The year before, in 1996, I had left here on an unmarked trail in the direction of White Mountain. After a few minutes I had noticed a head light far off, clearly looking in various directions. Mushing on over to investigate, I found DeeDee Jonrowe lost and searching about on the sea ice. I told her what I had been informed of on my way out of the last checkpoint:

"We can't take the regular trail, the water has risen and flooded it. It's too dangerous, but there is supposed to be an alternate route somewhere."

Now we were both lost, looking for the "new trail" together. Eventually we found a marked way leading off of Golovin Bay and bypassing the water danger. We continued to follow the distinct markers even though they led into unfamiliar territory – carrying us into the hills surrounding White Mountain, but also taking us further and further away from our checkpoint goal. At daybreak it had become obvious that this trail was headed in the wrong direction. Up and over a couple more hills and we decided to backtrack to the bay in hopes of finding the proper path. In front, I soon spotted the correct trail in the distance and asked my team, led by Blondie, to "Gee" on over. Blondie then turned without hesitation and porpoised through the deep snow. While trudging through the thick of it, a helicopter buzzed overhead – the fourth place Tim Osmar had pulled into White Mountain without having seen us anywhere, and as a result the media went out searching. Susan Butcher, sitting in that helicopter, and with her keen eyes, spotted Blondie breaking trail. The sight of my little cream-colored leader's ability and willingness to forge an unbroken path after nearly a thousand miles had impressed Susan to the point of nominating her for the golden harness award, which she ended up winning.

My trust in Blondie had only grown since that incident, and this time she wouldn't let me take a wrong turn. We still had a race on our hands. Doug Swingley had given chase immediately behind us as we pulled out of Elim, but nearing ever closer to White Mountain the once five-minute lead gradually stretched out into ninety. For four days and almost 500 miles we had successfully fended off any and all attempts to steal our lead. It seemed, this year, the stars had aligned in our favor.

When our mandatory rest approached its end in White Mountain, I hooked up Blondie and Fearless in lead and walked down the gangline, petting and giving words of encouragement to each of my dogs. Then I walked back to the sled and waited. We still had a minute left before we could go, but many of them began to lunge in their harnesses, impatient. *Good dogs.* As the final seconds counted down, I stood on the brake and bent over to pull the hook.

At about the same time, just across the street from the finish line, an Anchorage Daily News reporter interviewed Kathy, asking her how she thought my positive attitude affected the dogs:

"If they're happy, he's happy, and if he's happy, they're happy. As long as that cycle continues, there's no stopping him. He could go on to Russia."

I couldn't have agreed more, but we planned on stopping in Nome.

I finished the 1997 Iditarod in first place with a time of nine days, eight hours, thirty minutes, and forty-five seconds. The dogs that completed the race were Blondie, Fearless, Dave, Poydras, Ingot, Calvin, Decatur, Fisher, Riptide, and Lafite. The dogs not only were rewarded with the yellow roses for winning, but I was also honored with the Leonard Seppala Humanitarian Award – singling out the best cared for team – for an unprecedented fourth time.

HANGING OUT
WITH FRIENDS

KATHY CHAPOTON

MY TWO
LOUDEST DOGS

AL GRILO

BLONDIE

FEARLESS

BLONDIE
AND
FEARLESS
LEADING
THE WAY

MUSHING NEAR
RAINY PASS

CUTTING THE
RUG IN NOME

Low Tide
The 2001 Iditarod

2001.

I don't know exactly where things started to go awry, but as the off-the-rails ride down the barren and tussock-littered Dalzell Gorge catapulted me from one obstacle to the next – sending me bouncing against trees, falling over and dragging behind the sled, and smashing my knees and elbows – I knew that I had lost control of my race. I had always been pretty nimble on the sled, but this year bruises already covered every part of my body, from head to toe. I had dropped four of my best dogs, and we weren't even over the Alaska Range yet. To make matters more miserable, on the worst sections of trail, the dogs accelerated like they were running loose in a field in the summertime, impervious to my pleas to slow down.

In the Buffalo Tunnels, the dust particles kicked up by the dogs' feet irritated my eyes, and my headlight reflected off the dirty fog like high beams in a snowstorm. I couldn't see anything.

Across the Farewell Burn, my brake spring disconnected from the brake bar, rendering it useless as it ricocheted off of every bump. I repaired it well enough to continue down the trail by pulling down on and reinserting the coil end back into its designated hole, in the process slipping and slicing the knuckles on my right hand – which then bled profusely and painted the brake bar red.

I tried to stop the bleeding with the little bandaging material that I had, but the makeshift band-aids kept washing away with the seemingly unstoppable flow. Sticking some padding inside a tight glove liner under my regular gloves provided direct pressure and lessened the problem – the blood eventually soaked through, but at least it had stopped dripping. Two or three stitches would have been the fix of choice, but it is hard to stitch yourself up in the middle of nowhere, at night, with dental floss, so I let it be. Besides, the pain from my many falls provided enough distraction to take my attention away from almost anything else.

The trail stayed unforgiving. I only had eleven dogs. By the time I made it to Nikolai, the pain started to be mental as well as physical. My confidence was gone, and my team sensed it – you can lose the trail, lose a runner, even temporarily lose your team, but the last thing you ever want to lose is your confidence.

My depression persisted to the point of wanting to quit, and the dogs deserved a long break, so I deviated from my plan and pulled into Takotna for our mandatory twenty-four hour rest. It took four naps and a few phone calls home during the layover before I could honestly look at continuing. In my pocket I still carried the race schedule that would have gotten me to Nome in about nine days and three hours. At this point it functioned better as a handkerchief. I forced myself through the motions.

Outside Don's Cabin – the dilapidated shack that serves as the unofficial halfway between Takotna and Iditarod – I stopped for a rest. Rick Swenson and Paul Gebhardt joined me shortly after. Before tending to ourselves, we all went through our list of dog chores – in my case that also included rubbing the dogs' ointment on my left knee, right elbow, and right hand in a futile attempt to ease the pain. My mild cough – picked up from the dust in the Buffalo tunnels – had now amplified into a constant hacking, accompanied by a greenish discharge. Rick noticed my discomfort and delivered a dropper of his helpful – and disgustingly foul smelling – herbal remedy, Echinacea. I lay down on my sled, held my nose, and let the medicine hit my throat. Immediately the war between Good and Evil began within my body and I gagged and convulsed uncontrollably like Dr. Jekyll and Mr. Hyde in reverse. At the ceasefire my breathing felt easier.

The miles on the Yukon blasted a windy hell straight into my face, when I dared to show it. Already having sent home all the unnecessary (and some necessary) equipment to lighten the load, I tried to help the dogs as much as possible by pedaling with my feet and pushing with my ski poles, but the headwind nullified all of my efforts – efforts which were actually more of a burden than no help at all.

Hiding behind the back of the sled became the best way to reduce drag. Whenever I popped my head up and into the wind, the team slowed down. Running was out of the question because even on a punchy and newly snowed in trail, with the dogs moving about six miles per hour, I could not keep up for any length of time while wearing my arctic gear. Crouching for hours behind a twenty-inch wide sled at three feet tall or shorter sometimes sent debilitating cramps through my legs and shoulders, so I would stand up and lean over, sticking my head in the sled bag, ostrich-style – if you cannot feel, see, and hear the wind, it must not be all that bad, right? Wrong. Occasionally I lay flat on top of the load, melting into it to stay aerodynamic, but all steering ability was lost this way, and inevitably the sled would run off trail into even deeper snow. Then back behind I would climb, peeking out from under the handlebar to help us stay on course.

My mental woes again eclipsed my physical pains, and only the thought of my wife and boys kept me going. For years I had tried to instill a can-do attitude into those whom I love and now I needed to live up to those expectations myself. At least my situation, no matter how difficult it seemed, was self-imposed.

In Kaltag I convinced myself – after dropping two more dogs and resting for fifteen hours – that the headwind we battled all the way up the

Yukon meant there must be a tailwind on the next section to Unalakleet. With seven dogs I headed out on a smooth and lightly snowing trail.

The good conditions didn't last. A few miles out the wind picked up and the snow started flying horizontally, directly at us. Pretty soon we were fighting our way in a whiteout against a strong headwind. *Another headwind.* The odds for the wind direction to have shifted 180 degrees were astronomical and only the melting snow on my face hid my tears.

After what felt like a days-long battle, we approached the Old Woman Cabin. Often in the past, overflow had presented an obstacle to wade through just before arriving. Fortunately the overflow appeared absent this year, but I stopped anyway and walked to an open spot in the small river there to fill my cooler. Carefully I stepped my way to the waterhole, testing the ice with all of my considerable weight. I filled the cooler to the brim and turned around. As I began walking back to my sled, a large sheet of ice dropped about two feet, with me on it. Water spilled in every direction as the ice broke free and I scampered forward to safety, somehow staying dry. *Mother Nature.*

Back to step one. The watering hole sat much closer to the trail now. I refilled my cooler, drove three hundred yards to the cabin, and began cooking for the team.

Were it not for several friends – Jeff and Heidi Erickson, Tony Haugen and sister, and Pat Hahn and daughters – snowmachining out to commiserate with me and give me a "gentle kick in the rear," I may have declared an unofficial second twenty-four hour break at the cabin, as Charlie Boulding's tall tales captivated all those present. I took a short nap, and after waking up, my heart – along with the rate of snowfall and wind speed – felt a little lighter, so I packed up and headed out. *Maybe things aren't so bad after all.*

The trail to Unalakleet had just received a dusting of snow on top of the glare ice, making traveling swift and easy. When I pulled into the village, the checker delivered a message:

"The good news is that your backup sled is here. The bad news is that we accidentally ran over it with a forklift."

During my stay I found myself convincing one of the other mushers not to quit, and by doing so I reaffirmed in my stubborn mind that I, too, could actually reach the finish line.

Racing with seven dogs for hundreds of miles required extra rest and extra effort. The kids in Shaktoolik thought I looked crazy when I arrived in running shoes, but crossing the Blueberry Hills with a small team forced the mantra *Just don't stop moving*. I opted for an eleven hour break, dropping me from fourteenth down to twenty-first position.

A big group of mushers prepared to exit Shaktoolik at dawn. I wanted to rest my team longer but a storm had brought high winds overnight and threatened to worsen. We latched onto the outgoing wave of teams and headed out into yet another headwind. Being among other dogs excited mine, and we fought our way to Koyuk where we took a nine-hour break.

On the way to Elim another team caught up to me. I tried to pull over and wave them by, but for some reason they stopped and refused to pass. When I looked back I recognized the dogs and musher on my tail. It was Andy Moderow – my handler, on his rookie run – driving a mix of mostly my younger dogs – dogs that I had felt were either too inexperienced or not good enough to make my race team. *The student surpasses the teacher.* Andy felt uncomfortable passing and was just trying to be polite, but he was doing an incredible job with his own race. I wasn't about to hold him up on account of personal pride:

"You go right ahead, you are having a great run, there's no reason for you to have to wait for me," I said.

I watched as he and his dogs ran by. They looked great, which gave me a spark of hope for the future.

A day and a half later, we toodled on into Nome in twenty-fourth place – my second-worst performance in eighteen tries. To add salt to my wounds, I didn't see any of the frontrunners at the finish line, not even as a show of support. Come to think of it, I hadn't seen any of them for days. The critics called it the end of my career, the waning period before my inevitable retirement. They said I had lost the desire to win.

Were they right? Nobody could tell me I had lost the joy of raising, of running dogs, but had years of being on top and winning three Iditarods rounded off a few of my more competitive edges?

I needed to do some serious soul-searching.

I finished the 2001 Iditarod in 24th place with a time of twelve days, seven hours, forty-three minutes, and fifty-nine seconds. The seven dogs that finished the race with me were Kira, Inca, 4-Runner, Ranger, Aztec, Old Spice, and Cypress.

This Land Is Our Land
The 2002 Iditarod

After a bit of reflection – which included a family trip to the happiest place on Earth, Disney World – I concluded that I had stretched myself a little thin with all of my outside commitments. The training mileage and routine for the 2001 Iditarod had been the same as in the past, but it was the quality, not the quantity, that lacked.

We cut out the superficial stuff and went back to having fun with the dogs and focusing on their progress, and not much else. Training took on a new meaning, with the underlying attitude that there was nothing to lose, nothing to prove, and no old molds to follow. The seemingly endless list of points to change and improvements to make was implemented point for point. Though hard at first, letting go of so many things we had done in the past was ultimately very liberating. We enjoyed every day, and we trained with renewed determination. The new kennel mantra became "From worst to first."

Throughout the summer we regularly took up to twenty-four dogs at a time to the nearby hay fields and turned them loose, letting them race up and down for an hour or two. They loved it, and it was great for both strength and team building – learning to get along with each other's personalities was vital. The late summer rains soon unleashed a crop of birch bolete mushrooms and it grew into a regular exercise to try and beat my dogs to the newest sprouts out of the ground. These free runs intensified as the months progressed and jazzed up not only the owners and athletes, but all the visitors and friends that joined us. We turned the corner into September with momentum.

Tuesday morning, September 11th, 2001, started out like most days. My alarm clock sounded at five-thirty. I got out of bed, walked into the kitchen, and turned on the coffee pot. My first cup was enhanced by the background noise from the television – this part of my routine I never really paid attention to, it just helped me start the day. When I finished gulping down my coffee, I went outside and fed the dogs.

My weekly Rotary meeting started at seven. Around 6:30, I hopped in my car and began the twenty minute drive. I pulled out of the driveway and turned on the radio:

"A commercial airplane has crashed into the World Trade Center in New York City..."

I continued driving, but now I listened intently. Nobody knew what was going on. Most of the talk seemed like pure speculation. *Why would a plane hit the tower in the middle of the city? Could that really be just an accident?* Several minutes passed.

"We have some breaking news...a second plane has hit the World Trade Center."

I knew what that meant. I stopped the car, turned around, and sped home. The pieces of information that trickled in started to make sense but one thing was clear. We were at war.

When I opened the front door, Kathy was already watching the news:

"This is a big deal," I said.

We sat on the couch together and tried to absorb it all. When the kids woke up we informed them they had a day off from school. We told them what was happening in New York, but at eleven and thirteen years old, I'm not sure they fully understood the gravity of the situation.

As a teacher, Kathy decided that she needed to go to school and be there for any of her students that might show up. The boys and I stayed at home, and as the horrific pictures crystallized throughout the morning, a profound feeling swept over me. It had been a long time coming.

"Boys, your dad is going to become an American citizen," I said.

Up until that moment, I had felt like an Alaskan, and there had never been any need to be more than that. I had been honored to represent the state at a presidential inauguration in Washington, DC. I had met all of the state delegates and knew many of the dignitaries. Heck, Alaska was virtually a separate country anyway. My family, my friends, my passions, they were all Alaskan. But on paper, I was Swiss.

I had nothing to do with picking my parents or my place of birth. I simply lucked out by being born in a neutral country that had maintained a pretty good grasp on democracy since the year 1291. The need for an army in a neutral country might elude the minds of most, but you can only staunchly defend what you believe in, if you have the firepower to do so. The operative word for the Swiss is always "defense," and they had proven to have one of the strongest militias in the world, for a very long time.

As the buildings crumbled in New York, my first thoughts centered on defense. I wanted to be here, to stand my ground, to prove that this was my home turf. I wanted to defend this soil. To do that, I needed to become an American citizen. And so I set about making that a reality.

The weeks after 9/11 were hectic if you worked for the INS. After a couple of weeks, I made a trip to the Anchorage branch office:

"How are you doing, Martin?" said the man behind the desk.

"I want to become an American," I said.

"Oh, I didn't know you weren't one already. Glad to help, hold on just a moment," he said, before placing a stack of about 2,000 pieces of paper on the counter.

"Here is what you need to fill out. See you in a few weeks!"

Becoming an American citizen, the legal way, was an entirely new beast to tackle. I studied American history. I studied the Constitution. I studied our system of government. I swear I learned far more than your average high school student, but the paperwork took time. At one point I picked up the telephone and called Senator Ted Stevens for help:

"What legislation do I need to enact on your behalf?" he said, humorously.

"A simple letter of recommendation will suffice, thank you; there is no need for special legislation," I said.

In the meantime, we continued preparing for the 2002 Iditarod. The winter arrived early and catapulted us onto snowy trails in the middle of October. We trained with purpose, even if the purpose of some runs seemed to be just having fun. We went to new places, camped in unfamiliar spots, and ran along with other great dogs – DeeDee Jonrowe and her operation kept training exciting. We drove to each other's kennels and had head-on passes in unpredictable locations. We traveled together on the trails, resting and visiting with as many as six teams at a time, simulating race conditions.

On the citizenship front, I sat through a few interviews and passed the required exams. One of my last bureaucratic hurdles included being dictated a full sentence and then writing it down in proper English. My sentence was *She had a big dog*.

With all of the paperwork completed I inquired – provided I survived the scrutiny of the INS –about the possibility of a special swearing in ceremony at the beginning of the Iditarod. When word came back that they approved of the idea, I was elated.

As the race drew nearer I found myself in an unfamiliar situation, with only my team to worry about, extra dogs to choose from, and time to sleep every night before the start – Kathy had assembled some of the greats that helped Happy Trails kennel in the past. Larry cooked delicious meals, Kent ran every imaginable errand in and around Anchorage, Art built me a sled, and many other friends chipped in with encouragement and action.

The day of the ceremonial start, an INS representative delivered my completed paperwork and a tiny American flag to be carried in my sled, all the way to Nome, where a judge would then sign, deliver the oath of allegiance, and declare me a United States citizen. *Now I have some real motivation to get to the finish line.* I put the packet in my sled, starting what we called The World's Longest Naturalization Ceremony.

Our veterinarian, Dr. Beatsle, had suggested I leave certain dogs home and take others he deemed more fit. Reluctantly I adjusted my roster to give the team the best chance of making the long journey the most successful. The team was less than four years old on average, and I felt confident in their abilities, but if there was any concern it was the lack of stand-out lead dogs. In years past, "super dogs" such as Eleanor, D-2, Dave, Blondie, and Fearless had made such promising appearances in their initial Iditarods that a championship caliber team behind them seemed within reach.

As the race began, those worries disappeared. All eight of my leaders, fully half of the team, took turns up front and posted faster times than expected. There was Bronson, promoted from Andy Moderow's yearling team; F-150, a Fearless/Blondie pup with a lot of heart, who ran in lead but preferred to be back in the team somewhere; Fisher, the most experienced veteran and the only dog not yet retired from my 1997 victory; Inca, a main dog from Aaron Peck's yearling team in 2000 who had blossomed into one of the swiftest and smartest; Luna, the most reliable; Stealth, who had tired of being a wheel dog and gradually moved up the ranks; Kira, the second oldest at nearly six years old and the best known, with a second place finish under her harness; and K-2, daughter of Kira, and named after her.

The dogs worked together up and over the Alaska Range, staying at the front of the field and drinking and eating as insatiably as at home. We pulled into Rohn in second place after Linwood Fiedler. I rested the team for six and a half hours before departing at two in the morning, carrying a bale of straw.

Eleven miles shy of Nikolai, I steered the team onto the Salmon River and stopped at the fish camp, spreading out the straw and letting the dogs make their beds. I dug into the snow a little to try and find water but came up dry and had to melt snow instead. An hour of solitude passed, and I turned in for a nap. Other teams soon started to glide by – I heard the banging of approaching sleds, the soft rumble of paws on a packed trail, and even the panting of the advancing groups.

Kira and K-2 occasionally announced the coming of another team, sometimes resulting in a return bark or howl from those passing. Each of these boisterous events awakened me, and after checking my alarm clock to make sure I had not rested too long, I then buried my head even deeper into my sleeping bag in hopes of hearing less the next time. Sitting and waiting while other mushers streamed by in droves proved difficult. I wanted to give chase, but I also knew that sticking to the plan would make us more competitive later in the race.

Our patience was ready to be rewarded when we pulled into Nikolai. I wanted to leave right away, but first we had to wait five long minutes for the vet on duty – who needed to look over my dogs and sign my vet book – to exit the outhouse. The checker asked me to sign-in on the second sheet of paper, which meant the first twenty spots were already filled. We had fallen way back, and the dogs lunged into their harnesses as I stood on the brake. A well-meaning volunteer tried to help park my team behind the schoolhouse with the rest of the pack, but stopping was out of the question. In the midst of the misunderstanding we mowed the poor man over with the gangline as the dogs jumped over him to reach the outbound trail. *Sorry.* With all of the commotion I was unable to ask the most pertinent questions, such as who had left and when and with how many dogs.

I tried to make out how many sled tracks lay in front of us. One set looked very fresh and I studied them for awhile, attempting to determine who might have left before we did, but without any evidence of paw prints I realized they belonged to a snowmachine pulling a freight sled. I went back to focusing on the progress of my team.

An hour out, Kira looked tired. Like last year, she had missed many of the more serious training miles, and her selection to the team came strictly from her reputation from past race performances. The trip to McGrath ran across flat terrain so I decided to give her a ride all the way to the checkpoint. I stopped the team, walked her back to the sled, and made her a comfortable bed with my sleeping bag in the sled bag. When we took off again, she realized the team had started running without her, and she did not approve – she struggled and wriggled free, darting out of the sled bag, scattering some stuff on the trail, and running up to her rightful spot in lead. The leap to liberty spilled my mittens and mandatory vet book several feet behind us and forced me to stop and anchor the team before walking back down the trail to retrieve the items – a huge no-no. Generally speaking, you should never, ever walk behind your parked sled, lest you want to run to Nome, but both of these were difficult to replace and very much needed for the rest of the race. Luckily my team waited for me.

I repacked my belongings and tucked Kira in once more, petting her and assuring her it was okay to be on the receiving end of her pulling powers every now and then. This time she realized my intentions and relaxed with her head on top of the cooler as we raced to our next goal.

Periodically she looked out of the sled, and I continued chatting with her to keep her calm – I had a good feeling that she would benefit from the extra hours of rest.

My radio picked up the local radio reception. I kept my ears open amid the diverse programming for any race updates. Only in rural Alaska can you hear the most aggressive rap song followed by a church sermon. It took a couple of hours, but finally I heard the news I had been waiting for:

"Come on down to the checkpoint to meet the Iditarod mushers; Martin Buser should arrive first between seven-thirty and eight pm."

I'm in the lead. Apparently we had passed twenty teams while they rested in Nikolai, and none had left before we did. The radio also broadcasted which teams comprised the rumba line of chasers and how far back they were. I knew many of them would leapfrog us again.

We coasted into a welcoming crowd of townspeople in McGrath at 7:37pm. As the first team, PenAir CEO Danny Seibert presented me with the Spirit of Alaska award:

"PenAir is pleased to present you with this Native Alaskan Spirit Mask. It symbolizes the union of the spirits of the musher and the dog. Together they combine to make one spirit, and you have proven that here tonight. Congratulations," he said, before pointing out what all the various symbols meant.

The mask was beautiful, and at that moment it seemed fitting since I had made the pact with Kira to give her extra rest time. We stayed for six hours, during which thirteen other teams streamed through, but only two – Jeff King and Charlie Boulding – for more than a few minutes. We had the checkpoint almost to ourselves.

With the additional four hours in the sled, Kira appeared like she had taken a day off. She ate everything I put in front of her, slept well, and passed the physical exams by the veterinarians. As we prepared to depart, she stood up and started screaming to go. I put her in lead, and she lunged and loped as she pulled us out of town. *Intuition pays off.*

At Ophir we took a four-hour rest before heading for the halfway. Little trail intelligence was known on the new location of Cripple – the checkpoint only exists during the Iditarod – except that it was farther from Ophir than it had ever been by an undetermined distance. We ran through the day and into the early evening.

Eight hours of effort brought us within minutes of reaching the makeshift tent camp, where the GCI Dorothy Page Halfway award awaited the first musher. The heavy marble trophy, scale model dog sled, and silver cup containing jewelry-grade gold nuggets had long been one of the finest trophies in the race. This year an internet live cam trained on the incoming trail made it possible for the world to see the first team to arrive. Often I wore just the liner of my Northern Outfitters parka, and as luck would have it, my light blue liner also resembled DeeDee Jonrowe's. I learned later that for a few anxious moments there was some debating and worrying going on back home as the first musher in light blue approached the checkpoint. My family was split about fifty-fifty and was very relieved when it became clear that Kira was leading the race to the halfway mark.

Settling in for our twenty-four hour break, I unclipped all of my dogs and removed their harnesses. Once loose they chose their sleeping places and which of their buddies to lie next to. I fed and checked on them every few hours. The Iditarod volunteers had erected a heated wall tent with bunks inside for mushers to spread out and relax, and I took advantage. Several other drivers, also on their twenty-fours, soon joined me – DeeDee Jonrowe, Ramy Brooks, Linwood Fiedler, John Baker, and Jerry Riley.

As the clock wound down and the start differentials were accounted for, revealing everyone's relative position, I emerged once more in the lead. Bill Cotter actually left Cripple fifteen minutes ahead of me, but he had yet to take his long rest, leaving him essentially a full day behind in real-time.

We quickly caught up to the temporary rabbit and raced on to Ruby. My well-rested and eager dog team devoured the rolling hills to the mighty Yukon River like they were level terrain, reminding me of a conversation with my son Nikolai on the day of the start:

"How can you tell if you have a good dog team?" Nikolai had asked, ever inquisitively.

"Well, sometimes a strong dog team seems to flatten out all of the hills. Their combined power in pulling the sled overcomes all obstacles – hills, mountains, and punchy trails alike," I had answered.

We made it to Ruby in first place at four in the morning, two and a half hours ahead of the next team, piloted by Ramy Brooks. I fed and bedded down my dogs before walking over to the community hall to humbly accept the First to the Yukon award – the seven course gourmet dinner that this year included smoked chicken pecan salad, chilled roast pork tenderloin, prawns stuffed with lobster, grilled Portobello mushrooms, and fruit tart flambé. I sat down and shared most of it with several race officials and volunteers. Seven bottles of wine came with the meal, but at five a.m. and 500 miles traveled, I decided it better to save those for another day, when I could savor them with my wife.

None of my previous teams had ever looked this good this far into the race. We were sitting in a nice position, but the competition was keen, and it was a long way yet, with nearly another 500 miles to the finish line. After completing our mandatory eight-hour break, we headed west down the Yukon. Unlike last year, we enjoyed a tailwind.

Roughly twenty hours later, at 8:45am, we pulled into Kaltag. Ramy Brooks followed at 11:25am. In more than 150 miles of racing, we had picked up only ten minutes on our closest rival. I rested my dogs for five hours, then continued on.

The way to the coast revealed challenging trail. Loose snow drifted over the trail in twenty-five mile per hour winds. My team charged through it and held their speed, despite the conditions. A group of old friends greeted me at the Old Woman Cabin and gave me an American flag t-shirt they had covered with good wishes and signatures. I thanked them for the gift, but I was in a hurry and did not plan on stopping:

"You know, you were much more fun last year when you were in twenty-something place, feeling dejected and sorry for yourself and cracking jokes with Charlie Boulding to keep yourself from crying!" they said.

"I am truly sorry for the brief stay, but hopefully we can party together in Nome, and if not I will certainly see you the next time I come through," I said, as I let off the brake and the dogs pulled me down the trail.

Navigating the last couple of miles into Unalakleet, the wind kept up, and the polished river ice yielded no footing for the dogs – with all the slipping and sliding going on, it felt like we were running in place. The trail markers were few and far between, and the thought of taking a break in this wicked winter squall helped me devise an unprecedented resting procedure. I had a new sled waiting for me at Unalakleet and, assuming it did not get run over by a forklift, I planned on emptying both sleds – the new one and the one I was driving – of all their contents and bedding the team down inside the sled bags, which I would fill with straw. That would give the dogs a chance to sleep in peace.

The optimism for my new plan occupied my mind until we made it to the checkpoint at ten minutes after midnight. The volunteers directed us to the proposed rest area, and I did not believe my eyes when my headlamp beamed up and down on six huge snow berms. Bigger than any man, the towering snow walls blocked all the wind, allowing the team to rest in great comfort. Although they were not around, I openly thanked the "snow engineers," whoever they were, for constructing such perfect shelters with their front end loaders.

Ramy Brooks and team arrived at twenty past three in the morning.

We had gained half an hour in the last ninety miles, giving us a three hour and ten minute lead. With the weather brewing, however, I knew not to take anything for granted.

I let the dogs relax for six hours before packing up. Darkness lingered, and the winds away from the checkpoint now howled at forty miles per hour, making our departure as much of a challenge as our arrival. We plodded forward, but as daylight approached, the wind subsided, and the Blueberry Hills became mere speed bumps compared to last year.

We glided into Shaktoolik under calm blue skies – a moment so unexpected that the locals all grabbed their cameras and rushed outside to record the rare event. We stayed for five hours, and while still in town, a light breeze materialized again, but this time from the south. A tailwind. My favorite.

At the outset of the race I had been worried about the lack of a "super leader." As the race progressed, those worries had abated, as all eight of my leaders proved themselves along different segments. But now, as the slight southern gusts aided us in crossing the sometimes dreaded Norton Sound, one of them emerged above the rest as the unlikely hero of the team. Bronson.

Andy Moderow had suggested that I take another good look at Bronson after the 2001 Iditarod. I heeded his advice, and now the unassuming, quiet, and docile dog had come to shine through every mile of this year's race. Bronson had been picked on as a puppy by the other dogs, and even though he was still somewhat shy of strangers, he overcame his social anxieties and learned to lead a super competitive team. His nonaggressive behavior is in part what made him so special, as he always implemented the commands given and never tried to intimidate his co-leader, like Kira or her daughter K-2 would do. Bronson actively sought out and followed the trail stakes, a skill I had a hard time teaching at home since most of our trails were not heavily marked. After a few days of racing, the dogs typically tuned in to the marking system and often even implemented turns on their own. I always praised them when they showed that kind of initiative. Bronson was as good as any at making his own decisions, but he also drifted to the left when he ran. Given an open, hard-packed field, he would probably run in a five-mile circle. Luckily, most of the wooden markers on the Iditarod happened to be on the left, since the trailbreakers kept their right hands on the throttle of their machines as they rammed the trail stakes into the snow with their left hands. On the way to Koyuk, Bronson ran headfirst into a marker about every quarter mile. Each accidental impact alerted him to swerve a bit to the right to correct his bearing, but after a few minutes he was back on course for another collision. I certainly could not complain – Bronson was leading us ever closer to the finish line, and more than six hundred other dogs were chasing after him.

We made it to Koyuk at a quarter past ten at night. Ramy Brooks showed up almost three hours later at one in the morning. He had cut into our lead a little bit, so I took off at two-thirty to keep him on his toes.

My Achilles' heel – one of many – had long been Elim. Having always believed that the dogs would finish strong if allowed the luxury of a rest there, I decided once again to stop and give them a couple of meals at the checkpoint. I knew that with Ramy about three hours back, I could rest my team at least that long and still find myself in the lead – my poor family and friends must have grown a few gray hairs or even pulled their hair out as they followed the race updates and watched Ramy come within seven short minutes of our team when he pulled in and out of Elim, only stopping for two minutes. On the way to White Mountain, however, our lead grew again, and we had a cushion of more than an hour.

Ramy had played his last card, hoping that he would close the gap with his strong push and be able to trail our team into the last mandatory eight-hour break. Sometimes a dog team, like a pet dog at a park, is more apt to chase those in front of them when they are close behind. Had Ramy been able to do that, the outcome would have become far less predictable, but Bronson and Kira just set too fast a pace for anyone to keep up.

We left White Mountain at midnight and mushed the last seventy-seven miles through the moonlight and into a new day. My most important lead dogs had been Bronson, Kira, Luna, and K-2. I wanted all four to cross the line together, so I hooked them up in an experimental fan hitch just outside of Nome, but K-2 preferred to be in the team instead. Coming up onto Front Street, Kira, Bronson, and Luna ran in lead, Stealth and Cypress were in swing, then K-2 and Hunter, then Danny, with Daisy and F-150 bringing up the rear.

Nikolai met us at the beginning of the chute and handed me a large American flag as he ran next to the sled. I had already been clutching my tiny official flag from the beginning of the race, but now I gladly waved Old Glory to the excited crowd. The dogs must have sensed my pride as they trotted eagerly ahead, finishing our race in less than nine days.

The next day, amid a large group of family, friends, and fans, I returned to the burled arch. Many of us were decked out in red, white, and blue. With my wife and two sons standing on either side of me, I raised my right hand and repeated the words that Judge Ben Esh, the acting immigration official, provided:

"I hereby declare on oath, that I absolutely and entirely renounce and abjure all allegiance and fidelity to any foreign prince, potentate, state, or sovereignty, of which I have heretofore been a citizen; that I will support and defend the Constitution and laws of the United States against all enemies, foreign and domestic; and that I take this obligation freely, without any mental reservation, or purpose of invasion, so help me God."

We stayed in Nome and celebrated for several days, during which I made sure to shake hands with and welcome every other musher across the finish line, from second place on down to the red lantern. After that, Kathy, Nikolai, Rohn, and I all hopped on our own snowmachines – mine with an American flag attached – and left town, riding the Iditarod trail in reverse, all the way back to Big Lake. It took a week to make it home. For me, though, it felt much longer, like it had taken nearly twenty-three years.

I finished the 2002 Iditarod in first place with a new record time of eight days, twenty-two hours, forty-six minutes, and two seconds, but who's countin'? The dogs that finished the entire race with me were Bronson, Kira, Luna, K-2, Stealth, Cypress, Hunter, Danny, Daisy, and F-150.

FREE RUNNING

KATHY CHAPOTON

THE BEGINNING
OF THE WORLD'S
LONGEST
NATURALIZATION
CEREMONY

JOY BERGER

WAVING OLD GLO
ON FRONT STREE

JEFF SCHULTZ

RECITING THE OATH
H JUDGE BEN ESCH

PROUD TO BE
AN AMERICAN

Evolution
2004

The 2004 Iditarod saw more lead changes than any race I had ever entered. More than 100 mushers signed up, but a more manageable eighty-seven showed up to the starting line. We enjoyed no lack of competition, with five Iditarod champions, representing seventeen wins, all returning. 2003's winning dog team from Team Norway tried to repeat their performance, albeit being driven by a different musher. They almost did it, but Mitch Seavey came out on top. I ended up eleventh. Merely forty miles from the finish, while trying to untangle my team from a pile of driftwood after the wind had blown us across glare ice, I slipped and fell and suffered a hernia. The temperatures along the trail swung as low as forty below zero and as high as forty above Fahrenheit. It turned out to be a revolutionary year, but not for anything that happened during the race.

Christmas morning I opened one of my gifts from Santa and discovered an iPod inside. It could store thousands of songs, which meant that I could listen to music for the entire Iditarod and never repeat a single track – a far cry from the early days.

Some races I had purposefully tackled in radio silence, but not most. My first real struggles had come in 1981 when I spent hundreds of miles reading candy wrappers. Part of that desire to read stemmed from running with a slower, noncompetitive team, but once I got my own dogs, that was no longer a problem, because I liked to go fast. So I turned to music.

The first portable entertainment system was the tape deck. The Walkman. Each cassette tape stored ten or fifteen songs on it, which lasted maybe an hour – thirty minutes on each side – and got you about ten miles down the trail before you had to repeat it. My favorites included The BeeGees, Elton John, The Rolling Stones, and Aretha Franklin. Being weight conscious I would just send one new cassette in my drop bags to last between each checkpoint, but after ninety miles I would get pretty sick and tired of listening to Aretha's top hits and was more than ready for some BeeGees or Rolling Stones or whoever. How long could one person realistically listen over and over to the same songs on a thousand mile trail without going insane? Sending the tapes out with the food drops caused many of them to be loose and partially unwound from all the shifting and jostling that occurred during transport to the checkpoint. I always took a little twig to make sure the tape spooled up properly before I put it into my tape player, otherwise they might jam or snarl or even break.

Frequently when I caught up with another musher, or someone passed me, we switched tapes. "Hey, do you have a tape you want to trade?" That was the custom. I listened to whatever tapes I could get my hands on.

Once I found an unlabeled cassette lying on a table and popped it into my player on the way out the door. Not wanting to waste battery life, I didn't press the play button until I got out on the trail. That proved unfortunate, because it contained some of the raciest, nastiest, ugliest lyrics I had ever heard – some kind of low quality rap crap. It sounded so terrible that I decided to be its last listener. As I went down the trail, I pulled the end of the magnetic tape out and hooked it on a little bush, holding on as it buzzed and unreeled until I heard it pop. Seeing the demise of that particular album gave me real pleasure. I considered it a humanitarian action.

A few years went by, and then compact disc players came on the market. The Discmans. At the time it seemed like the ultimate, as they could store twenty songs instead of only ten or fifteen. You didn't have to wind them up anymore, but you did have to keep really still if you wanted to hear anything because of all the skipping. If you were on a rough trail then you had to change how you drove the sled and become the suspension system for your music player. Once the no-skip feature debuted we thought we had it made, even though it only helped for a few seconds at a time.

By then I had made all of my gear user-friendly. Instead of having wires hanging around everywhere I took all my winter hats apart and inserted and sewed a speaker on either side at ear level, running a single wire out of the back of the hat that I could plug it into whatever audio platform was popular at the time. That allowed me to not have to deal with headphones or earbuds, which became painful after wearing for a day or two.

When Rick Swenson upgraded to the minidiscs, everybody rushed to retool yet again. They were half the size as CDs – saving weight – and could store as much or even more music. I went out and bought them, but I only used them for a single year, as they ended up being like the eight track – a temporary fad. The MP3 player arrived not too long after.

The first thing we noticed about the MP3 players was that they never skipped, no matter how rough the trail. They started out with the same amount of storage as CDs, but as time went on they kept getting smaller and smaller while being able to hold more and more songs. It was hard to keep up with the early iterations. The iPod, or high memory MP3 player, pushed the evolution even further, because you could choose your soundtrack, and it lasted for days. It quickly became the panacea of portable entertainment.

The second innovation of the winter resulted from a sled redesign. Historically, the musher occupied the back portion, standing on the tails of the runners, and could pedal or run behind. The basic style hadn't changed much in centuries. Then during this year's Kuskokwim 300, Jeff King unveiled a new sled that allowed the driver to sit down on part of the load. He had shortened the traditional area in the front and added about a third of the storage space to the back. He called it a tail dragger, or a caboose. I jokingly called it an O.M.S., or Old Musher Sled, because anybody that physically needed to drive one must have run at least fifteen Iditarods or been fifty years of age. It was a major departure from the sleds of the past.

In my racing career I thought I had seen almost every sled design known to man. In the 1988 Iditarod, the famed Shishmaref Cannonball, Herbie Nayokpuk, had somehow, with special connections, managed to fly a special sled out to Shaktoolik. He had probably done it for years. We were racing near each other, and when I pulled into the checkpoint I saw the sled with my own eyes. It was an old-timey birch sled, made probably out of driftwood, and lashed together by hand. Something about it seemed quite different, however, and looking at the bottom I realized what it was. It had ivory runners. Thinking about it, I knew that no walrus existed with tusks long enough to make that, nor would you want to have a solid ivory runner. The Eskimos dealt with that by carving little pieces of ivory, about an inch and a half wide, the width of the runners, and about four to six inches long – it didn't matter how long they were so long as they were straight. Then they beveled each piece at a forty-five degree angle and made little holes through the ends and lashed them to the bottom of their sleds, one piece after another, all the way down the running surface of the sled. The result was something super strong that slid easily on ice. Herbie took that sled all the way to the finish line, but the ivory runners were not the only feature, or non-feature, that caught my attention. The sled didn't even have a brake. There were still some hills between Shaktoolik and Nome, but he had his dogs so well trained that they would slow down, they would stop, and they would listen to him, using only the sound of his voice.

Around the same time period, many mushers started the race with a big, heavy, indestructible sled to get up and over the Alaska Range, through the Farewell Burn, and across any of the rough terrain until McGrath. There were different ways of dealing with or hoping that you had built an unbreakable sled. One of those ways was to use material perceived to be indestructible. That's when the first generation of aluminum runners came out, although any metal, if you flex it for long enough, however little that may be, will eventually break. Another school of thought used runners made of something really flexible, like a ski or laminate material, because their ability to bend meant they were less likely to break. But that became expensive. My school of thought for awhile was to overbuild the sled, make it super strong, and take all the flex out of it completely. In essence, I took a ten foot long 2x6 board and fabricated an ultra thick runner out of it by cutting the front three feet and holding it with fasteners to bend the wood into the proper shape. The drawback of driving such a strong, simple sled without flex was that I felt the bumps. I became the shock absorber, because there was no give whatsoever while going down the trail. We called them "stone boats" or "beater sleds." When I was young that type of rough riding presented no problems, but as the years progressed I gradually converted back to sleds with more flex. The aging body can only take so much.

Design tinkering by somebody occurred every year. I had tried my hand at it more than a few times, but my most innovative and well-known feature had been the sail. The idea for the sail came from a natural evolution of working with nature, the trail, and the spirit of whatever goes. Probably because all of my early Iditarods had a big blow that often affected the outcome of the race, I learned to be prepared for anything.

The first version of the sail was a simple trapezoid, about two and a half feet wide at the bottom and five feet wide at the top. I made it out of typical sailing cloth and sewed long pockets on either side for inserting the telescoping aluminum poles I used to hold it upright. Going down the trail, I would hold it by the poles wherever the wind was coming from, steering the sled into the same direction. The wind would fill that sail and help propel us forward. Clearly it helped the dogs, and they certainly didn't mind if they had to pull a little bit less, but the earliest sail was very fatiguing on my hands.

The next generation had a very similar design as well as handles that allowed me to hold it easily while still wearing mittens. Since the sail could only be employed under certain conditions, I continually challenged myself to find lighter fabrics and poles in an attempt to justify carrying the extra weight in my sled. A friend of mine who had been sailing every free moment in his life helped me both find an extremely light sail cloth and improve the design even further. When I told him that I had to peek around the corner to watch my dogs, he suggested inserting a round window. We ended up finding a workable size hole, with a suitable material, that let me see the team when I held the sail up. There was very little trial and error other than successive Iditarods, because at home we hardly ever had sailable wind conditions and always had a well-rested dog team that needed no help in speeding up.

The last generation of sail was strong and light and could be rolled up in a tiny tube that I tucked away in the sled and forgot about. It could harness about 100 degrees of wind, so long as it was behind me. I used it for a few years in the Iditarod and came up with plans for more improvements, but then it got outlawed by the rules committee, even though I stumbled upon a century-old picture of a Gold Rush era musher using one. I could still use it – and still do – on the Kuskokwim 300, as their rules are based solely on practicality and whether they help or hinder the dogs.

In 1994, in my first "Kusko," I had encountered the perfect wind conditions for sailing, and my dogs that year had basically run the entire race while free running, setting a speed record in the process And now, ten years later, on the same trail, Jeff King had decided he would test out his new prototype design. I followed him for many miles, peeking, looking, and evaluating the way that he was driving that sled. Every now and again he would sit down on his seat, put his hands behind his neck, stretch out his arms, and put his feet up on the handlebar like he was watching TV from an easy chair, just to rub in the fact that he could sit while I had to stand for 300 miles. It certainly made an impression, so much so that right then and there I determined it to be a game changer.

When I arrived home after the race, I modified one of my sleds and within a couple of hours had gone on a training run with a very similar design. In the 2004 Iditarod, Jeff and I were the only mushers driving them. That gave me a chance to properly try mine out and think about how to better customize the design for my own needs. It was a good thing, too, because the very next year, although I didn't know it yet, I would need it more than I could have ever imagined.

THE SAIL,
NOW OUTLAWED

ERIK HILL

A BASIC SITDOWN S

JEFF SCHULTZ

An Unplanned Weight Loss Program
The 2005 Iditarod

Rohn was working in the garage on a pinewood derby car project for high school. Feeling competitive, like always, we discussed the potential differences of higher weight versus the lack thereof and decided that lighter was better. Faster.

As Rohn sat there, cutting, sanding, and whittling away every unnecessary gram of wood, of course, per my fatherly duties, I had to get in on the act:

"What do you think about gouging out a significant amount of wood from the underside of the car, between the two axles?" I asked.

"Yeah, there is a fair amount of mass there," he agreed. "It might take awhile to cut out but it seems like a good idea."

"No need for it to take a long time, if only we can get the proper tool set up to do that," I said.

We settled on the table saw and the blade of choice became the dado blade – a carbon-tipped saw blade with deliberately offset teeth to chip out the maximum amount of wood at high rpms, also called a wobble blade in some shops. In retrospect, it was overkill, but it provided more power, and I couldn't resist.

I turned the saw on and held the car over the humming blade, slowly lowering the belly of the body towards it. The instant the wood made contact, my right arm jerked forward and the little car flew across the room with a hiss. In its place a thin red line of blood now streamed to the ceiling.

In shock, my eyes followed the flow and I saw the word "Challenge" printed on the poster that had become the point of contact with the wall. I grabbed my right hand and applied direct pressure to try and stop the bleeding. I had no idea how badly my hand was cut up, but I knew that I needed medical attention immediately.

"Go get your brother; he is going to drive me to the hospital," I said, "Then clean up the garage as best you can and tell mom I need to get some stitches. Sorry about your car."

Rohn was too young to drive, but he reacted quickly and ran out the door. Moments later, Nikolai, holding the car keys, came running in as I was wrapping my hand with some clean rags.

I opened the passenger door and hopped in. Nikolai, already in the driver's seat, started the car and backed down the driveway.

"Drive as fast as you feel comfortable," I said, secretly hoping that we would get stopped by the police, which would result in an even faster arrival at the hospital.

Nikolai, then sixteen years old, obliged. We set course for the nearest hospital in Palmer. I unflipped my cell phone and called a local doctor friend of mine, waking him up:

"Can you meet me at the hospital?" I said.

"No, I can't, I just got back from South America a few hours ago and need some sleep. You should go to the emergency room," he said, in the midst of a serious bout of jetlag.

Back at home, Kathy felt the disturbance in the Force and questioned Rohn while he cleaned up the messy garage:

"Did dad cut off a finger?" she asked.

"I think so," he replied.

That started the cell phones whirring. Kathy called me. I told her the story. Then she tracked down the number of our friend Mike McNamara, a hand surgeon. I talked to him on the phone:

"We are on our way to the ER. I put my hand in a table saw and I think I cut a finger off."

"Come to the Alaska Regional Hospital in Anchorage instead. I will meet you there when you arrive."

I told Nikolai about our change of plans and reminded him that he should try and make good time. *Where are the police?*

We drove and drove. Direct pressure and elevation kept the bleeding at bay until we were a half a mile from the hospital. Turning right on the corner of the Glenn Highway and Airport Heights, less than a minute away, I felt a steady trickle running down my arm and elbow – the rags on my right hand had completely soaked through. As I exited the car, I took one look at my shirt and pants. They were drenched.

Dr. McNamara met me at the door and in a blur a bunch of folks rushed me into a room.

"Martin, Martin, Martin, what have you done now?" Mike said.

"I'm doing the Iditarod in four days. Do whatever you have to, to allow me to do the race," I said.

Surgery was imminent; it was just a question of what could be done. The tip of my middle finger was gone, never found, disappeared somewhere in my garage, and the top half of what was left Dr. McNamara referred to as mangled – injured so badly that it was not very reconstructable. A tiny fraction of my index finger had also gone missing and my ring finger suffered five deep triangular gashes.

"Martin, you're not going to make it," Mike said, "You can't do the Iditarod with this bad an injury to your hand."

"You leave that up to me, doctor. You do your part, and you leave the rest to me," I insisted, as the anesthesia kicked in.

When I awoke, an inch and a half of my middle finger had been amputated and sutures now lined the length of my ring finger, with two more on my index finger. The surgery had taken two and a half hours. Dr. McNamara then tried to persuade me not to race.

I decided to go anyway. The way I saw it, I couldn't do any more damage than I already had, and I still had three reasonably good fingers on my injured hand to do chores with. I could still drive the sled, although it would be difficult. I knew that it couldn't be a completely one-handed race, but I am left-handed, and that had to count for something. The Iditarod had always been a proving ground for me, my dogs, and my entire operation, and we had worked towards it for an entire year. It would be foolish to stay home and feel sorry for myself if I thought the race was at all humanly possible. I had finished twenty-one times before, and I knew every inch of the trail. It was my livelihood. And when you only have one paycheck a year, missing your one shift at work is not an option.

I didn't want to jeopardize my health, however. My post-surgical prescriptions included antibiotics to stave off infection and anti-inflammatories to keep down any swelling. I had pain medicine as well, but those caused drowsiness, and making myself even more tired during a nine-day ultra endurance event was not my highest priority. I didn't plan on taking them. Maybe the pain would help to keep me awake. My hand sat snug and immobilized in a bandaged splint that I then stuffed into a mitten to keep warm. For functionality I rigged my parka with Velcro on the left chest to hold my hand stable and pointing up. When I needed to steer or use it, pulling free from the Velcro would be simple and easy and uncomplicated. Dr. McNamara put together a special emergency kit – should a rogue situation arise where I required it – with sutures, medical tapes, betadyne, and a lidocaine gel to numb my injured fingers if the pain intensified.

The forecast called for relatively warm conditions. Had it been the opposite, I might have changed my mind. My dogs were strong, fast, seasoned, and ready. With my injury, I knew I wasn't at 100 percent, but sometimes awareness of your shortcomings can help you focus on your strengths. I planned on racing to win, with the realization that if my health deteriorated I would have to regroup. Nobody ever said the Iditarod was supposed to be easy.

The end of the week vanished in the blink of an eye. At the starting line on Sunday, I made my annual mental transition to just react to whatever came my way and keep pushing forward. I listened to the announcer on the loudspeaker for my cue:

"Martin can leave in one minute…he and his family live in Big Lake…he is a four-time champion of the race…his hobbies are carpentry and woodturning."

This year the race committee had changed the traditional restart time from ten in the morning to two in the afternoon. Mushing folklore believed that sled dogs ran at their most optimum outside of the heat of the day, meaning that between about noon and five o'clock the extra few degrees of mercury would slow their average pace ever so slightly. To try and account for this I had waited until the last minute to sign up in order to secure one of the absolute rearmost starting numbers – I drew bib number seventy-eight, the third to last, ensuring that I left in the late afternoon. Normally I didn't adhere to such reasoning and ran right through that timeframe, but for the first day of the biggest race of the year I felt it was worth a shot to try and take advantage. Over the course of a thousand mile race those seconds might add up to something significant.

I held on like glue with my left hand, and we took off down the orange-fence lined chute. Making our way for the first few miles, waving to the fans, person after person kept sticking out and pointing to their own seemingly shorter fingers and limbs as we passed by, cheering and encouraging us on. It took me a minute before I realized that these fans were also amputees, and that I had inadvertently stumbled on a new group of supporters.

We passed sixteen teams on the way to Yentna. By the time we pulled into Skwentna, we had passed forty-two more. Not bad for the first seventy-two miles. My race continued smoothly to the top of Rainy Pass.

Descending down the backside of the pass, my handicap made itself known. The side hills, ravines, and steep drops relentlessly swung my momentum in every direction. In my struggle to keep upright, my left hand just couldn't hold on – each time I lost my grip, my right arm would then slip out from under the handlebar and my body would get thrown backwards, giving way to freefall. In those moments I expected to crash and tumble on the ground, but then, every time, like a dip net scooping up a salmon, here came the caboose to catch and keep me from losing the team. Typically the split load sled design afforded the driver a break from standing up only on flat and smooth trails, and I had no intentions of ever sitting down on this precarious section, but since I found myself one-handed, in pain, and scared for my safety, I had no choice but to discover yet one more redeeming quality of the year-old design – with such a low center of gravity, these "Old Musher" sleds were more stable while sitting down, even on horrid trails. Using the occasional boot-based outrigger to avoid obstacles, I drove like that the rest of the way to Rohn.

Somehow we arrived in second place behind Robert Sorlie. I took care of the dogs and inspected my bandaged hand. Unwrapping it, I saw that the turbulent trip had exacted a toll. The wound looked swollen and slightly infected. Several of the stitches had torn loose and a nerve now stuck out that needed to be clipped. The only medical personnel present were veterinarians. As I approached the nearest one for help and explained my situation, a raspy voice barked from behind me:

"Why don't you take the other two off?" I heard.

"I'm already hurting enough, don't you think!" I shouted back in anger.

Turning my head around to find out who it was, I saw Rick Swenson talking to one of his dogs, who happened to be biting at their booties.

Rick heard me, and when we caught each other's eye, we realized the misunderstanding and laughed it off.

The vet, on the other hand, wanted no part in helping the human species. But I really let him have no choice in the matter. It was either him or me who would have to handle it. After both agreeing he was more qualified, we walked into the one room cabin.

We stood across the table from each other. A news camera hovered above us both to capture the moment. The vet unfolded his surgical kit on one side of the table. I unfolded my hand on the other. The sight of the wound impressed the otherwise calloused professional and he let out a few expletives:

"You are one tough S.O.B.," he said, among other things.

He then proceeded to take care of my finger, snipping off the loose nerve and suturing it shut again. The pain subsided immensely without anything dangling anymore.

"Thanks for the patch job. I guess I'm back in business," I said, before swallowing a few more antibiotics.

Come five in the morning and a few miles after leaving the checkpoint, I caught up to John Baker. His sled sat askew in the trail and his dogs rested barely inches out of the way – not your regular method to let another musher pass. I pulled up and parallel parked beside him.

"What's going on?" I asked.

"I busted my sled and need a hand fixing it," he answered.

"I can give you a hand, but that is all I can give you," I said, pointing to my right hand, now bandaged to the size of a catcher's mitt.

Three-handed, we spent twenty minutes repairing his rig with makeshift parts, while our dogs visited and discussed the shortcomings of their respective drivers.

I gave the dogs a break at the Salmon River fish camp because that's what I did when I broke the record in 2002 and I was superstitious. I only stayed long enough in Nikolai to drop a dog – my team now fifteen strong – before continuing on to McGrath.

Five and a half hours of rest and we pushed ahead, blowing through Takotna and stopping again at Ophir. Race leader Robert Sorlie arrived nine minutes before us but left four minutes after. I suspected he would stop at Don's Cabin. I rested my team for another five and a half hours and dropped one more dog before heading out.

We made the twelve-hour dash for our twenty-four hour break at Iditarod and signed in third behind Sorlie and Ramy Brooks. Accounting for the start differentials, however, would put us in second place, merely twenty-eight minutes back, once we left.

I had been doubling up on the antibiotics since Rohn, and now I ran out. Luckily, via the veterinarians checking on me, the word had spread, and Dr. McNamara flew out to meet me during my layover, bringing with him a long-lasting shot of antibiotics.

"Okay, Martin, I have to give you this shot in your rear end, and it's really going to hurt," he warned.

"Do you think it's going to hurt more than this?" I said, as I politely showed him my injured middle finger.

"Oh, well, when you put it that way, I guess not," he quipped back while drawing the needle.

The injection alleviated most of my worries about my hand getting infected, but it did nothing for the phantom pains.

In the Iditarod you have to be strategic about every run. You can run shorter and rest more often, hoping to keep your speed up and stay fast, or you can run longer and rest less, moving at a slightly slower pace but hoping not to slow down too much while building a lead or chasing. There are countless combinations and conditions to consider. Rarely is it feasible to run faster and for longer, but one of the best stretches of the race to attempt it is right after the mandatory twenty-four.

We made an eleven-hour effort to Anvik and took our required-somewhere-on-the-Yukon eight-hour break. By sandwiching a long push in between two lengthy rests, I put us in a position to catapult up the Yukon River in two runs and pressure the race leader Robert Sorlie while nipping at his heels.

My team – now eleven strong, after dropping my slowest couple to try and keep our speed up for the chase – pulled me into the night on a sticky and soft trail. We stopped in Grayling for two minutes, just long enough to grab some food and supplies, and then departed into a developing snow squall. I settled down on my seat to get out of the storm and admired how well my two lead dogs, Luna and Quebec, worked together. Then I fell asleep, but not on purpose.

A bump in the trail, or at least one imagined in a dream, rattled me awake. I looked over the team again and noticed Luna powering away flawlessly in single lead. *Wait a minute, single lead? Didn't I have two leaders? How many dogs am I driving? Am I missing something?*

The effects of having shed some body parts before the race had finally accumulated, sending me into a state of utter confusion. I forgot how many dogs I was supposed to have, and I couldn't remember when or where or even if I had dropped any dogs at all. I debated who had led me out of the last checkpoint, but I suspected that Quebec, one of my best, was still supposed to be hooked up.

I stopped the team on the trail and walked up to Luna:

"Have you been in single lead this entire time, or was Quebec with you earlier?" I asked.

Her brown eyes squinted and she just smiled, panted, back at me. This little black-haired leader had been with me since her birth, and since our love was mutual I thought I could read between the lines.

"Okay, thanks for the information," I said, petting her on the head.

If Quebec had come loose from the team, he might have kept running down the trail and should be waiting ahead of us somewhere, maybe even at the next checkpoint. That meant I should be able to read his tracks, finding his footprints inside the runner marks of Robert

Sorlie's sled, as it was simply impossible to run for miles and avoid stepping on them.

I parked and walked ahead of the team, scrutinizing every inch of the trail with my eyes. For a half a mile I followed the untouched sled marks until I convinced myself that no loose dog had darted in that direction. *He must be behind me.*

I hoofed it back to my dogs, turned them around, and we began to retrace our steps. Being sleep deprived in a storm can make every driftwood log appear in the shape of a dog, but each one will turn out to be only a twisted root ball. After thirty minutes of backtracking I pledged to go no further than fifteen more minutes. If I didn't find Quebec by then, I would camp and wait for the next team to give me a report of any sightings.

And just like that, there he was, curled up on the trail, asleep, waiting for us as if nothing had ever happened. *Silly boy.* Quebec had a not so flattering habit of backing up and off the trail to relieve himself, and in all probability that had been the cause of our separation – none of this should have been a surprise, as Quebec came from the same family, now four generations apart, as Highway, the dog who had sent me on a similar search in 1986. Quebec wagged his tail when I woke him up and put him back in the team. Then I turned the whole outfit around once more and we headed up the trail, this time in the right direction. The search party had taken more than two hours.

When I finally neared the checkpoint of Eagle Island, a welcoming committee immediately approached me wanting to know what had caused my delay, the primary inquirers of which were two highly influential women – my wife, who had flown out to make sure I was okay, and the woman she teamed up with, my former archrival and top Iditarod contender, Susan Butcher. Between the two of them there was nothing they couldn't figure out about either me or my team from just a few seconds of simple observation, so when I spotted them I tried to sway the score in my favor by doing a hula dance to prove that I still felt alright. I knew that the costs of dealing with my hand, the phantom pains, the meds, and prolonged exposure were starting to weigh me down, but I hoped I might be able to convince my wife, or at least convince Susan, who could then convince my wife, that I looked no worse for wear than anybody else.

The quest for Quebec turned what had been an hour and a half lead for Robert Sorlie into almost four, allowing him some strategic leeway in how long he could rest after my arrival. His options were to take off early and attempt to become a ghost or to give his dogs more rest and ensure his speed on the next stretch. He chose to rest for eight hours, leaving four hours after my arrival. The extra time and energy it took us to catch up had already dictated my next decision, which was to give my dogs, and myself, a solid seven-hour break – during which I slept on the straw with my dogs, right next to Quebec. Any chasing before the next checkpoint would have to be done on the move.

We pursued to Kaltag and maintained our second place standing. Now we sat only two hours and forty-five minutes behind, having traveled slightly faster than Sorlie on the way. Most of our gain had come from resting an hour shorter in Eagle Island, however, and I knew that with comparable run times our best chance to catch him, unless he made a mistake, came in cutting rest. But only to a certain point. Sorlie pulled his hook again after five hours of downtime, and I called my dogs up after four and a half. Nine other teams watched me leave Kaltag, and each one looked ready to take advantage, should the opportunity arise. The race was heating up, and I knew the margin of error from then on out would be small.

We shaved exactly one minute off the lead in our twelve-hour push to Unalakleet, arriving at eleven at night. In other years I could have ski-poled the entire portage, making up more than a minute, but as the one-armed man I needed to hold on with my good hand.

Sorlie made his next move by departing a few minutes past midnight, after just three and a half hours of rest. With 250 miles remaining, I wasn't prepared to rest my dogs less than that, because too little time off would slow us down, and that would have played right into Sorlie's hands. Were I in his position, I would have wanted the same. I intended to wait until two-thirty in the morning to chase, but before I could sign out, as I was putting booties on my dogs, Ramy Brooks appeared and vanished down the trail. He had been camping outside of the checkpoints on a secretive schedule for the last few days, and up until that moment had remained elusive. I left minutes later in hot pursuit.

If we were going to make up ground, it had to be now. I paid attention to every bump, every change of direction of the sled, maintaining our heading as straight and as smooth behind the dogs as possible. I ran up the Blueberry Hills and hopped back on for the downward slopes. Muscle memory took control, and my mind summoned back the motivation to never, ever stop moving. Most of the race had been warm, around or slightly above freezing, but now, after a stretch of rain leaving Unalakleet, the night turned cold. I felt the wind slowly seeping through my parka, through my sweat and rain soaked liner, and down into my skin, chilling my bones. Chilling my hand. Signing in at Shaktoolik, shivering, I looked at the times on the clipboard and saw that we had made up thirty minutes on Robert Sorlie. But I was cringing in cold-induced pain, so I quickly parked my dogs and for the first time in my career did something that I swore I would never do. I took care of myself first.

In dog mushing it is anathema to attend to your own needs before those of your dogs. A good musher always gives their dogs food and water, takes care of their feet, beds them down, covers them with blankets, and pays attention to their individual needs before even thinking about any human-related wants. You take care of your dogs before you take care of yourself, it's that simple. Coming into Shaktoolik, I was dehydrated, exhausted, fearful of frostbite, and found myself in a situation where I knew I had to break the rhythm of dogs first. I spent about forty-five minutes inside, dealing with my hand and warming up, before I could go back out and tend to my team. It wasn't a proud moment, and it was one that I refused to repeat. Right then I pushed any thoughts of trying to win out of my mind. *Time to regroup.*

We left Shaktoolik behind Sorlie and Mitch Seavey and started to cross the windswept Norton Sound. Ramy Brooks soon caught and passed us, even after I had so graciously lent him a backup pair of boots to save his wet feet. We arrived in Koyuk in fourth place, rested for five hours, and then left in fifth place. More teams started to pass me as I cruised comfortably towards the finish, and by the time we reached Elim we had dropped to seventh. I rested my dogs there for six hours – an eternity at this point in the race – during which time three more teams took off in front of us. When we left Elim, we were in tenth place. Only twenty-four hours before, we had been within striking distance of the lead, sitting two hours back. Now we trailed by nearly ten.

Lance Mackey, a rising star this year after winning the Yukon Quest, and Jessie Royer, mushing's version of Annie Oakley, both blew by me on the slushy trail en route to White Mountain. When I approached the village for the last mandatory break, I thought I might be hallucinating, as the checker, standing on the frozen river, looked exactly like my wife:

"Hi honey! What's your bib number?" she said.

There was no mistaking her voice, hallucination or not. Kathy had become the checker.

"You know, just when I thought the best part of this race was behind me," I said, "you show up and prove me wrong."

"Bib number, please," she said.

A windstorm had prevented race personnel from flying to White Mountain. Kathy and our friend Paul Claus, a pilot, had in turn been flying to Nome but were forced to retreat to White Mountain when ice began building up on the wings of their plane. Running out of options, the race marshal then drafted and deputized them over the phone as the official checkers. They would have to stay and do the job until the entire field arrived, a days-long task, unless the weather subsided. It looked like I would be racing my wife to Nome, if not anyone else.

The ice fog shimmered in the path of the beam from my headlamp when my dogs and I embarked for Front Street the next morning. Aliy Zirkle overtook us just before the ascent up Topkok. We eclipsed Jeff King on the way to Safety, but he passed us back and pulled away right after leaving the roadhouse, thus guaranteeing me what I considered a rather appropriate finishing position: Lucky number thirteen.

The race may not have ended how I wanted, but from the starting line until Shaktoolik, all my chips were on the table. At the very least I think I upped the ante. And just like in Vegas, when you win, you win big, and when you lose, you lose big. Sometimes even a finger.

I finished the 2005 Iditarod in thirteenth place with a time of ten days, two hours, thirty-two minutes, and forty seconds. The six dogs that finished the entire race with me were Colonel, Corporal, Godzilla, Luna, Quebec, and Ranger. At the finisher's banquet, I was given the Most Inspirational Musher Award and the Sportsmanship Award.

WITH DR. MCNAMARA

MARTIN BUSER

Y CAREER AS A HAND MODEL IS OVER

MICHAEL MCNAMARA

EPING WITH THE DOGS
AT EAGLE ISLAND

JEFF SCHULTZ

SUSAN BUTCHER AND KATH▸

MICHAEL MCNAMARA

JUST KEEP MOVING...

JOY BERGER

The Wrong Way
March 2008

M y love-hate relationship with technology needed immediate refinement. It was January of 2008, and I was on a training run with my dogs near Lake Louise. The various pockets inside my parka were filled with a cell phone, an MP3 player, a handheld GPS, and extra batteries. In an outside pocket I stowed my headlamp. Everything but the headlamp required warmth to work properly, or the batteries would drain quickly, sometimes within minutes, rendering them useless; I called them "electronic parasites." Keeping them close to my body alleviated the temperature issue, but I was in a region where the phone and GPS likely wouldn't work anyway because there was little, if any, service or satellite connection. Who could I call, and why would I call them in the middle of nowhere? The reality of mushing is that you have to deal with and solve your own problems – help is almost always hours away, with rare exception. As far as the GPS, I used it to gauge our speed and distance, but I could also just as accurately gauge our speed by watching the gait of my dogs – a skill that comes with experience and knowing how your team moves.

Mushing while constantly glancing back and forth at the GPS readings felt a lot like texting and driving, and as we covered ground on that training run, I thought of the mushers in the early Iditarods – they barely had flashlights, let alone anything modern. That thought made me disgusted with all the devices weighing me down; it was like trying to run a marathon with a brick in each pocket. The headlamp had its worthwhile uses, but the rest of the gadgets I thought about throwing into the woods and letting them freeze to death. But I was too cheap to do that, so I tossed them into the sled bag and carried on. All I needed was a headlamp. *Back to the basics.*

"Martin, would you be willing to carry a GPS tracker on your sled during this year's Iditarod?"

"What's the benefit?"

"We're testing out a pilot program for making the race more virtual for the fans. We think it will bring more exposure to the race."

"Sure, I'll be your Guinea pig."

I agreed, but with some reluctance. Only the top ten teams from the year before were going to carry trackers. Everybody with a computer would know whether we were moving, how fast we were going, and how cold it was. The little kid in me appeared once again, and I figured I could inject some mischief into the equation.

On the way to McGrath I wrapped the tracker with air-activated hand warmers, in the hope that I would show up on the computer going ten miles per hour in sixty-degree weather. I thought that would be funny – and that people would think *Oh look, Martin must be in the tropics* – but it wasn't very funny because we were already racing in higher-than-normal temperatures, ranging from thirty to forty degrees. The prank just didn't have the impact that I desired.

As I progressed down the trail, it began to gnaw at me more and more that other people would know how fast or how slow I was going, where I was stopping, and for how long. Only one musher held the record for fastest Iditarod ever. That musher was me, from my victory in 2002. I knew that my competitors wanted to know how that was done, but since I was presently trying to equal or better that performance, and I was the only who had the knowledge and documentation on how to achieve it, I had to figure out a way to prevent that from happening.

The bush planes kept landing and taking off from the Cripple checkpoint. My dogs were resting on beds of straw, nestled in the trees, in the middle of our twenty-four hour layover. It was still warm out, and to try and take advantage of the relative heat wave I was wearing a red Hawaiian shirt, with white flowers all over it, as my outer layer. As I massaged my dogs one by one, a light bulb went off in my head. I knew exactly what to do.

I detached the white plastic brick that was the GPS unit from my sled and marched out to the landing strip, where one of the pilots – he who shall remain unnamed – was loading his plane and preparing to leave.

"Do you mind taking this package for me?" I asked, "I'm pretty tired of it."

"Oh yeah, no problem. Any special instructions?" he said.

"Well, how about whenever you land, you give it to another pilot, along with the message for them to do the same whenever they land the next time," I said.

"Sounds like a plan," he said.

I heard the plane takeoff, and then I walked back to my dogs and took a long nap. While I slept, the little blue dot that represented me on thousands of computers around the world showed that I was moving, and fast. The newspaper headlines read *Buser Going 130MPH In The Wrong Direction*. Soon after I woke up, the race officials figured it out, and they were not amused, but by then it was time for me and my dogs to head back out. I roared with laughter as I rode the runners on the way to Ruby. If anybody wanted to know what I had been doing on the trail all these years, they would just have to wait for me to write a book.

The Greatest Journey
The 2014 Iditarod

A week before the 2014 Iditarod, I hooked up twelve dogs and went for a leisurely forty-mile outing. I wanted the dogs to have a chance to stretch out, and I kept them at an easy pace. A ribbon of ice ran the length of the route to the Big Susitna River, but the snow had been lacking for months and it was the best, the only, option.

A band of birch trees separated the open tundra from the turnaround point on the river. The wind stood up on our approach and I leaned into it to counter. It was nothing unusual, just a regular run on my home trails. Then on the last turn leading to the descent onto the river, I tipped over.

As I dragged downhill on my back, grasping the handlebar, fully expecting to slide all the way to the bottom, my gloved left hand scraped and wedged against a fallen tree, halting the team.

I jerked the sled upright, set the snowhook, and pulled off the glove. My pinky finger now sat crooked as it pointed directly towards its own thumb. It looked like there might be some bone sticking out of the top joint. The gears in my head started spinning and memories of my accident in 2005 returned. *What have I done?*

I stuffed my glove back on, ran the rest of the descent to the river, swung the team around, and headed back. On level ground again, I assessed the situation closer – my left pinky was no longer where it should be, but the foreign piece of flesh on top of it looked more worrisome. I decided to leave the hand alone, race back home, and then pay another visit to Dr. Mike McNamara in Anchorage.

My wristwatch read two in the afternoon. I would need two hours to cover the twenty miles to the kennel, and the drive to Anchorage would take an hour and a half – that put me in the doctor's office at five-thirty. They would be closed by then. I reached into my parka pocket and pulled out my phone. Two bars. Still on the move, I called Rohn:

"Hey dad, what's going on?" he answered.

"I need your help," I said, describing my predicament.

"You have to be joking," he said.

"I'm not. If this is what it looks like, you might have to run the Iditarod after all. Please meet me out here as fast as you can, I can save at least an hour with a snowmachine," I said.

Rohn – now twenty-four years old and having recently rejoined the family business – knew this particular group of dogs as well as I did. They had just pulled him to an undefeated season, winning both the Knik 200 and the Kuskokwim 300. Having Rohn as a co-racer had freed me up to continually look at all my dogs in the hopes of sorting out the diamonds in the rough, and together we also emerged victorious in the Denali Doubles Invitational – a 300 mile race with two drivers instead of one. Three wins out of three races entered. Only one other team in either Alaska or the Yukon Territory had fared as well, and that team belonged to Aliy Zirkle and Allen Moore in Fairbanks. They had also won three – the Yukon Quest, the Copper Basin 300, and the Quest 300. Our dogs had yet to face each other in any race. Would the Iditarod be the tiebreaker? Maybe, but many of the best teams only showed up for the big one. And what about my hand?

When the snowmachine came flying up the trail, I called out "whoa!" and stepped on my brake. Rohn slowed down, jumped off, and took control of the team. Without words, I hopped on the iron dog, grabbed the right handle, pressed the throttle with my thumb, and hurried home.

The next transportation change put me in the passenger seat of Kathy's car, replacing my mushing clothes with street wear while she stomped on the gas pedal, sending the studded tires reeling into the road. We arrived at the doctor's at four-thirty – from the river to town in two and a half hours without an airplane must have set a record. Dr. McNamara's greeting felt all too familiar:

"Martin, please tell me I am not the only one having déjà vu."

The water washing the blood off the wound revealed only a minor cut on top of my little finger, with no bones sticking out anywhere, and the X-rays displayed a severe dislocation but no fractures. *What a relief.*

I held out my hand and Dr. McNamara pulled and tweaked my finger back into place. After some splinting, taping, and anti-inflammatories, Kathy and I walked out of the office feeling lucky. I called Rohn with the news, and he was more than happy that he didn't have to fill in as an emergency driver – he had a point, as this was no ordinary year. Staring out of the window on the drive home, looking towards the Alaska Range, I pondered the circumstances.

This winter had been challenging. Freezing rain and icy trails alternated with thawing temperatures and spots of impassable open water. Snow stayed minimal for months, and conditions were so warm and dry in January that the state issued a wildfire warning. We rode out the roughest weeks by employing more creative training methods – namely, by running the dogs on the Alaska Zoo's former elephant treadmill, now housed at my kennel.

In the last few weeks, the race committee had faced a tough choice whether to use the traditional start in Willow or to begin the race further north in Fairbanks. A late snowfall helped them decide to go with the traditional route and crews went out to improve the worst sections. Mother Nature then rebelled, raising the mercury and melting much of the already marginal snow cover. Plenty of mushers proclaimed the trail as "impossible," and there was no shortage of discouraging perspectives. I expected the conditions to be well out of the ordinary but I would never judge the race undoable. The Iditarod itself had once been thought to be impossible. An eleven day race was once impossible, and then ten, and then nine. Only one question mattered: Did I plan on going to Nome? If so, then I needed to adapt and react and overcome whatever came my way, just like always. Anything else was counterproductive.

I had never seen a group of dogs move as well as mine this year, and I had seen a lot of dogs. Equal parts fear and excitement simmered inside me. *If I can just hold it together, we have a chance.*

The prerace hysteria hit a fever pitch by start day. The tide of fans carried us through Yentna, after which my nerves began to dissipate. My team pulled us into Skwentna with enough power that two volunteers had to grab my sled while I stood on the brake to keep us stationary. We signed in fifth and left nine minutes later in first.

Civilization still tries to follow you for the first hundred miles, but the further to the front you are, the faster you and your dogs can move past the early distractions and get into a rhythm. The last encounter with large groups comes at Shell Lake, where we approached and cut through a crowd of variably sober revelers hooting and hollering to welcome us as the first team through.

"Welcome to the Shell Lake bonfire, Martin," one reveler said, sticking a coffee can towards me.

The can held a pile of tickets for their annual Iditarod raffle. I stuck my hand in and pulled out the winning number and everyone yelled some more. Somebody handed me an envelope containing a wad of cash. As I stashed it in the glove compartment of my sled, I could tell that this had been a busy raffle year. The envelope felt thick, but I didn't count it.

We resumed racing and left the party behind. My headlamp swept over my dogs, and several of them looked over their shoulders at me. Translation: *What was that all about?*

The smooth trail so far had instilled hopes of better-than-reported conditions in the days to come. We conquered the first 112 miles at a brisk clip, cruising into Finger Lake at two in the morning. On the way in I noticed that the markers – guiding us toward the lantern hanging under the wooden tripod signaling the checkpoint – stood stabbed into oversized snow bricks, clearly manmade. Usually the markers stayed upright while sticking into the natural snowpack, but the snow looked thin here. I took it as a sign that the good trail was coming to an end – most of the places I wiped out on an annual basis waited for me over the next 100 miles. I gave my dogs clear, cold water and a salmon snack before heading back out into the night.

Immediately a sharp drop provided a booster shot of energy. The dogs meandered uphill for the next hour, and then we flew down and around the Happy River steps without incident. We pressed on through the forest and across lakes, skipping over ice bridges and leaning into side hills. The Rainy Pass checkpoint came into view. I checked in and bedded down the team for our first real break of the race.

The weather reports in the days leading up to the race had convinced me that sleds would take a beating and runners would wear out faster than normal, so I built a flexible sled with runners made completely from black plastic as thick as ten sets of regular runner plastic stacked together. I tried to make it indestructible. The next section – the most infamous – would put the design to the test.

Sunrise broke through at nine-thirty and we left under clear skies, venturing out onto the wide white expanse of the Ptarmigan Valley. Ahead, the wind collided with the craggy peaks, forcing the air to roll away into visibility as clouds. Exposed rock reached high on either side and the trail narrowed. *Time for the hard part.*

We launched down Mother Nature's pinball course on an icy chute that gave way to a dirt path devoid of snow but full of ruts and rocks. On this type of terrain, I typically wouldn't have dared take a dog for a leashed walk, let alone an entire team. I managed to avoid most of the boulders on the trail and not fall into any of the gaping holes in the creeks – much of the ice in the middle of the creeks was "drum ice," so named because it sounded like a drumbeat when you ran over it. Time and again I stopped my team just milliseconds before smashing into immovable granite canyon walls. Over thirty Iditarods I had learned how to drive a sled pretty well, but whipping around tight turns and knocking bark off a few trees challenged that theory. I lost count of the close calls. When we emerged out of the woods and rumbled down the barren runway before Rohn, I felt fortunate to still be in one piece. At the checkpoint I pulled the race judge aside and urged him to fly in a doctor, knowing from experience that some mushers would not be as lucky.

As bad as the trail had been, I also knew the next section could be equally treacherous, if not more so. I was not about to give the dogs much rest, for fear of bounding through the Buffalo Tunnels and the Farewell Burn with a fresh team. I wanted a tired, easily controlled group. I pulled the hook after three minutes.

Slanted hills of frozen black dirt. Downed trees and stumps sticking up where the sled was supposed to glide – normally snow filtered down into these low spots and filled it in, making the trail somewhat passable, but I saw none of that. Exposed tussocks ranging from golf-ball-sized clumps to mounds as big as medicine balls, spaced four to six inches apart. Rocks. Sleds weren't made to race over obstacles like that, but I didn't have a choice, and there was no time to dwell on it.

I danced from one runner to the other. My left foot stood on the right runner while my right leg acted as an outrigger, hanging way out to the side, with my right foot sliding steadily against the ground as I balanced the sled around a left-hand turn. In a split second I changed position and jumped on the drag pad with both feet to slow the team. Then a sharp right hand turn forced me to balance everything to the left. And so on.

Steep descents and side hills required the metal brake, but on this mix of ice and frozen dirt, it was useless, maybe even counterproductive. Most brakes have a foot-activated metal bar connected to the sled with at least two protruding claws. These brake claws are intended to dig into the snow, and when combined with the musher's voice command of "easy" or "whoa," to slow or stop the team. But on this killer trail, the brake became the Devil. When engaged, the claws scraped against the frozen ground, making tons of noise. Instead of slowing down, the team – now scared by the screeching sound wave – would speed up. *Reverse training.* With my full two hundred pounds of force on the brake, and my arms pulling the handlebar upward for leverage, the sled lifted off the ground so that the entire rig perched on the two sharp steel points, like an Olympic skater performing a pirouette.

During one of these moves, my left foot slipped off the brake and became trapped under the sled. The dogs failed to notice my mistake and kept happily chugging on down the trail, my ankle notwithstanding. I cried out in pain, tears streamed down my face, and I careened out of control. The sled tipped over, and the tundra absorbed my fall.

This was the worst I had ever seen this section of trail, and I had mushed through it when it was on fire. With bare ground in every direction and limited snow to melt for water, wherever we found a creek crossing I stopped and let the dogs get a good drink. Over the rest of the run, I managed to hurt my ankle several more times while trying to be overly careful – slowly it swelled to the size of a two-liter bottle of soda. To add to the challenge, my left pinky finger kept jumping out of its joint, aggravating my prerace injury.

In Nikolai I parked my team and sat down on my sled to assess my bodily damage. I removed my boot, pulled off my sock, and stared at my injured ankle. Then I rubbed my face with my good hand, trying to massage it back to reality – runs like that were the kind that gave you wrinkles. I had earned all my wrinkles. A cameraman with the Iditarod Insider crew walked over.

"How bad was it out there?" he asked.

"If I had known it was going to be this rough, I would have sent my son instead," I replied.

True to my race plan, I took my mandatory twenty-four hour layover here. Team after team spilled into the village with horror stories of stranded mushers, injured bodies, and broken sleds. The dogs all looked better than their drivers – all sixteen of mine were without issue – and my starting sled still appeared drivable, even after all the wrecks.

Hoping the worst of the trail lay behind me, I asked my friends the Runkles if they would be willing to snowmachine to McGrath and bring my backup sled to me – it was lighter and faster but less sturdy – before my rest ended. PJ, the son, volunteered.

50 miles there. 50 miles back. Six hours later, when PJ returned with my sled in tow – not expecting anything more than money for gas, which cost nine dollars per gallon in Nikolai – I reached into my sled bag, grabbed the envelope I had received at Shell Lake, and handed it to him as payment for the delivery.

"Thank you," he said, pocketing the money without looking at it.

Then he walked straight over to his father and paid it forward.

"Grandma isn't well, and this will help you get to see her."

What a good kid. I choked up.

I packed my new sled and took a nap. After waking up, I joined the other mushers in the school gym where we swapped trail stories and displayed our various injuries.

At midday, I limped outside to see snow falling and Kathryn

Keith – another musher, also an Ironman triathlete – pulling into the checkpoint, surfing a pile of sticks. Her dogs didn't seem to mind. She needed a spare rig, so I offered my starting sled. She accepted.

I continued the cycle of feeding and caring for my team. A doctor assessed my ankle and diagnosed it as sprained. No broken bones.

Danny Seavey – a veteran musher who had flown up from Florida a week before the race to be a last-minute substitute, also the brother of Dallas and the son of Mitch, both recent Iditarod champions – arrived and parked next to me as I prepared to depart.

"Martin, I haven't driven a sled in years. Am I out of practice, or was that really hard?"

"If you're here, you're a hell of a sled driver."

I zipped up my parka.

"Have a good run," he said. "Like third place good."

"You mean behind-your-dad-and-brother good? At least you're honest."

My dogs lunged forward and we left.

After a lifetime at sea, a salmon swims a thousand miles or more, trying to return home across the wild ocean. He outruns the fisherman's net, the one that tries to bring him up for air, as he drives on, motivated by instinct, by the one desire that all can relate to. He recognizes the freshwater from where he came, and he fights upstream toward his spawning grounds. He knows that he is on his greatest journey. He avoids all that stand in his way, from bears to bald eagles to baited hooks. Some waterfalls, some heights seem too high, but he climbs them anyway. He grows tired and hungry, yet he keeps going, challenging himself as he races the momentum of the other salmon around him. Some may swim faster, and some may swim slower, and not all of them will make it, but all will try. He keeps swimming because the current won't allow him anywhere to rest. The closer he gets to his goal, the more exhausted he becomes, yet the more he feels alive. His gills are working at their capacity, but he can't stop now. Biology begins to take a toll. He ages with every inch gained, and his body changes shape, changes color. His skin goes limp, and his once silvery-bright scales sag into splotches of gray and green and red. Like fall leaves. He gives everything he has to keep moving, because in his mind there is no other way. He presses onward.

My left ankle started looking like the discolored pattern of a spawned-out salmon, and the swelling ballooned to pachydermic proportions. Copious amounts of "vitamin A," or Advil, helped manage the pain, but I worried that my skin might stretch to the point of bursting.

The trail was hard and fast to Ophir. When I left there, the volunteers put together a little care package that contained a few snacks to help me get to the next checkpoint, including two cold beers, which I declined to take. Those would have put me to sleep, and drinking a cold beverage at twenty below was never ideal. I gladly accepted the rest.

We carried on to Cripple, with the temperature dropping every step of the ten-hour run, and we arrived in the middle of the night. My left pinky finger refused to stay aligned, so I slid a dog booty over it and my ring finger and Velcroed them together.

Four and a half hours later, we pushed on. Traveling along the old mining road to Ruby, one of my dogs, Suzette, put on the brakes to go to the bathroom. I cringed, worrying that she might hurt herself. This was a bad habit of hers, as most of my dogs had learned to "do it on the run," since I preferred to run and train without using necklines – every musher trains differently, and all methods have their various idiosyncrasies that need to be refined. I eased on the drag pad to slow the team, but sure enough, when Suzette started running again, her gait changed ever so slightly. I stopped the team, unhooked her from the gangline, and put her in the sled bag to evaluate the situation.

Whenever something like this happens, I always do the same. While the dog rests in the sled, and while I am driving, I remove their booties and harness. Then I start palpating them as I search for any problem areas. If I can determine what's wrong, I can massage out a cramp or rub ointment into any sore spots.

Looking over Suzette, I couldn't find the source of her discomfort, so I let her rest in the sled for a couple of hours until we approached a severely-slanted section of trail – overflow seeping down from the hills had sent water glazing across the road, most of it freezing at a forty-five degree angle, making it slippery and difficult to maneuver. The one positive was the water that still streamed ran clear and clean. When I stopped the team for a drink at one of these crossings, Suzette hopped out of the sled. As she skipped about I noticed that both of her hind feet had swollen substantially. I could relate. She showed no pain, but I handed her a ticket for a free ride to the next checkpoint, with a direct flight home from there.

We made it into Ruby in third place behind Jeff King and Sonny Lindner, both about halfway done with their mandatory twenty-four hour breaks. While my dogs slept, Aliy Zirkle sailed through the checkpoint like an apparition and disappeared into the night. No surprise there. The competitive wave began rolling.

The freshwaters flowed deep under the four-foot-thick ice as we charged down the Yukon River after her. The temperature sank to somewhere just above absolute zero, and I unpacked my sleeping bag and draped it over me to try and stay warm. Occasional echoes of cracking trees – dotted along the hilly banks, with sap frozen so solid as to expand beyond the tree's own structural capability – shot across the frostbitten air. I shriveled into the fetal position in the hope that my cocoon of clothing would sustain me until morning, but I couldn't stop shaking.

When the musher hasn't eaten well, the temperature drops, and the wind picks up, they risk "circling the drain," or becoming uncontrollably cold. The only recourse is to drink something hot out of their thermos and to eat calories, calories, and more calories. Oil-rich and high-density foods stoke the fire best. For this reason, I always carry salmon strips and *muktuk* – the traditional Inuit/Eskimo snack of buttery-soft whale skin and slippery blubber – in the fabric glove compartment on my sled.

I forced some food down and hydrated. By the time we turned up in Galena, my spirits were soaring again. Aliy and team had arrived before me, but two hours later I headed back out, seizing the lead.

We shuffled down the Yukon, making an S-curve around the three-hundred-foot-tall Bishop Rock – a bluff jutting out along the north bank, notorious for ice jams and overflow. The weather then warmed enough that I didn't need to wear my parka. As the river made a southerly sweep, we closed in on Nulato.

Riding into town, I parked between a snow bank and a string of reporters and tended to my dogs. I limped inside the school, sat down at one of the cafeteria tables, and experienced a moment of true joy when a friend delivered what looked to be a four-course meal – two Styrofoam trays flexed under the weight of steak, shrimp, corn, peas, potatoes, and a slice of homemade blueberry pie. I fueled my body and retreated to the wood shop for a nap.

When I woke up, Sonny, Aliy, and Jeff had all joined me. I took it as a sign, and four hours after checking in, I re-bootied my dogs, clicked my heels, and we left.

It was nighttime, and we followed the trail as it slalomed around several islands on the way to Kaltag. We jumped the bank and coasted quietly down Main Street.

One of the advantages of being first into any checkpoint is having your choice of camping spot. At Kaltag the best place is hugging the border of the eight-sided, log-cabin community center. I signed in with the checker, and then my fourteen dogs chased a jogging volunteer to our chosen real estate. I fluffed up enough straw for each of them to build the perfect nest. After distributing dishes of kibble, I stuffed my sleeping bag under my left arm, snatched a vacuum-packed meal from my drop bag with my right hand, and walked inside.

With suspicions that Aliy would do a "grab and go" move and blow through the checkpoint, I lay down on the wooden bench against the wall and rested my eyes.

A "grab and go" is when a musher stops only long enough to pick up supplies, and then presses on to camp out along the trail somewhere. One of the main purposes of such a move is to disrupt their competitors' schedules, since nobody knows how far the passing team will travel before they stop. They might go a mile, or they might go 100 miles. In this case, Aliy would probably stop thirty miles away at the Tripod Flats cabin, forty-five miles away at the Old Woman cabin, or maybe not stop at all and instead run all the way to the Bering Sea Coast.

My suspicions were confirmed when I stirred from my slumber – Aliy had signed in and out in just seven minutes. At five-thirty in the morning, after three and a half hours of rest, I said goodbye to the good trail on the Yukon. The word floating around said the portage was covered in glare ice and dirt, with slivers of snow here and there.

The trail reports were right, but we also encountered little speed bumps created by short-track snowmachines, causing an inconsistent jerking of my sled that tugged on the gangline and disrupted our momentum. I did my best to smooth it out, trying to pedal or push along at the right moments, but my left ankle wasn't strong enough, and I had to stop. Within a few hours, my dogs Lindsey Vonn and Vesuvius developed sore triceps muscles. To err on the conservative side, I stopped and loaded them in the sled, massaging them as we went. Our pace dropped, but the two aching dogs were better off.

We passed Aliy and her team while they rested at Tripod Flats.

They passed us back while I fed and watered mine at Old Woman. The pendulum stayed put for the rest of the run, and we pulled into Unalakleet in second place.

The first village on the Bering Sea coast always welcomes the mushers with the utmost hospitality. If you can just make it here, the weather might not warm you up, but the people will. The locals know what it takes to arrive by dog team, as their ancestors traveled, hunted, and subsisted with dogs. Many also pick their favorite musher and make a point to welcome them when they reach town.

For many years, a little girl would greet me upon my arrival, with her mom walking her out to the checkpoint even if my timing got me there at two in the morning. The little girl faithfully saw me arrive every year, and every year I watched her grow up a little bit more until finally she went off to college. The year that she left, a friend of hers with a young son started the routine all over again, and an adorable little boy began greeting me when I arrived.

The manmade and windproof berms of chunky snow at the checkpoint parking lot spanned hundreds of feet in length and piled ten feet tall – ideal for kids to clamber on top to view the dogs and mushers, as well as slide down and chase each other around. The grownups stood on the level ground, observing dog care and visiting with each other. While pulling my cooker out of my sled bag, I spotted the boy – my fan, escorted by his father – as he stepped forward a few inches from the crowd and quietly raised his mittened hand, holding a ziplock baggie in my direction. Immediately I recognized what was in the bag and reached out to grab the offering – word had gotten around that I enjoyed the traditional Eskimo diet, so this little boy had brought me the choicest cuts of muktuk.

"Thank you very much, this is my favorite," I said, giving him a hug.

Without hesitation, I opened up the bag and chewed down the first tidbits. I bedded down the dogs on straw. I ate a little muktuk. I took all the booties off, and then I ate a little muktuk. I prepared a meal for the dogs. I ate some more. As I kept on with my chores, big smiles and cheers erupted from the spectators each time I took a bite of the tasty treat that had kept the local population alive for millennia. Once the dogs were cared for, I wandered inside for a nap.

With Lindsey Vonn and Vesuvius boarding a plane home, I soon readied my twelve dogs for our land-based departure. We left in third place, an hour behind Aliy, but only a single minute behind Jeff King. We followed a brown and snowless seam to the Blueberry Hills and began to climb. I had my tennis shoes on to help the dogs ascend, but helping might be an exaggeration. Hobbling along was more like it – it is amazing how much the human body can take, especially when you are foolish enough to believe that a better trail awaits you.

The grassy patches alongside the path looked more like old piles of straw, confusing Pineapple, one of my younger female dogs. She kept running wide and lowering her head to inspect the soft clumps, as if she was window shopping for a bed. After reaching the top, we began the three-mile descent to the beach. Usually this section was not much of a hurdle, but the one-legged, one-armed paper hanger version of me had lost all downhill coordination. Even at walking speeds, I wiped out a few times.

We hit level ground again and emerged onto a lagoon of glare ice. The wind began blowing, sweeping us to the side. Dunes accumulated to our left, fifty meters wide, and just over the dunes, open water. The dogs quartered into the gale, but they had little traction, with or without booties. We persisted, the team faring better than their driver. As they pulled me into Shaktoolik, they yapped like coyotes.

My hopes of better trail had been dashed so many times, with such an abundance of bodily pain, that somewhere along the way my mind switched to autopilot mode, honed by years of experience. Still, I feared the Norton Sound crossing more than normal. At the end of a three-hour rest, with the sun breaching the mountains on the eastern horizon, we set out for Koyuk.

The light grew, reflecting off the sea ice as the day wore on. My fur ruff flowed back, and the dogs' ears flopped about while we ran straight into a headwind that refused to let the temperature rise – the team was decked out in their black jackets and me in my white wind anorak, hiding my hands inside the sleeves. Scabs of snow stuck to the ground. The breeze tried to vacuum them away. The crunch of booties on ice chips, where the trailbreakers had scratched down the rough spots, announced our travel, though nobody else was nearby to hear it. We rambled briskly for hours, curving around jumbled ice craters and crossing over swollen, cracked pressure ridges.

I ran up the last hill into Koyuk, entering town on a trail that reminded me of a skateboard park made entirely of glare ice – all the roads, ordinarily covered in snow this time of year, were raised sheets of frozen glaze with bowling-lane bumpers of abrasive gravel at the shoulders. We slid from one edge to the other like drunken sailors as eight or ten local kids ran after us on the stronger footing found along the sides. In front of the checkpoint location, volunteers had spread out straw and then deliberately spilled water on top to provide better grip. After I parked and finished taking care of my team, I let myself believe, for the first time in the race, that I might actually survive this Iditarod – I had been hobbled and hurt, my mind had been blown, and I had felt sorry for myself in quite a few prior years, but this one had been the most difficult by far, and it wasn't even over yet. *It can't possibly get any worse.*

During the break, my son Rohn and his friend Tim, a pilot, flew in on a prop plane – the sight of familiar faces, especially ones that understood the difficulty of the trail without words needing to be spoken, gave me a boost. I watched them takeoff, and as I imagined the boys averting their eyes from the conditions on the ground, their airplane tilted and appeared like it was covering itself up with one wing, as if to say: *If I don't look at it, it won't be so bad.*

Four and a half hours of rest and it was time to go again. I checked out in third place, just before nine at night. The leaders, Aliy and Jeff, had already pressed on, and they seemed to be pulling away, slightly out of reach. But there was only one finish line, and it wasn't in Koyuk. I heaved my sled up and over the road crossing, and we slithered over the tundra and around the trees while descending the mile and a half to the shore.

The route wound across slabs of ice and driftwood for ten miles. Dallas Seavey soon caught up, and then the trail cut inland, giving way to a slightly snow-covered climb into the hills separating Koyuk from the long spit beginning at Moses Point. From there, in the dark, we ran past a chain of abandoned houses and continued west on a hard-packed road to Elim.

The fire hall in Elim – population 341, with an airstrip that measured longer than the village – had long served as the Iditarod checkpoint. It was also the morgue, and an elder of the community had just passed away. Mourning was in full swing, so there was no room for the Iditarod at the regular spot, but a local resident had kindly offered up their own home instead for race personnel to use. The veterinary team met us as we glided in at three a.m. They carefully looked over each of my dogs, and once done, they assessed my own condition and let me go inside. The Spartan accommodations didn't have much, but it did have a flush toilet and a table topped with a smorgasbord of snacks collected from the drop bags of scratched mushers. The volunteers encouraged me to take whatever I wanted from the pile, but what I really needed were both of the veterinarians to help me restabilize my hand. I watched like a spectator in the stands, feeling detached, as we fashioned a plastic knife into a splint, and then all five of our free hands bandaged up my left in an attempt to again immobilize my now thumb-sized pinky finger. Then

I laid down for a twenty-minute nap, sharing the same sleeping surface as the owner of the house: the linoleum floor.

An hour and thirty minutes after our arrival, I pressed the button on my headlamp twice to beam at full brightness, and we departed Elim. The trail leaving town ripped around the eroding, boulder-strewn coastline for much shorter than in most years, and only a few minutes into the run we skimmed over a small sheet of glare ice and jumped back onto land. Hill after hill came and went, and we found ourselves climbing Little McKinley at daybreak. Matchstick-like markers tilted at various angles along the left-hand trim of the shaved rut leading down the brown and pitched backside of the mountain.

As if in a cartoon, my twelve dogs slid out onto Golovin Bay and started doing the splits and triple salchow in unison. The figure-skating quality ice looked like a polished plate of glass, extending for miles in every direction. A stiff wind blew from onshore and wanted to blast us out into the middle of the bay, making it difficult to stay upright, much less follow the trail.

I struggled to cling to the wooden markers. Scratch marks in the ice, spaced ten dog-team lengths apart, provided grip enough to take two or three steps – I used these scratch marks to drag the sled upwind to stay close to the marked trail, knowing full well that we would drift dangerously away from our wooden lifeline before reaching the next strip of footing. The arduous task proceeded at a crawl, and once the town of Golovin came into sight – halfway up the eastern border of the bay on a narrow, quarter-mile-wide peninsula – I promised the dogs a well-deserved rest. I needed the break more than they did.

We scraped off the ice and onto the dirt and gravel road. A small crowd had gathered.

"How do I get to the laundromat?" I asked one of the onlookers.

They pointed me in the proper direction. We headed that way, hanging a left at the next street.

"No, the trail is that way," several people yelled, flailing their arms to the right.

Golovin used to be an official checkpoint, but many years had passed since then, and it was now only a brief hello and goodbye for most mushers. Considering that White Mountain sat only eighteen miles further down the trail, it came as no surprise that my stay was unexpected to the locals. But at my travel speed, and with my body rebelling, it would take another three or four hours to get to White Mountain. The Laundromat had water and warmth, and I wanted both.

Once parked out of the wind along the side of the building, more people appeared in droves and began asking questions.

"Are you hurt?"

"I'm hurting, but I'm going to be okay."

"You need to go to the clinic up on the hill."

"I have no time to go there, and no need."

"Oh, they will come to you then."

Excitement filled the air. A few kids wanted to assist with my dog care, so I had them pull grasses from across the road to help bed down the team. One family brought water to the dogs, and other bystanders asked to lend a helping hand in snacking and distributing kibble. Somebody ushered me into the building.

Three health aides approached seconds later.

"Where do you hurt?"

"Everywhere. My fingers and ankle hurt the most, but I will be fine. I just need to warm up and rest a bit."

I sat down in a chair, and they slipped my boots off.

"Ooh, does this hurt?" one lady asked, pointing to my ankle.

"Yes."

"We have a splint for that; let's see where it might be."

"I don't need a splint."

She gave up on my ankle, but for good measure started giving me a shoulder massage.

"I'm not really good at this," she said, kneading away on my concrete-knotted back.

One of the aides then remembered the importance of paperwork.

"What insurance company do you use?"

"I don't know."

"Have you ever been to the Nome hospital?"

"I'm sure I have."

"Okay, they will have your records."

Next of kin, phone numbers, where is your wife – on and on, the questions came with urgency. The one in charge of paperwork realized she had yet to take my temperature, so she stuck a digital thermometer in my mouth and continued with the questions.

"On a scale of one to ten, how would you rate your pain level?"

Anywhere else in the world that question would be applicable, but this was the Iditarod with 100 miles left to go. There was no scale; there was only mind over matter.

"I'm fine," I mumbled, with the sound of the thermometer raking against my teeth.

Beep. She checked the reading.

"He has no temperature, he must be hypothermic!"

A new probe went in, and this time I registered something better. There were six hands working on me, and my dazed mind found the entire situation amusing.

"You should go across the street and visit with Mary. She is getting old, and she would like that. She'll feed you."

"Thanks, but I have my own food."

A couple of older Eskimo ladies walked in and introduced themselves.

"We are the ones that gave you your Eskimo name, *Ayhup*, a long time ago. You should come over and have breakfast with us!"

At least fifteen years prior, I had been honored with the name *Ayhup*, pronounced "I-up," a shortened derivative of the mushing command "hurry up."

The invitations poured in left and right. I could have stayed for days, making my visiting rounds and probably gaining a lot of weight at the same time, but all I really wanted was to rest. When a little girl retrieved my sleeping bag from my sled and brought it inside, that was the ticket. As quickly as the commotion had started, everyone respected my need for a nap. I plopped down on the floor, set my alarm, and chuckled as I dozed off. *What a race.*

An hour and a half later – one full sleep cycle – I woke up to the loud, scheduled chime. At the head of my sleeping bag, I found a tin-foiled egg sandwich with a note attached:

"I have been following you all my life, and now me and my husband and our three girls are following you still. Safe travels."

I devoured the sandwich, and then I ventured back outside to ready my team. A convoy of three four-wheelers soon appeared and led us back onto the glare ice. The north end of Golovin Bay, filled at the top by the three branches of the Fish River, beckoned.

The second half of the bay showed us the same glassy conditions as the first half. Because of that, we followed the middle branch of the river to White Mountain – a different and slightly longer route, but the one the local people had been traveling all winter, which made it the safest. Despite racing with the hood up, we arrived for our last mandatory eight-hour break in seventh place.

While I slept, a massive coastal storm woke up. I couldn't believe the flurry of news.

"Winds are forty-five miles per hour, with gusts reported as high as sixty-five."

"The GPS trackers show several mushers off course, as far back as Shaktoolik."

"Conditions between White Mountain and Nome are very, very, very, very, very dangerous. If you do leave, be prepared for the worst."

"Jeff King hunkered with his dogs for hours in the worst of it, but then he tried to walk to Safety to request help rescuing them. A couple of snowmachiners picked him up on the way. He scratched."

Jeff King had scratched? How could that be? He was leading the race, having an incredible run, and on the verge of victory. All of the information we received in White Mountain came second-hand or worse, but hearing that a fellow four-time champion had asked for help – while knowing full well that it would nullify his chances for a fifth win – grabbed my attention. Aliy Zirkle had fought her way to Safety, where she was stopped, and the other top teams were now venturing out into the storm. It felt like 1991 all over again.

Get with the program. I knew that if the first few teams had it tough, that I would too. It scared me. I procrastinated for half an hour beyond my required layover, and at one-thirty in the morning, my dogs and I finally shoved off into the unknown.

The villages on the Bering Sea coast were all established near a good food source, like a big river, near good firewood for heating homes, and near good shelter to be out of storms. That is not to say it doesn't get windy in a place like Shaktoolik, but if it is blowing thirty miles per hour in Shaktoolik, then it is blowing fifty everywhere else. The shelter cabins built along the route to Nome have some of the same characteristics. The Dog Musher cabin – where Rick Swenson holed up in 1991 before securing his fifth Iditarod win, and where he scrawled on the inside wall "3-14-91, R.A. Swenson stops here to dry out on his way to Idit. V!" – comes first, then six miles later sits Tommy Johnson's, and last is the appropriately named Safety Roadhouse. All were put up to provide refuge from a storm, and I had visited each of them in prior Iditarods.

As we climbed into the Topkok Hills, the wind began to howl at the highest points. Bands of ice and snow thinned out into wide swaths of exposed tundra. The dogs strode forward with power, driven by the instinct to chase. Briefly we spotted Sonny Lindner's headlight in the dark distance. At the base of the last hill, I stopped to feed my team a full meal and put on their jackets. Then I tied down all of my gear and made sure my head was screwed on properly. We coasted across the top at five-hundred feet above sea level, and then we took the plunge into the abyss.

The wind picked up as we passed the Dog Musher cabin. The dogs charged ahead, with the fox-furred and floppy-eared Shaun White at the helm. Driftwood logs augured permanently into the ground, with reflective, four-inch metal plates nailed into them, depicted the safe and only path along the coast. The gusts grew strong enough that they pushed the entire team sideways in short bursts. When we veered too far towards the Bering Sea, we ended up in driftwood piles, tangled in sticks and ice chunks. Correcting our direction, we then veered too far on the upwind side, wrapping around the twenty-foot-tall trail marker trees. Untangling proved harder each time. The wind swelled, toppling the sled over, again and again, with me still standing on the runners – it felt like a storm on the surface of the Moon. My headlight barreled forward to beam the way, but after a few hours of bucking the wind, it stopped making sense to the dogs.

I need to be the lead dog. When the going gets tough, great lead dogs emerge. When the going gets impossible, the two-legged leader needs to take over. The complexities of this challenge had simply become too much for the dogs, and I needed to assume the leader position. I willed my body to the front of the team and wrapped my fingers around the gangline. Leaning into the wind, I took a step forward. Inches. I took another step. Inches again. A gust of wind threw an uppercut my way and I was on my back, gangline in hand. I mustered all my strength and stood up. Stepping on the bare tundra, I discovered some traction underfoot, so I zigged and zagged in hopes of staying near the trail, but the wind kept knocking me off my feet. Mother Nature had always been the most formidable competitor, and this time was no different – this was a bareknuckle boxing match between Life and Death. For thirty agonizingly-long minutes I tried in vain to lead the dogs along the trail. The all too palpable intensity of the wind blew forcefully enough that we could only head out to sea, but that wasn't part of the plan.

Forward progress became impossible. I simply could not stand up in the wind and walk; it had nothing to do with my injuries and pain but everything to do with the strength of the storm. If anything, the pain kept me alert. It occurred to me to try and crawl to Nome, but crawling for thirty-five miles did not make much sense. I laid the sled down and gathered the team into a doggie pile on the leeward side. They cuddled together as if they were puppies. Some actually whined to tell me they were scared. I unfurled my down sleeping bag and huddled with them, stroking each dog to comfort away not just their fears, but also my own.

From my now several days long out-of-body experience, I marveled at how little space twelve sled dogs, the sled, and musher could occupy when everyone wanted to stay out of the wind. We stayed like that for several hours, the wind sucking away at our body heat. When I had to leave the group to relieve myself, I stashed my sleeping bag in the sled to make sure it would not blow to Russia. *What a mess.*

While outside of the huddle, both the wind and I agreed to use this opportunity to explore the idea of going downwind and out on the sea ice to determine if things had improved. In less than a hundred feet my question was answered. Travel was not yet possible, and I had to get back to my team. Venturing away from the dogs was easy in a thirty-knot wind; venturing back only reaffirmed my decision not to try and crawl to the finish. I gave everything I had to get back to them. Once returned to the huddle, my down bag again proved its worth after I draped it over the team.

I decided not to try and move until full daylight in the hope that either the storm would die down or daylight would help clarify the trail to the dogs. Our only option was to wait; we were going to "rest" here for a while longer.

How long can we last? I took a mental inventory of the situation: We were still reasonably warm, well hydrated, and had enough food with us to last a day or two. And there was that button on the tracker.

Shivering in the screaming winds several miles from Safety, I entertained the thought of pushing for HELP. But who was going to come and rescue us? Who was going to travel *into* this impossible situation? If we couldn't move, who could? I didn't want to jeopardize any potential rescuer attempting the impossible. I needed to remain focused, but I was drifting in and out of sleep...

I thought of everything.

Martin's family and friends gathered around the kitchen counter at a house in Nome, two hundred feet past the finish line. Their eyes were glued to the blue GPS tracker dot on the computer, and anxieties ran high as they speculated the reason that Martin had stopped moving. Was his tracker malfunctioning? Had he hunkered down? Could the battery have gone out? How fast was the internet connection? Pat Hahn, Martin's Nome host and veteran member of the Nome Rescue Squad, convinced everyone, whether by belief or by altruism, that Martin must be holed up at Tommy Johnson's cabin and waiting out the storm. What they didn't know was that the wind had surged and pinned Martin and his dogs down less than two miles from the shelter. Kathy, adhering to a gut feeling honed by years of experience, continued her morning with trepidation.

Sunrise came, and the fast-floating current of fog still tore horizontally across the ground, but streaks of yellow and orange struggled to be seen, revealing a trail marker ahead. The wind had died down to a degree, and I thought travel looked possible. I rousted the dogs, letting them loose to stretch their legs – some of them wandered around a little ways, but they all soon returned to the huddle. I righted the sled, strung out the gangline, and hitched the dogs at the positions I knew they could handle.

I climbed on the footboards, and we crept forward on a vein of ice. Within twenty minutes we passed Tommy Johnson's cabin. The trail swung westward, and with each step I felt the wind more and more from behind, rather than from the side. Snow began blowing wildly. I reached into my pocket for a fresh felt facemask, and then I attached it by slapping the sewed-on Velcro strips onto the sides of my red, plaid hat – before the race I had dabbed a drop of Kathy's perfume on all of my facemasks, simply because it was nice to have a little bit of home out on the trail.

I connected my headphones and turned on the radio. As I listened, the picture of the frontrunners became clear: Jeff getting stuck, walking to Safety, scratching; Aliy making it to Safety not knowing what happened to Jeff, then resting upon learning his fate; Dallas pulling in and out of Safety, pressing on thinking he was in third; Aliy chasing after Dallas, gaining on him; Dallas believing it was his dad Mitch behind him, and then running, pedaling, and ski-poling to the finish, where he collapsed, not realizing that he had won; Aliy arriving two minutes later. *Incredible.*

The last twenty miles blurred together. We moved up and onto Front Street, the dogs trotting right down the middle between parallel rows of parked cars. Cheering spectators on either side of us held a yellow rope that led to the orange-fenced chute. I balanced on the right runner as my left foot hovered over the brake bar. When my dogs crossed under the burled arch, I dropped the hook, walked to the front of the team, and crumpled down onto my knees in a heap, covering my face with my hands and crying. I couldn't control my emotions. A minute later, after a deep breath, I stood up and dissolved into Kathy's arms as she whispered into my ear:

"You don't ever have to do this again if you don't want to."

I was empty, bone tired, and in pain, but I was also happy to be alive. Could this be how my story ended? Could I leave the Iditarod behind? Could I really walk away from the life I had built over the last thirty-five years? In our formative era, Kathy and I had often said to each other "Well, we didn't win, but at least we had a happy bunch of dogs." We had even named our kennel "Happy Trails" as a reflection of our approach that the dogs really do come first. And that had always been my vision, to win the Iditarod with a happy group. I had achieved it four times. Was that enough, and was it time to hang it all up? For a moment, I felt lost. As any good musher knows, when you are lost, when you don't know which way to turn, you have to be able to trust your dogs. So I looked to my team for the answer.

They were wagging their tails.

I finished the 2014 Iditarod in sixth place with a time of nine days, fifty-eight minutes, and fifty-eight seconds, the second-fastest time of my career. The twelve dogs that finished the entire race with me were Baloo, Banana, Heath, Ivar, Michael Phelps, Payton, Pineapple, Rigid, Rock, Roll, Seattle, and Shaun White. At the finisher's banquet, I was given the Leonhard Seppala Humanitarian Award for outstanding dog care – my fifth.

ON THE WAY TO NIKOLAI

CROSSING THE NORTON SOUND INTO KOYUK

THE ICE OF GOLOVIN BAY

ALL ROADS LEAD TO NOME

Acknowledgements

My dogs are who I am and what I do. A thousand dogs have blessed me with their companionship, taught me to be in the moment, forgiven my mistakes, and greeted me daily with wagging tails. No amount of thanks would be enough for nor is expected by my dogs.

Thanks to my parents, adventure seekers in their own right, who instilled freethinking, independence and self-reliance in me. The groundwork was tilled a long way from where I am now because of them.

My wife and sons provided the backdrop to much of the story and the writing of this book, and I thank them for their daily indulgence and positive enthusiasm for my unique career.

This book has been many years in the making and Charles Chapoton deserves special recognition. "The keeper of the book" encouraged me almost from the very beginning to keep track of my trials on the trails, and he in fact preserved many of the stories included.

Lindsay Nyquist and Chanler Holden are especially appreciated for the design work of the book. Lindsay transformed the text into a book, and Chanler worked her magic on the photo layout and cover.

Sean Patrick Williams, my editor, took on this book as a side project and became immediately engulfed in the details of the story. I thank him for choreographing my "English as a second language" recollections into a cohesive chronicle. He was the "detail master," checking, verifying, clarifying, and researching, and without his perseverance and encouragement you would not be reading *Dog Man*.

About The Author

Born in Winterthur, Switzerland in 1958, Martin became fascinated with sled dogs while still a teen. He came to Alaska in 1979 to enhance his knowledge of care and training of sled dogs. He began working and training with long-time Alaskan mushers Earl and Natalie Norris and ran his first Iditarod in 1980. Martin and wife Kathy Chapoton, a retired teacher, reside in Big Lake, Alaska, where the family owns and manages Happy Trails Kennel and B&B. Their sons, Nikolai and Rohn, both named after Iditarod checkpoints, have been involved with dogs at various times in their lives. Nikolai currently resides in Seattle. Rohn lives near the kennel and is currently an integral part of the kennel operation. Rohn completed his first Iditarod in 2008, as a senior in high school.

Martin spends a great deal of time speaking in schools on the humanitarian care of animals and the spirit of the Iditarod. A favorite celebrity of the children of Alaska, Martin treats them with surprise visits from his dogs and puppies.

Martin runs the race each year with his dogs to test the success of their breeding, training and physical endurance. He regards his racers as true competitive athletes and prides his team on their longevity and spirit of competition. Says Martin, "I run the Iditarod to prove that my dogs, bred, trained and raced by Happy Trails Kennels, are the best amongst the world's long distance athletes." For nine years, Martin's

2002 team held the record for the Fastest Iditarod by completing the race in 8 days, 22 hours, 46 minutes and 2 seconds.

As tribute to his treatment of his racers, Martin was awarded the coveted Leonhard Seppala Award an unprecedented five times, in 1988, 1993, 1995, 1997 and again in 2014 for the most humanitarian care of his dogs. The award is named for the most famous Alaskan musher who ran the longest and most dangerous stretch of the 1925, 674-mile diphtheria serum run from Nenana to Nome, which saved hundreds of lives.

Following Martin's 2002 Iditarod victory, the process for his becoming a naturalized citizen of the United States was completed under the burled monument. He then turned around in Nome and made the trip from Nome to Big Lake with his family by snowmachine.

Upon completion of the 2005 Iditarod, after a woodworking accident four days prior to the race start had resulted in the amputation of a part of his finger, Martin was awarded both the Sportsmanship and Most Inspirational Awards by his fellow mushers.

Martin is an honorary member of Rotary. He is always involved with some project around the kennel or house. While he and Kathy moved into the retirement home that Martin built, they are still working on finishing all the details, your typical Alaskan self-built home that is never quite finished.

In the summer, Martin and his family give tours of their working kennel. The tour begins with a DVD trip from Anchorage to Nome narrated by Buser and includes his unique anecdotal stories gathered over 31 Iditarods. Visitors are offered a glimpse of a mock up of the Cripple Checkpoint complete with campfire and wall tent. Veterinary and dog care topics are discussed and of course, there's the cuddling of puppies. The tour ends with a riotous symphony of dogs barking as a team is hooked up and taken on a demo run to show folks the dogs in action.

Sprocketheads, LLC produced a DVD featuring the unique lifestyle made possible by training and racing sled dogs. The DVD, *For the Love of Dogs*, is available from www.buserdog.com along with other Happy Trails Merchandise. The DVD captures a sled dog's life from puppyhood to racing and Martin's interaction with his athletic friends. *Mile by Mile: Martin Buser's Iditarod* is a new release DVD. In partnership with Jeff Schultz and Sprocketheads, LLC, a unique journey from Anchorage to Nome with some of the most spectacular images ever assembled in a DVD was created. With a combined 54 years on the trail, Jeff's photos and Martin's trail stories make it possible for you to "be there" on the back of the sled!

Martin tailors motivational speeches on many topics to large and small audiences in and outside Alaska. Some titles include:

- "You're Only As Fast As Your Slowest Dog: Elevating the Entire Team for Maximum Performance"
- "Capitalizing on Extreme Challenges"
- "Travelogue Alaska: Negotiating 1000+ miles with a Dog Team", "Work Hard, Never Quit, the Mantra for Life in the Last Frontier(or anywhere else for that matter)"

Martin is currently the musher with the most consecutive Iditarod finishes, 29 races completed in row, 31 total finishes. We are looking forward to many more and working diligently toward a fifth Iditarod win. While the race is always the final exam, the year-round interaction and relationship with the dogs is the most valuable aspect of this lifestyle. On a daily basis, we are amazed by the stamina, loyalty, honesty, and joy of our dogs. Author Brian Jacques went on a ride with Martin and the team many years ago and described the dogs as "eternal children." We couldn't agree more. It is our good fortune to be able to take care of them.

CPSIA information can be obtained at www.ICGtesting.com
Printed in the USA
BVOW11s0628200215

388388BV00003B/3/P